UNHINGED

UNHINGED

EXPOSING LIBERALS GONE WILD

MICHELLE MALKIN

Since 1947
REGNERY
PUBLISHING, INC.
An Eagle Publishing Company • Washington, DC

Library of Congress Cataloging-in-Publication Data

Malkin, Michelle.
 Unhinged : exposing liberals gone wild / Michelle Malkin.
    p. cm.
 Includes bibliographical references and index.
 ISBN 0-89526-030-1
 1. Liberalism—United States. 2. United States—Politics and
government—2001– I. Title.
 JC574.2.U6M25 2005
 320.51'30973—dc22

                                        2005028199

Published in the United States by
Regnery Publishing, Inc.
One Massachusetts Avenue, NW
Washington, DC 20001
www.regnery.com

Distributed to the trade by
National Book Network
Lanham, MD 20706

Manufactured in the United States of America

10 9 8 7 6 5 4 3 2 1

Books are available in quantity for promotional or premium use. Write to
Director of Special Sales, Regnery Publishing, Inc., One Massachusetts Avenue
NW, Washington, DC 20001, for information on discounts and terms or call
(202) 216-0600.

For J.D. and V.V., who keep me sane

Contents

Introduction: Liberals on the Couch...1

Chapter 1: Stark Raving Lunatics...13

Chapter 2: The Party of Paranoia 31

Chapter 3: When Angry Democrats Attack 53

Chapter 4: They *Don't* Support our Troops 69

Chapter 5: Campus Moonbats on Parade 97

Chapter 6: "You Are One Sick Gook."..................................113

Chapter 7: The Hollywood Walk of Hate..............................135

Chapter 8: Assassination Fascination..................................153

Afterword: The Road to Recovery 167

Acknowledgements 173

Endnotes 175

Index 213

Liberals on the Couch

What makes unhinged liberals tick—and why are they so ticked off?

They're mad about losing the past two presidential elections. They're mad about losing the mainstream monopoly on how news and information are disseminated in the 21st century. They're mad about minority conservatives in the Republican Party. They're mad about patriotism, capitalism, and the War on Terrorism.

And they're bleeping mad about being called mad. (Just ask Anger Management Poster Boy, Howard Dean.)

If ideologically biased members of the American Psychological Association weren't so desperately preoccupied with proving that we conservatives are crazy,[1] they would find a gold mine of research material waiting in the Bush-bashing enclaves of the anti-war movement, academia, and the Democrat leadership. I am not a licensed medical professional, but after compiling case study after case study, I do know this:

The American Left is unwell.

1

I know this from both professional and personal experience—and I'm not just talking about the time MSNBC caveman Chris Matthews frothed at the mouth and kicked me off his train wreck of a show because I dared to defend the Swift Boat Veterans.[2] Every day, my mailbox teems with seething, spiteful, and incoherent rants from left-wing crackpots who make Matthews look like a Zen master on Morphine. Granted, some of the correspondents are probably half-baked homeless people logging in from taxpayer-subsidized Internet accounts in San Francisco and Berkeley. But many are supposedly respectable students, homemakers, legal secretaries, and retirees whose hatred of President Bush and the conservative media has driven them over the edge.

How is it, you may wonder, that a reasonable Democrat mutates from quietly sporting a faded Gore-Lieberman bumper sticker on his Volvo, to bellowing across the dinner table about yellowcake (uranium, not Duncan Hines), to e-mailing profanity-laced screeds decrying "Chimpy McHitlerburton!"

How is it that you can take a seemingly normal person, add a dash of left-wing sanctimony, and voila, create an instant lunatic?

Many private citizens are emboldened by the shields of presumed anonymity and invincibility bestowed by the Internet. And many Democrat officials are bolstered by the smug knowledge that their sympathizers in the mainstream media will not hold them accountable for their actions. Liberal racists, for example, who insist that Hispanics, blacks, and other minorities "betray" their skin color if they don't embrace liberalism, almost always get a pass.

Like the hideous creature in the movie *Alien*, gestating in the stomach of a seemingly benign human host, the unhinged liberal feeds off the illusion of normalcy until he can no longer tolerate his artificial confines. This book is a forensic examination of the extraterrestrial creature exploding from the Democrat Party's gut. Like any good horror movie, it's scary and silly at the same time. You cover your eyes, but you can't help gawking through the cracks between your fingers at the nightmarish scenes of haywire leftists on the loose.

Actually, the unhinged liberal phenomenon isn't entirely novel. The Left's hatred of President Bush today is not all that different from its hatred of President Reagan a quarter-century ago (although Helen Thomas was somehow able to keep her anti-Republican suicidal thoughts[3] to herself during the

1980s). And just as there are tinfoil-hat-wearers today who claim that President Bush engineered the September 11th terrorist attacks, there were crackpots two decades ago who asserted that AIDS was cooked up by government scientists.

What is new is how readily these crazy ideas are now accepted by the highest echelons of the Democrat Party and liberal establishment. And with the advent of the Internet as an engine for political activism, the radical left's attack dog politics have only been accelerated in momentum and maximized in volume. The scariest part is, these Internet crazies aren't just riding along in the Democrat bus—they're driving it.

Dems Gone Loco

You could see this clearly in the aftermath of the 2004 presidential election, when Democrats needed their heads examined.

Literally.

Waves of acute anxiety, depression, helplessness, grief, and denial spread from Hollywood to Manhattan. A few days after the election, Renana Brooks, a Washington, D.C., clinical psychologist (and Bush critic), told the Los Angeles Times: "People are in absolute post-traumatic stress and total despair and pretty much believe American society is permanently destroyed. That's what I've been hearing all day...It looks to me like a worse trauma than 9/11."[4]

Democrat Tony Sears broke down in an interview with the Los Angeles Times: "'I felt,' he said, his voice cracking, 'like someone had died.'"[5]

Countless blue-staters wallowed in victimhood as never before—and sympathetic psychologists (many of whom confessed to being miserable Democrats themselves) pounced. The Boca Raton branch of the American Health Association was quick to capitalize on the Democratic pity party and coined a new term for liberal dyspepsia: Post-Election Selection Trauma (or PEST).

According to the AHA, PEST symptoms include:

- feelings of withdrawal,
- feelings of isolation,

- emotional anger and bitterness,
- loss of appetite,
- sleeplessness,
- nightmares,
- pervasive moodiness, including endless sulking, and
- excessive worries about the direction of the country.[6]

The medical professionals might have added "complete loss of perspective and common sense" to the list. But to addled liberals on the couch, the nausea of election-induced sickness was no joke.

Mike McClure of Fort Worth, Texas, became physically sick. The day after the election, he told the *Fort Worth Star Telegram*, "I had a stomachache ... It's more than mental—it's a physical drag on me."[7]

On a website dedicated to bashing the Fox News Channel, poster Jim B. fumed: "I need to see a shrink. I am losing it. I quit my job, a job I love and a boss to die for. I broke down after giving notice. I am crying almost every day. I can't snap out of it. There are deep, dark thoughts in my head."[8]

Manhattan psychoanalyst Sherman Pheiffer told the Associated Press: "My patients were incredulous, depressed, angry, very frightened ... Everyone talked about feeling frightened [about] the future of this country."[9] In Pennsylvania, Elizabeth Marshall, a volunteer at the Centre County Democrat headquarters, reported that people there exhibited "bereavement, almost. People feel that something they had, which was hope for imminent change, has been taken from them."[10]

In Madison, Wisconsin, area therapists were "flooded" with patients suffering from post-election depression, according to the *Capital Times*. Psychologist Suzanne Drennan was overwhelmed by the demand for counseling services and expressed shock at the number of people affected by the Democrats' loss. "I've never had an experience like this before. Never. Never. Never," she told the *Capital Times*. Temporarily forgetting the admonition, "Physician, heal thyself," psychologist Roger Garms told the newspaper he shared his patients' pain: "I'm too depressed myself to speak about it."[11]

Heartbroken in Des Moines

Karen Emmerson, a 20-year-old University of Iowa student, president of the College Democrats, and campaign volunteer for the John Kerry presidential campaign, was "heartbroken." She told the *Des Moines Register* that after the election, she "sat in her U of I bedroom for hours, dressed in a bathrobe and wearing a towel on her head. She clutched her stuffed donkey, watched Kerry deliver his concession speech on television, and then flipped to the soap operas instead of watching the relentless news coverage. 'It was crushing. I couldn't focus on anything,' Emmerson said. 'I lost my appetite for a few days.'"[12]

Sharon Malheiro, president of the Lesbian, Gay, Bisexual, and Transgender Community Center in Des Moines, suffered even greater PEST paralysis: "I couldn't work."[13] Somehow, Iowa's economy survived.

In Florida, during counseling, one Democrat moaned: "I haven't been able to sleep since this whole election."[14] Palm Beach County psychotherapist Douglas Schooler treated Kerry supporters using "intense hypnotherapy." His patients were "threatening to leave the country or staring listlessly into space. They were emotionally paralyzed, shocked, and devastated." Schooler balked at the suggestion that the illness was hype. "The problem is out there, and it's not going to go away anytime soon," he told the *Boca Raton News.* "Conservatives are calling me to say these people are weak-kneed kooks, but they're not acknowledging that this is a normal psychological response to a severe and disillusioning situation."[15]

Normal?

"Any suggestion that this is not a serious problem arises from a political agenda," Schooler huffed. "The Republicans don't want this talked about."[16]

Ah, another Republican cover-up! But wait—why would conservatives want to cover up liberals' admitted inability to deal with reality?

The Democratic mental health crisis was so severe that writer Gene Stone rushed to print his "Bush Survival Bible"—not only to help others afflicted with post-election trauma, but himself as well. "I was so bummed out by the election," he told United Press International, "so I thought that all that anxiety, depression—all those negative emotions I felt—I thought, hey I've got a channel to do something about it."[17] Stone helpfully refers stressed-out readers to "Mark Liponis, M.D., who writes on how to fight panic and monitor blood pressure."[18] The book also provides suffering liberals "tips to maintain your sanity," "five antidepressants to consider," "nine prayers to get you through the nights," and "seven countries to move to."[19]

Showing classic symptoms of "feelings of withdrawal," thousands of PEST-y Democrats seriously considered abandoning the country altogether. The left-leaning online magazine *Slate* posted a how-to immigration guide for people looking to cross the northern border.[20] Another lefty publication, *Harper's*, offered a "reader's guide to expatriating" for disgruntled Democrats looking to renounce their citizenship.[21] In the week after the election, Canada's Ministry of Immigration and Citizenship noted a record-shattering spike in visits to its website, most of them via American internet service providers.[22] A "hard-core" Democrat volunteer, Maia Fourmyle, told the *New York Sun* she would be moving to Guatemala or Spain as soon as her lease was up. "I can't be part of a country that would elect such an ass," Fourmyle seethed.[23]

Exhibiting similar classic PEST symptoms of "emotional anger and bitterness," Lancaster, Pennsylvania, Democrat city councilman Nelson Polite (yes, that's his name, ironically enough) lashed out at a Bush-supporting baker who had photos of the winning president hanging at his little farmers' market stand.

The baker, David Stoltzfus, displayed the picture next to photos of his grandchildren. It was too much for Polite to bear. According to Stoltzfus, Polite admonished him for featuring the "offensive" pictures and told the baker that

Democrats were mad about it. Recounted Stoltzfus: "He then informed me that the picture must come down, or he will take his request to higher authority. 'One way or another,' he said, 'That picture will come down.'"[24]

When Stoltzfus refused, Polite threatened to enact a city ordinance banning all political material from public places (the market is on city property). "Bush didn't win here [in Lancaster City]. It is like rubbing salt on a wound," the Democrat councilman fumed.[25] After a national uproar, Polite backed off his demand but refused to apologize. "This country is angry," he told the city council. "This community is angry. We need to do something about it."[26] Like banning pictures of the President of the United States? It must be another impulse of the liberals' Post-Election Selection Trauma.

Liberals to the World: "Sorry!"

Embodying the classic PEST symptom of "pervasive moodiness, including endless skulking," James Zetlen, a junior at the University of Southern California, helped left-wingers cope by creating a post-election website too goofy to parody. On "sorryeverybody.com," Zetlen posted photos of forlorn and angry Democrats apologizing to the world for the re-election of President Bush. Zetlen's own photo showed him holding a notebook page with a sketch of the globe and the words "Sorry World (we tried)—Half of America." By mid-November 2004, Zetlen had received 15,000 photo submissions and more than 50 million hits.[27]

One apologist gripped his head in his hands, his mouth covered with duct tape sporting the word "SORRY" in black marker.[28] Another photo showed a woman in total meltdown, her hands covering her face.[29] "Cathryn in Arizona" posted a distorted image of herself with the message: "I'm SO bent out of shape over this! Sorry, World."[30] One angry apologist with issues held up a sign reading: "DEAR WORLD, I ALSO HATE THAT MONKEY-EARED, WAR-MONGERING, TEXAN JACK-HOLE. I'M SO SORRY. SO SORRY. LOVE OHIO."[31] Zetlen marketed this bizarre form of photo-therapy through t-shirts, a book, and a CD collection of "swell protest songs" to soothe tortured Democrat souls. A year after the election, the site continues to receive and post new submissions from grieving Bush-haters in America and around the world.

What a truly sorry lot.

Sadly, they aren't alone. If tummy aches, crankiness, and Internet sob story collections were the end of it, we might be able to laugh off these losers. But there is a dark and dangerous side to their behavior that cannot be dismissed as harmless eccentricity.

Losing It

This book is not about liberals being liberal. It is about Liberals who've lost their grip on sanity and reality.

The traits that distinguish today's unhinged Left are the pervasiveness of its pathologies, the intensity of its hatred, and the sanctimony of its self-delusion. From the grass roots to the top suits, Democrats have abandoned arguments in favor of *ad hominem* attacks and conspiracy theories. They now routinely indulge extremism, rampant campaign vandalism, and assassination fantasies. The holier-than-thou Left has become the crazier-than-thou Left, and needs to be exposed—for its own good. By holding up a mirror to the flipped-out face of the metaphorical donkey, we can help Democrats better understand themselves, and try to figure out how the party that once was home for Adlai Stevenson, John F. Kennedy, and Daniel Patrick Moynihan became the party of Michael Moore, Al Franken, and Howard Dean.

The greatness of liberal tolerance and compassion, perhaps always more myth than reality, has been exchanged in favor of leftist vitriol and political mania. You know the portrait of today's leftists is a picture of the absurd when anti-military activists are driven mad by the mere sight of yellow ribbons; when award-winning liberal newspaper cartoonists pen racist attacks on minority conservatives; and when top Democratic leaders celebrate conspiracy-mongering Bush-haters.

This book provides an unflinching and uncensored look at the Left's foul-mouthed bigots in Hollywood, its pie-throwing lunatics on college campuses, and the fetid swamps of the liberal blogosphere. Together, we'll examine the Left's berserk record of attacks on Republican women, people of faith, troops, and veterans.

And while the Left's knee-jerk response to these stories will doubtlessly be to trot out well-worn examples of unseemly behavior on the Right—Dick Cheney swearing, or mean-spirited conservatives' Internet jibes about Democrats—the truth is that it's conservatives themselves who blow the whistle on their bad boys and go after real extremism on their side of the aisle. Though no one in the mainstream media depicts the GOP as the party of peace, tranquility, and civility—preferring to cast those of us on the Right as angry, destructive, bigoted, and off the rails—it is, in fact, the Left that now embodies that unhinged caricature.

If the mainstream media devoted equal time and outrage to unhinged liberals, there would be no need for this book. But witness the disproportionate attention that "objective" reporters paid to Pat Robertson, who called for the assassination of Venezuelan dictator Hugo Chavez on his Christian Broadcasting Network program, *The 700 Club.* Cable news programs gave the story wall-to-wall coverage. Every network morning show featured Robertson's remarks. In the mere five days between August 23-28, 2005, the *New York Times* ran eight news and opinion articles mentioning the incident, including an inflamed editorial criticizing the Bush administration for not condemning Robertson to the newspaper's satisfaction. "[C]ommon decency, not to mention a rational sense of the national interest, demands condemnation of his remarks," the editorial raged.[32]

When a liberal makes far more reckless suggestions about assassinating our own leader, however, the *New York Times* loses its commitment to "common decency" and "rational sense of the national interest." The editorial board had nothing to say when left-wing radio talk show host Randi Rhodes of Air America recklessly advocated the assassination of President Bush—not once, but twice. Indeed, we'll see that anti-Bush assassination chic is all the rage among unhinged elites in media and literary circles.

Why that Muttering Street Person is Probably a Liberal

After a close study of these creatures in their native habitats, it's clear that being unhinged isn't an exception for today's liberals—it's the norm.

It's now conventional wisdom that *Bush v. Gore* was a coup; electronic voting, implemented in response to the Florida 2000 election debacle, is a tool for electoral fraud; Ohio was stolen in 2004; Iraq was invaded for its oil; the bin Laden family and the Bush family are in cahoots. Belief in the conspiracy theorizing of modern Democrats has one prerequisite: the total denial of reality.

The Democrats even officially embraced one of the looniest of the loonies—and a bona fide loser to boot—in Howard Dean, the newest Chairman of the Democratic National Committee. In tribal Africa, the man who brings bad fortune and shame is shunned from the village. Democrats make him their leader.

Where conspiracy theories and Nazi comparisons were once found only at wacko rallies and amongst the muttering class, they've now become par for the course for leaders and elected officials. The Democrats have taken the Rorschach test to uncharted territory: in every picture of George W. Bush, they see Hitler. And in every closet, they see Karl Rove.

The average unhinged Democrat today is the man who stubs his toe getting out of bed, cuts himself shaving, arrives late to work, finds no coffee left in the break room, and blames Bush's war in Iraq.

As I finished the first draft of this book, an iota of uncertainty lingered in my mind: *Maybe, just maybe, I'm being unfair.* And then, on cue, along came anti-war zealot Cindy Sheehan and her unhinged minions to remove any doubt in my mind that the Left has truly lost it.

Sheehan, the Bush-bashing mother of a soldier who died in Iraq last year, is far more extreme than the mainstream media has made her out to be. In an August 9, 2005, interview on Fox News Channel's *O'Reilly Factor*, I pointed out Sheehan's unseemly alliance with the likes of Michael "Iraqi terrorists are the new Minutemen" Moore and the Marxist anti-military activists of Code

Pink. I also questioned whether Army Specialist Casey Sheehan would have agreed with his mother's loopy accusation that he was murdered by his commander-in-chief rather than by the Iraqi terrorists who ambushed his convoy.

Then all hell broke loose.

Ex-conservative David Brock's media watchdog goons and other members of the anti-war public relations machine accused me and other conservatives of "smearing" Sheehan by accurately reporting her inconsistent accounts of her meeting with President Bush in 2004 and her radical statements calling the Bush administration "the biggest terrorist outfit in the world."[33] Duncan Black, "senior fellow" for Brock's "think tank," Media Matters, fumed: "I'm sure there are serial killers and other horrendous criminals who probably actually deserve the prize, but when it comes to taking our political discourse as far away from the American ideal as possible, Malkin might actually be America's Worst American."[34] (For the noble Mr. Black's idea of "ideal" political discourse, see Chapter Six.) Clara Frenk, an ex-Fox News Channel employee who runs a website called "DC Media Girl," declared "Open war on the self-hating racist bitch Michelle Malkin. OPEN. WAR."[35] A Democrat activist registered my maiden name at a website that redirected web surfers to a Google.com search for "Michelle Maglalang whore."[36]

Thousands of insane and profane messages nearly crashed my e-mail box.

Patrick Mitchell, a legal secretary at the Los Angeles office of Ogletree and Deakins, wrote a typical response to my remarks about Sheehan: "YOU STINK you nasty CUNT! Eat Shit and DIE bitch!!" Tolerant liberals are such charmers, aren't they? And geniuses, too. Mitchell, no doubt thinking himself immune from any consequences, sent his e-mail from his workplace. Two hours after I published his message on my website, he was fired. Yet the haters remain undeterred.

Do not fear—as Senator John Edwards told us in 2004, help is on the way. I have peered into the Democrats' psychological abyss and offer this unflinching and uncensored portrait of Liberals Gone Wild as a public service—as an intervention, if you will. And the next time your sanctimonious neighbor, co-worker, local newspaper editor, or favorite Hollywood celebrity starts railing about angry/racist/sexist/violence-prone/mentally unbalanced conservatives, give them a copy of this book, along with a handheld mirror.

Just be sure to do it with a smile. That always drives them nuts.

Now, let the healing begin.

Michelle Malkin

August 31, 2005

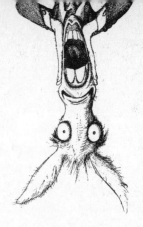

CHAPTER ONE

Stark Raving Lunatics

A picture is worth a thousand words. Here's Liberals Gone Wild Exhibit A:

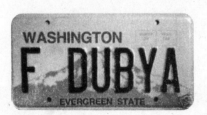

The "F" in "F DUBYA," needless to say, does not stand for "From" or "Feed" or "Free," but the Washington State Department of Licensing was a little slow to catch on. Tacoma-area resident Dan Kaiser had registered the irate plates the day after the 2004 presidential election and attached them to his PT Cruiser as an anti-Bush protest in January 2005. Four months later, after receiving numerous complaints, the licensing agency recalled the plates because it realized the message was "offensive to good taste and decency."[1]

Now, it's one thing to wear your politics on your sleeve. Or on your front lawn. Or on your rear bumper. But what would you call someone so consumed by political animosity that he'd proudly display a profane slur against the president on the front and back of his family car—for every drive to the neighborhood grocery store, the office, the kids' soccer matches, and Sunday services at church?

That, dear reader, is unhinged.

"I figured eventually it would upset enough people," Kaiser confided to the *Tacoma News Tribune*. The father of three (such an exemplary role model) then had the nerve to complain: "I have been flipped off more times in the last four months than in my entire life."[2] What do you expect when your obnoxious license plates are flipping off the commander-in-chief?

In the left-wing commune of Santa Monica, California, a Volvo was spotted in the fall of 2004 sporting plates with the same message: "F DUBYA." The California Department of Motor Vehicles revoked the plates after conservative talk show host Larry Elder called attention to them and his listeners protested.[3] But while the obscene sentiment may have been banished from sight on California and Washington highways, it was by no means out of mind.

Despite the abysmal behavior of liberals gone wild during the 2004 election (liberals set fire to Republican homeowners' lawns, slashed GOP voters' tires, fired shots into Bush-Cheney headquarters, and assaulted their political opponents), CNN executive Jonathan Klein continued to deride *conservatives* as inflamed social miscreants. Fox News Channel's right-leaning audience is full of "angry white men, and those men tend to be rabid," Klein told liberal PBS talk show host Charlie Rose in April 2005. "They tend to like to have their points of view reinforced," Klein sneered, and they are "people who like to get worked up over things."[4]

Liberal comedian Bill Maher's like-minded assertions that "Republicans need anger management" and are possessed with a "vein-popping, gut-churning rage that consumes the entire right wing" overlook the pathological wrath and fury on the Left.[5] Instead, it is clear that liberals have what pop psychologists call "serious issues." Jonathan Chait, a senior editor at the (once-) respected *New Republic* magazine, demonstrated how warped the Bush-haters have become when he wrote a lengthy screed in September 2003. The piece began:

> I hate President George W. Bush. There, I said it. I think his policies rank him among the worst presidents in U.S. history. And, while I'm tempted to leave it at that, the truth is that I hate him for less substantive reasons, too. I hate the inequitable way he has come to his economic and political achievements and his utter lack of humility (disguised behind transparently false modesty) at having done so. His favorite answer to the question of nepotism—"I inherited half my father's friends and all his enemies"—conveys the laughable implication that his birth bestowed more disadvantage than advantage. He reminds me of a certain type I knew in high school—the kid who was given a fancy sports car for his sixteenth birthday and believed that he had somehow earned it. I hate the way he walks—shoulders flexed, elbows splayed out from his sides like a teenage boy feigning machismo. I hate the way he talks—blustery self-assurance masked by a pseudopopulist twang. I even hate the things that everybody seems to like about him. I hate his lame nickname-bestowing—a way to establish one's social superiority beneath a veneer of chumminess (does anybody give their boss a nickname without his consent?). And, while most people who meet Bush claim to like him, I suspect that, if I got to know him personally, I would hate him even more.[6]

After venting his spleen for 3,800 words, Chait concluded: "There. That feels better." But he wasn't done yet. A year later, he penned yet another 1,000 words sustaining his defense of Bush hatred. With malignant snark, Chait mocked George W. Bush as "basically the Fredo Corleone of the Bush family."[7] Fredo Corleone, you may recall, was the clumsy, slow-witted character brutally executed on the order of his brother Michael in *Godfather II.*

Meanwhile, liberal comedian/author Al Franken abandoned his Stuart Smalley costume for his new role as the unhinged Left's Stone Cold Steve Austin. In April 2003, he stomped over to the Fox News table at the annual White House Correspondents Dinner and verbally abused Fox News host Alan Colmes for not being liberal enough. In January 2004, for a similar reason, Franken literally tackled a Howard Dean supporter at a John Kerry rally in New Hampshire. "It was unbelievable. He was really into it," NBC News host Tim Russert told radio personality Don Imus the morning after the incident. In a letter to *Time* magazine, Franken bragged that he was a "hero" for wrestling the pro-Dean heckler to the ground.[8] At the 2004 Republican National Convention, he nearly came to blows with Laura Ingraham's radio talk show producer, whom he publicly called an "asshole," over a booking dispute. And at the 2005 Conservative Political Action Conference in Washington, D.C., Franken went ape during a radio interview with talk show host Michael Medved—gesticulating wildly and calling fellow interviewee John O'Neill, the Swift Boat Veteran and co-author of *Unfit for Command*, a "disgrace." One witness, Internet journalist Robert Cox of the Media Bloggers Association, reported that Franken was so angry at O'Neill's presence that his "eyes [were] literally bulging out of his head. I was 3 feet [from] Franken and the corner of his mouth was twitching and his hands were curled up in close to a fist." Franken, unprepared to debate O'Neill, left in a huff—knocking over a chair as he stalked off the stage.[9]

If this is a hint of how Franken would conduct himself on the campaign trail in his oft-rumored Senatorial candidacy, Republicans in Minnesota should be cheering: "Bring. It. On." Who was it again that Jonathan Klein and Bill Maher accused of having anger management problems?

Profane Thoughts

While Franken and his ilk are certainly entertaining, they're positively tame compared to some of the other members of the unhinged Left found in the wild. Bush-bashers across the country went much further in venting their R-rated hatred and rage. You'll have to forgive the extreme vulgarities that are printed here and throughout the book, but I must spell them out when the liberals do, both for accuracy's sake and to illustrate the true depths of Democrats' unhinged nature. No hiding behind asterisks or dashes that downplay their crassness. No camouflage allowed.

On the Internet, liberal entrepreneurs launched "FuckYouBush.com" and "BitchAboutBush.com." The first site sells "FUCK BUSH" hats, thongs, and teddy bears. The latter site allows angry leftists to leave uncensored, incoherent messages for the president, whom they refer to as a "fucktard." A sample:

> **fuckabuncha:** fucktard is my new favorite word. a friend read it in a book, and we adopted the term. I am loving seeing it so aptly applied now. the fucktard IS a fucktard.

> **ishouldbefuckinpresident:** like I said in my name. . . . I know jack shit but I would still make a better president than fucktard!!

> **nighthawk45750:** That FUCKTARD(love that word) needs to be anal raped a few million times. His religious motherfuckers too. BURN IN HELL, FUCKTARD

> **Bushisapieceoffuckingshit:** Fuck you the fucktard and yours. Iraq is becoming vietnam and all you and your bitches care about is money. Goto hell you fucking cunt.

> **BushKiller:** Listen to me people, the fucktard is a fucking virus.

Enraged at Republicans in the South, who voted overwhelmingly for George W. Bush in both 2000 and 2004, a furious blue-stater created a website called "FucktheSouth.com." Here's the introduction to the raving diatribe posted on the site:

> Fuck the South. Fuck 'em. We should have let them go when they wanted to leave. But no, we had to kill half a million people so

they'd stay part of our special Union. Fighting for the right to keep slaves—yeah, those are states we want to keep. And now what do we get? We're the fucking Arrogant Northeast Liberal Elite? How about this for arrogant: the South is the *Real* America? The *Authentic* America. Really? Cause we fucking founded this country, assholes. Those Founding Fathers you keep going on and on about? All that bullshit about what you think they meant by the Second Amendment giving you the right to keep your assault weapons in the glove compartment because you didn't bother to read the first half of the fucking sentence? Who do you think those wig-wearing lacy-shirt sporting revolutionaries were? They were fucking blue-staters, dickhead. Boston? Philadelphia? New York? Hello? Think there might be a reason all the fucking monuments are up here in our backyard?

No, No. Get the fuck out. We're not letting you visit the Liberty Bell and fucking Plymouth Rock anymore until you get over your *real* American selves and start respecting those other nine amendments ...

Satire? The liberals who cheered the site and mass e-mailed the profanity-laced essay to friends and family didn't think so. The *LA Weekly* and *The Stranger*, Seattle's left-wing alternative rag, gleefully reprinted the "Fuck the South" article in full. Liberals who gave voice to a "secession" movement following the 2004 election were not joking either. Nor was another unglued graphic artist who posted a post-election map divided into blue and red regions, with the heartland and southern states labeled "Dumbfuckistan."[10]

Meanwhile, Teresa Heinz Kerry—demonstrating the class she would possess as First Lady of the United States—giddily wore an anti-Bush "Asses of Evil" button and passed them out to loyal supporters on the campaign trail.[11] While Democrat activists exulted in Ms. Kerry's outspoken nature, one still has to wonder how a national party went from First Lady Jackie Kennedy to Crazy Lady Teresa Heinz "Asses of Evil" Kerry in a mere four decades.

Failed Democrat presidential contender Howard Dean didn't spew any memorable public profanities, but his infamous scream (a guttural sound best reproduced in print as "YEAAARGHH!") was a harbinger of eruptions to come.

On the campaign trail and later as Democratic National Committee chairman, Dean launched vein-throbbing tirades against Republicans as "evil," "corrupt," "mean," "brain-dead," "not nice people" who "have never made an honest living in their lives," "are not very friendly to different kinds of people," "are all about suppressing votes," and "always divide people."[12]

Sometimes a fad comes along, the juvenile absurdity of which is apparent only to those not swept up in it—and to history. There's the Chia Pet, Roos, the Macarena, pet rocks, and the Hampster Dance. Howard Dean's Democratic National Committee cannot be far behind—in the end, his speeches translate easily into a license plate: F REPUBLICANS.

"Don't Get Well Soon"

The Left's fanatical hatred of President Bush often extends to all prominent conservatives—even those who are ill. Consider the treatment talk show king Rush Limbaugh received at the hands of liberal media critic Er Eiic Alterman, who vented to *Esquire* magazine:

> **Esquire:** As a liberal who do you find more objectionable, Bill O'Reilly, Chris Matthews, or Rush Limbaugh?
>
> **Alterman:** No question it's Limbaugh. He has an army. O'Reilly and Matthews are entertainers. I don't think anybody would follow the other two into a fire, but Limbaugh is different. The lack of civility that he demonstrates toward liberal politicians is really dangerous to our political public. I hate to say it, but I wish the guy would have gone deaf. I shouldn't say that, but on behalf of the country, it would be better without Rush Limbaugh and his 20 million listeners.[13]

Hint: When an unhinged liberal says he "hates" to say something, he loves saying it.

After controversy erupted, Alterman petulantly "apologized" on his MSNBC blog:

> I'm sorry. I should not have said, even in jest, that I thought we'd all be better off if Rush Limbaugh had gone deaf. I wish Rush the best of luck with his medical problems, though I do think it would be OK if he lost his voice. Moreover, I think the man is awfully sensitive for a guy who shows a photo of a 13-year-old Chelsea Clinton on television and asks, "Did you know there's a White House dog?" But that doesn't make it right and what I said was silly.[14]

As former CBS newsman Bernard Goldberg observed, Alterman represents "a new kind of liberal: smart, well educated, articulate...but mostly angry—the kind that is doing far more harm to liberalism in America than Rush Limbaugh could ever do."[15]

Alterman has plenty of company. When former Attorney General John Ashcroft revealed that he was being treated for pancreatitis in March 2004, liberals showed an outpouring of twisted "compassion." During his HBO talk show monologue, the aforementioned Bill Maher speculated that Ashcroft contracted his unimaginably painful and potentially deadly illness from "wiping his ass with the Bill of Rights."[16] The audience roared with laughter.

On the web, members of the Democratic Underground discussion board echoed Maher's sentiments—in eloquent form:

> "He has it coming. He is utterly sub-human and evil. Suffer, bastard."

> "[T]he world would be better off without him."

> "I hope he is in the most severe pain a human being can suffer, and after that, I hope he remains in constant pain with no hope of relief."

"ohhh...that's pretty painful... good...that a.h. deserves it."

"I believe it's related to....the amount of vasoline he slathers on his scalp each day. That and the fact that this anal retentive idiot probably hasn't taken a dump in months. Couldn't happen to a nicer fella'. Don't get well soon, John."

"Just desserts (deserts?)...Couldn't happen to a more appropriate person."

"HE'S GOT A LOT OF GALL...F***ING A**HOLE."

"As my mama used to say "God don't like ugly"...Apparently God saw the ugly in Asscroft and decided to take action."

"Pray for Pain...We need to let the AG know what pain I and others have everyday and the pain killers we need that he makes hard for our docs to write."

"Good...I hope it's slow, I hope it's painful, and I hope that he suffers greatly right before he dies. But not before regretting everything he's done to our country."

"Cound not happen to a more deserving bastard."

"It feels good.Just deserts, I say. I will never wish this SOB well."

"we should continue to bash the little Nazi S.O.B. unmercifully, because he deserves everything he gets."

"So, what you're saying is that he might live?...Aw, fuckity-fuck..."

"Let's keep our fingers crossed. I could play the adult and claim to not wish harm on anyone, but he's too destructive. It would be like saying one wouldn't have wanted harm to come to Hitler. Ashcroft is a purulent, malignant pustule, and the world would be better off without him. His blatant disregard for the welfare of the disenfranchised is disgusting."

"I just think: hey, couldn't've happened to a nicer guy. I doubt it'll kill him, but can't say I'd shed tears if somehow it did."

"Suffer . . . @sshole . . . Lets all hope for the worst."

"The Hills Are alive . . . With the sound of Music!"

"Reap what you sow, asscrap. Sorry, no pity here. He's caused so much suffering to others. Scum." [17]

The reaction at the Democratic Underground was just as hate-filled when former president Ronald Reagan died.[18] The first comment:

"i don't care what killed him, alzhiemers or the black plague, i'm glad he's dead and i don't care how many times i'm scolded or chastised for it. the day he took office was the most depressing day of my life, and i swore, that on the day he died, i'd drink a toast of celebration and figuratively piss on his grave and have said so to several gingrich sucking reagan worshipping dickheads. fuck ronald reagan, and i hope in some small way my fuck you counteracts all the bullshit we are going to be hammered with for a fucking month after the fall of this 'graaaaaat human being'. fuck you ronnie, here's to ya pal. see ya in hell." [19]

This was followed by hearty applause from other Democratic Underground members:

"woo woo!"

"Raise my glass too!"

"Yup, one less Nazi terrorist in the word, w. the death of Ronald Raygun . . . "

"If because of his Alzheimer's he was not of sane mind, he was still complicit in the murder of 200,000 Guatemalan Indians and others, because beforehand he gave consent and promulgated policies that lead to such genocides . . ."

"I second that!"

"I third it!"[20]

Those were just the first seven posts. The discussion railed on, with more than 100 comments delighting in Reagan's passing. Meanwhile, left-wing newspaper cartoonist Ted Rall cackled on his website:

How Sad . . . that Ronald Reagan didn't die in prison, where he belonged for starting an illegal, laughably unjustifiable war against Grenada under false pretenses (the "besieged" medical students later said they were nothing of the sort) and funneling arms to hostages during Iran-Contra. Oh, and 9/11? That was his. Osama bin Laden and his fellow Afghan "freedom fighters" got their funding, and nasty weapons, from Reagan. A real piece of work, Reagan ruined the federal budget, trashed education, alienated our friends and allies and made us a laughing stock around the world. Hmmmm . . . sounds familiar. Anyway, I'm sure he's turning crispy brown right about now.[21]

When conservative radio talk show host Laura Ingraham disclosed that she was being treated for breast cancer, the DUers uncorked another bottle of fermented bile.[22] One DU member tried to intervene:

> I have been a Democrat for a long time, and part of the Democratic principles that attracted me as a young person and kept me a Democrat all these years is our compassion. Democrats are simply good and decent people. And good and decent people want everyone to do well—those who agree with them and those who do not. We fight for the right of voices with which we disagree to speak out, for the right of people to say things we don't believe to be true, even for the right to be malicious and mean-spirited. If we fight for the right for LI to say what she says, how in the world can we use our disagreement with those words as an excuse not to be compassionate in her fight with cancer? Being willing to have her voice muted by illness is the same thing as not wanting her voice to be heard. It is not Democratic or democratic.[23]

Huh? Someone at DU asking fellow liberals to be considerate to an ailing conservative? Clearly this was an impostor—perhaps a Republican posing as a Democrat?

Nope, it turns out that this voice of civility and compassion was none other than Elizabeth Edwards, wife of failed vice presidential candidate Senator John Edwards.

Alas, Mrs. Edwards' admirable attempt to stop the madness was futile. After a few commenters applauded Mrs. Edwards' post, it was back to spewing as usual:

> "I don't pray for Nazis or other Totalitarian Scum."

> "I hope she goes into remission and fucking chokes to death."

> "She Probably Gave it to Herself... All that Hate, Lies, Anger..."
> "I'm sure that in her case it's because of all the hate she carries...."

around—it must be eating her up! (No pun intended.)" "She's another Ann Coulter. David Brock wrote much about Ingrahm in "Blinded by the Right." She is part of everything evil in the GOP since the revolution in the late 80s. Fuck Laura Ingrahm. Fuck her." "I hope she goes bankrupt. And they take her house and slap a lien on all her future earnings to pay off all the medical bills. And I hope the doctor operating on her is one of the gay students she outed at Dartmouth and he remembers her and makes little jokes about scalpels slipping... you get the idea." "I'm Not Surprised. Judging by the amount of hatred she spews on a daily basis, I'm surprised her body has lasted THIS long." [24]

And those were comments that passed the DU filter.

In June 2005, the malevolent unwell-wishers surfaced again—this time on political chameleon Arianna Huffington's blog, after she published an unsubstantiated rumor that Vice President Dick Cheney had been hospitalized for heart problems. Here's a sample:

"Hasn't he had his 'last throes' of chest pains yet?"

"I wonder how many regular readers to this pathetic, self-important blog are hoping that Cheney comes out with a sheet over his head...?"

"His heart is listening to all the lies coming out of his mouth. It can't take much more of this drivel."

"I wish the evil zombie would stop leaving his underground bunker. Surely, there's a medical ward where he lurks below the surface, near Washington, D.C."

"You bet we losers want him dead. And I'm glad to be a loser. If I were a winner, I'd have to be around the kind of assholes who like Bush and Cheney."

" 'Last throes,' does one suppose? Here's hoping."

"You're all assuming he actually still has a heart. I don't think so. I think it was replaced by a teflon pump a long time ago. Therefore he can no longer feel any pain."[25]

Huffington later deleted the offensive posts and published a statement condemning them—but only after conservative blogs, including mine, called attention to the hate-mongering.

There is a tendency by even-handed observers to assume that hatred on the left and the right are equivalent. But comparing posts for the conservative Free Republic to the posts for DU shows otherwise. Yes, some conservative posters cracked jokes when Elizabeth Edwards was diagnosed with cancer, as they did when Bill Clinton had to undergo coronary bypass surgery.[26] A few unhinged Free Republic commenters were happy when Paul Wellstone was killed in a tragic plane crash.[27] But the majority responded to these incidents with compassion. Few, if any, wished for Edwards or Clinton to suffer or die (or go deaf). A couple of rare, honest, and rational liberals e-mailed me acknowledging the imbalance. As Kenneth Bacon of Seattle wrote:

Admission: I'm a liberal who posts now and again on several left-leaning blogs.

I see that you've posted a large sampling of comments posted by "moonbats" about V.P. Cheney and his reported visit to a Vail cardiac unit. These comments can best be described as vile, dark, and nasty. Truth be told, my first reaction to the news was less than charitable. But, you know, I figured that I would be able to find similar posts at Free Republic during the time Clinton was first admitted to the hospital with his heart problems. However, I must report that what I found was not what I expected. Almost every post I saw had a similar message: "My prayers are with Clinton and his family."

So, taking their example:

> I sincerely hope the Vice President's condition is not serious and
> that he heads home soon feeling better. [28]

Bacon's refreshing candor notwithstanding, the perception that Republicans = mean and Democrats = nice persists. The media seems determined to reinforce the myth—even if it means fabricating the evidence. Thus, the Associated Press reported that a crowd at a Bush rally in West Allis, Wisconsin, booed when President Bush offered Clinton best wishes for a speedy recovery from his heart surgery. When Free Republic members and conservative bloggers who had audio of the event debunked the reporter's assertion, the AP was forced to run an embarrassing retraction: "This is a correction to an incorrect story posted by AP on Friday stating the crowd booed the President when he sent his good wishes. The crowd, in fact, did NOT boo."[29]

Taking it to the Grave

During the 2004 campaign season, the Cox News Service reported on a hot trend among unhinged Democrats who had passed on, but refused to Move On: anti-Bush death notices.[30] Various media outlets traced the beginning of the fad to Sally Baron, a Wisconsin Democrat whose August 2003 obituary requested that mourners send donations to any organization dedicated to defeating Bush, rather than sending flowers. An anti-Bush death cry was born.

Naturally, Republican-bashing New Yorkers joined in and the national media fueled the polit-uary craze further. Anemona Hartocollis reported in the *New York Times* in February 2004 that similar notices started sprouting in the paper of record "like a chain letter. Although dead people voting is a hoary tradition in places like Jersey City and Chicago, this kind of posthumous attempt to influence elections seems new, a creature of the Internet age and an indication of the intensity of this political season."[31]

The *Times'* paid death notice for Mary Jean Tully, "a pioneer of the feminist movement," directed mourners to make donations in her name to the

"NOW Legal Defense and Education Fund, Veteran Feminists of America, Alvin Ailey Dance Company, or any organization dedicated to the defeat of George W. Bush."[32] The notice for Virginia R. Shanahan's passing in the *Chicago Tribune* in October 2004 carried things further with the inclusion of the following line: "Virginia's last wish was for everyone to vote for John Kerry."[33] Some newspapers tried to cast this morbid phenomenon as bipartisan, but, as the *Tribune* pointed out, the vast majority of politicized obituaries were anti-Bush.

One Bush-hater, Corwyn (Cory) William Zimbleman, passed away in June 2005. According to his death notice:

> He had strong political opinions and followed Amy Goodman's radio broadcast "Democracy Now." Alas the stolen election of 2000 and living with right-winged Americans finally brought him to his early demise. Stress from living in this unjust country brought about several heart attacks rendering him disabled.[34]

At least Zimbleman's relatives had the good taste not to throw any profanities into their eulogy. But given the breakdown of liberalism in America, it's really just a matter of time before we see a headstone etched with the Left's unhinged *cri de coeur*:

F DUBYA.

Top 10 Unhinged Leftists

10 Antiwar rollerblader **LYNDA RAGSDALE** of Carpinteria, California, who skated through her town chopping yellow ribbons off trees and poles, brandishing her scissors.

9 Kerry supporter **MICHAEL HUSAR**, who was arrested for making a drunken attack on a female Bush supporter during a Northwest Airlines flight.

8 College student **AJAI PRASAD RAJ**, who disrupted an Ann Coulter lecture with a sexually obscene rant and simulated masturbation.

7 **KERRY-SUPPORTING APPLE VALLEY HIGH SCHOOL STUDENTS** in Minnesota, who beat a Bush-supporting student with a baseball bat.

6 Protester **BRUCE C. CHARLES**, who was so angered by a debate featuring Howard Dean at Pacific University in Portland that he took off his shoe and threw it at 64-year-old former Pentagon adviser Richard Perle.

5 Gainsville, Florida, Democrat **DAVID PHILIP MCCALLY**, who was charged with barging into a local GOP office, assaulting a cardboard cutout of President Bush, and punching a local Republican chairman.

4 **ANTI-BUSH VANDALS** in Madison, Wisconsin, who burned swastikas into Republican homeowners' lawns and destroyed their Bush-Cheney signs.

3 **DEMOCRAT STAFFERS** in Milwaukee, Wisconsin, who slashed the tires of 20 Republican get-out-the-vote vans on Election Day.

2 Democrat **BARRY STELTZER** of Sarasota, Florida, arrested for trying to run over former Florida Secretary of State Katherine Harris with his Cadillac.

1 Democrat **NATHAN WINKLER** of Tampa, Florida, charged with trying to run down a mother and her children after spotting a Bush-Cheney bumper sticker on their car.

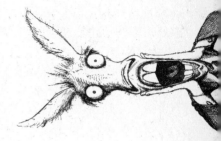

CHAPTER TWO

The Party of Paranoia

Liberals have taken a roller-coaster plunge into political lunacy. It's not just Hollywood crackpots such as Oliver Stone and Michael Moore. Democrat Party leaders, their loyal soldiers, and their liberal media allies have succumbed to what historian Richard Hofstatder famously dubbed the "paranoid style" in American politics—a pathological state of mind marked by "heated exaggeration, suspiciousness, and conspiratorial fantasy."[1]

This condition afflicts every region of the collective Democrat brain, not just its remote corners.

According to the *Washington Post,* at the Democratic National Committee headquarters in Washington, D.C., in June 2005, activists handed out documents suggesting Israel was behind the September 11, 2001, terrorist attacks.[2] Four years after thorough debunking of such baseless beliefs, the Democratic Party still encompasses countless screwballs who believe that September 11th was orchestrated by the Jews; that the war in Iraq was engineered by Halliburton; that the capture of Saddam Hussein was staged; that the Bush administration has Osama bin Laden secretly stashed away somewhere; that Bush has secret plans for a draft; that the 2004 election was rigged by voting machine manufacturer, Diebold; and the list goes on. It's still unclear how the faked moon landing fits in to all this, but it's got to be there somewhere.

And don't forget that Karl Rove is the evil genius behind all the liberals' ills.

Yes, Darth Rove. Lord of the Sith. Master of the Universe. Invincible infiltrator of the mainstream media. Creator of all Democratic Party problems. Throughout the 2004 election season and beyond, the Rovian Death Star loomed large in the overactive imaginations of warped liberal minds.

So many Democrat officials floated cuckoo conspiracy theories that the "D" after their names has come to stand for "deranged." Not just one or two Dennis Kucinich staffers, mind you, but enough high-ranking Democrats to fill an entire hospital ward.

The Democrats' Tinfoil Hat Club

Madeleine Albright, secretary of state in the Clinton administration, waded into the fever swamps in December 2003. It was a fertile month for conspiracies. In a conversation with centrist journalist Morton Kondracke, executive editor of *Roll Call* and a Fox News Channel political analyst, Albright reportedly suggested that Osama bin Laden had been captured by U.S. forces and would soon be trotted out for the Republicans' political gain. "Do you suppose that the Bush administration has Osama bin Laden hidden away somewhere and will bring him out before the election?" Albright asked in the Fox News Channel makeup room with Kondracke present. "She was not smiling when she said this," Kondracke said.[3]

He recounted the rest of the conversation on *Special Report with Brit Hume*: "I said you can't seriously believe that. And she said, well, she thought it was a possibility. I mean, you know, that is just unthinkable. That's irrational. It's—but they will believe anything about George Bush, the Democratic Party. And this is not some kid in sandals, you know, working in the [Howard] Dean campaign. This is the former secretary of state."

Albright claimed afterwards that her comments were "tongue-in-cheek." But two other witnesses backed Kondracke's version. After Albright issued a statement lashing out at Kondracke, he gave her the benefit of the doubt—but also noted that Democrat sources told him "they're concocting worst-case scenarios and this is one of them."[4]

Keep in mind the timing of Albright's remarks. Just three days earlier, American troops had captured Saddam Hussein. The day before Albright made her comments, Democrat Congressman Jim McDermott of Washington suggested, with deadly seriousness, that the capture had been staged. As the Associated Press reported:

> [McDermott] told a Seattle radio station Monday the U.S. military could have found Saddam "a long time ago if they wanted." Asked if he thought the weekend capture was timed to help Bush, McDermott chuckled and said: "Yeah. Oh, yeah." The Democratic congressman went on to say, "There's too much by happenstance for it to be just a coincidental thing." "When interviewer Dave Ross asked again if he meant to imply the Bush administration timed the capture for political reasons, McDermott said: "I don't know that it was definitely planned on this weekend, but I know they've been in contact with people all along who knew basically where he was. It was just a matter of time [until] they'd find him." "It's funny," McDermott added, "when they're having all this trouble, suddenly they have to roll out something."[5]

Howard Dean dished out his own paranoid conspiracy that same month during an interview with National Public Radio talk show host Diane Rehm. Discussing what President Bush knew about the terrorist conspiracy and why the September 11 Commission report had not yet been released, Dean rolled out this doozy:

> **Diane Rehm:** "Why do you think he [Bush] is suppressing that [Sept. 11] report?"

Howard Dean: I don't know. There are many theories about it. The most interesting theory that I've heard so far—which is nothing more than a theory, it can't be proved—is that he was warned ahead of time by the Saudis. Now who knows what the real situation is? [6]

For taxi drivers, Hollywood nitwits, and third-rate rappers to engage in such reckless rhetoric is one thing. But for the frontrunner in the race for the Democratic nomination for President of the United States to pander to that crowd is truly nuts.

When offered a chance to explain his tinfoil-hat musings on *Fox News Sunday* with Chris Wallace, Dean gave this disingenuous response using the old I'm-not-saying-it-I'm-just-posing-the-question card:

Wallace: The most interesting theory is that the president was warned ahead of time by the Saudis. Why would you say that, Governor?

Dean: Because there are people who believe that. We don't know what happened in 9/11. Tom Kean is trying to get some information from the president...

Wallace: Do you believe that?

Dean: ...which doesn't—no, I don't believe that. I can't imagine the president of the United States doing that. But we don't know, and it'd be a nice thing to know. [7]

What leading Democrat in his right mind would lend even a shred of credence to the baseless theory that Bush "was warned ahead of time by the Saudis" about September 11th? What would cause him to do so? Charles Krauthammer, the Pulitzer Prize-winning syndicated columnist and former psychiatrist, astutely diagnosed Dean with "Bush Derangement Syndrome: the acute onset of paranoia in otherwise normal people in reaction to the policies, the presidency—nay—the very existence of George W. Bush."[8]

The week after Dean donned his tinfoil topper, liberal blogger Markos Moulitsas Zuniga wrote that the establishment in the Democratic Party was lining up behind Dean for the highest office in the land. "We're seeing most of the outright opposition to Dean evaporate, and this week proved the turning point," Moulitsas wrote. "The establishment wants as much of that Dean magic as they can capture."[9]

Days later, failed 2000 Democratic presidential candidate Al Gore announced that he was "proud and honored" to endorse Dean for the presidency. "I think people realize that he sometimes speaks off the cuff, but they realize also that this is a result of him speaking from the heart. And he doesn't hold back."[10]

Such ill-advised lack of restraint was not, however, unique to Dean. Among other voluble Bush Derangement Syndrome sufferers in the Democrat Party:

- Senator Ted Kennedy of Massachusetts, who railed that the case for war against Iraq was a "fraud" that President Bush "made up in Texas" because it "was going to be good politically."[11]
- Congressman Cynthia McKinney of Georgia, who preceded Howard Dean in peddling wild-eyed "Bush knew" theories about September 11th, including this rant on left-wing Pacifica radio: "What did this administration know and when did it know it, about the events of September 11? Who else knew, and why did they not warn the innocent people of New York who were needlessly murdered? What do they have to hide?...What is undeniable is that corporations close to the administration have directly benefited from the increased defense spending arising from the aftermath of September 11th."[12]
- In July 2005, Rep. McKinney convened an 8-hour crackpot-fest in which participants concluded that the Bush administration wanted the attacks to occur for "power."[13]

➤ Rep. Maurice Hinchey of New York, who blamed CBS News's "Rathergate" debacle—in which anchor Dan Rather and his producers relied on obviously faked National Guard memos to attack President Bush's Vietnam War record—on none other than Bush senior advisor Karl Rove.

And that's just for starters.

Karl Rove did it!

In the kids' cartoon, *Family Circus*, an imaginary character in the form of a tot-sized ghost appears whenever the children in the family get in trouble. The character's name: "NOT ME." Spilled milk? "NOT ME" did it! Crayon scribblings on the wall? Broken toys? "NOT ME" did it!

Bush advisor Karl Rove is the "NOT ME" phantom haunting the liberal family circus.

Take the scandal we now know as Rathergate. In September 2004, bloggers and conservative Internet forum board members blew the whistle on CBS News's attempted sabotage of the presidential campaign. The web watchdogs provided crushing evidence that CBS's Dan Rather and staff relied on obviously bogus military documents for a September 8, 2004, *60 Minutes II* hit piece challenging President Bush's National Guard service during the Vietnam War.[14] Two weeks later, the network was forced to admit that "CBS cannot prove that the documents are authentic."[15]

In January 2005, an independent internal report excoriated Rather and company for their "myopic zeal" in recklessly pursuing the story—an arrogance that was compounded by the news executives' "rigid and blind" defense of the *60 Minutes II* segment. The debacle resulted in the firing of three executives and the piece's producer, Mary Mapes, as well as the premature semi-retirement of Rather, the veteran CBS anchor and liberal icon.

The unhinged Left's response: *Karl Rove did it!*

Then-Democratic National Committee Chairman Terry McAuliffe initially denied that anyone in his party or on the Kerry campaign staff had anything to do with the CBS News fiasco. Instead, he pointed to the GOP. "I can unequivocally say that no one involved here at the Democratic National Committee had anything at all to do with any of those documents. If I were an aspiring young journalist, I think I would ask Karl Rove that question." [16]

McAuliffe's denial of Democrat involvement in the CBS story was subsequently undermined by the network's own internal investigators. They determined that one of CBS producer Mary Mapes' sources, retired Texas National Guard officer Bill Burkett, had "pressed her to arrange for him to be put in touch with someone from the Kerry presidential campaign so that he could provide the campaign with strategic advice on how to rebut the attacks by the 'Swift Boat Veterans for Truth' group." Mapes contacted Joe Lockhart through Chad Clanton, a Kerry campaign official who had been quoted by Mapes' husband, a newspaper reporter, in an article on an unrelated matter. The panel found Mapes' "contact to be highly inappropriate." [17]

The investigators noted that the fake National Guard memos segment "had a strong political focus and it was to air in the middle of a hotly contested presidential campaign. While it is certainly proper to receive information from a variety of sources, this contact crossed the line as, at a minimum, it gave the appearance of a political bias and could have been perceived as a news organization's assisting a campaign as opposed to reporting on a story." [18]

The panel's conclusions didn't stop Democrat Congressman Maurice Hinchey of New York from echoing McAuliffe's theory even more explicitly. A month after the CBS News internal report was published, Hinchey was still blaming Rathergate on Rove and his shadowy Republican operatives. The indispensable blog Little Green Footballs was the first to report on Hinchey's remarks at a constituent town hall in February 2005:

> **Hinchey:** They've had a very very direct, aggressive attack on the, on the media, and the way it's handled. Probably the most flagrant example of that is the way they set up Dan Rather. Now, I mean, I have my own beliefs about how that happened: It originated with Karl Rove, in my belief, in the White House. They set that up with those false papers.

Why did they do it? They knew that Bush was a draft dodger. They knew that he had run away from his responsibilities in the Air National Guard in Texas, gone out of the state intentionally for a long period of time. They knew that he had no defense for that period in his life. And so what they did was, expecting that that was going to come up, they accentuated it; they produced papers that made it look even worse. And they—and they distributed those out to elements of the media. And it was only—what, like was it CBS? Or whatever, whatever which one Rather works for.

They—the people there—they finally bought into it, and they, and they aired it. And when they did, they had 'em. They didn't care who did it! All they had to do is to get some element of the media to advance that issue. Based upon the false papers that they produced.

Audience member: Do you have any evidence for that?

Hinchey: Yes I do. Once they did that—

Audience: [murmuring]

Hinchey:—once they did that, then it undermined everything else about Bush's draft dodging. Once they were able to say, "This is false! These papers are not accurate, they're, they're, they're false, they've been falsified." That had the effect of taking the whole issue away.

Audience member: So you have evidence that the papers came from the Bush administration?

Hinchey: No. I—that's my belief.

Audience member: OK.

Hinchey: And I said that. In the very beginning. I said, "It's my belief that those papers, and that setup, originated with Karl Rove and the White House."

Audience member: Don't you think it's irresponsible to make charges like that?

Hinchey: No I don't. I think it's very important to make charges like that. I think it's very important to combat this kind of activity in every way that you can. And I'm willing—and most people are not—to step forward in situations like this and take risks.

Audience: [clapping and cheering]

Hinchey: I consider that to be part of my job, and I'm gonna continue to do it. [19]

Congressman Hinchey, whose salary has been paid by U.S. taxpayers since 1992, was at least a man of his unhinged word. Four days later, he repeated the unsubstantiated allegations on Fox News Channel's *Hannity and Colmes*:

Hannity: Where is the proof, sir?

Hinchey: The proof? There's a whole host of proof.

Hannity: Give it to us right now. Where's the proof?

Hinchey: A host of circumstantial proof. You say you don't want to talk about the past, but the past is indicative of the present and the future. And if you look in the past here you find that Mr. Rove has a history of dirty tricks ...

Hannity: History of dirty tricks? Congressman ...

Hinchey: ...going all the way back to the 1970s right on up to the present.

Hannity: What evidence do ...

Hinchey: And—and besides that ...

Hannity: Wait. Let me finish the question. What evidence do you have that Karl Rove manufactured the CBS scandal? Because if you don't have direct evidence in this case, sir, you owe the man an apology. You owe your constituents an apology. And you owe America an apology for your bizarre conspiracy theory.

Hinchey: That's your opinion, but it's a very bad opinion. I don't owe anybody an apology.

It's my responsibility as a representative to go to Washington, represent my constituents and come back and tell them what's going on there and also my interpretation of what's going on there.

Hannity: So let me get this. So you ...

Hinchey: ...Sean, and I think you know that.

Hannity: Without any proof, without any evidence or substantiation, you can accuse the president's top advisor of conspiring to bring down a network. And you have no evidence that you can bring this audience right now, none whatsoever, except he's played dirty tricks before? That's your evidence?

That's embarrassing, Congressman.

Hinchey: I know it's embarrassing...

Hannity: To you.

Hinchey: It's embarrassing to you.

Hannity: To you.

Hinchey: It's embarrassing to you because of what you think you represent. It's not embarrassing to me.

My theory is that the White House political operation was behind the development of those false documents, those forged documents...[20]

The almighty and omniscient Karl Rove has certainly been a busy man. Kennedy assassination conspiracist James Fetzer speculated that Rove and other GOP leaders may have had a hand in murdering Democrat Senator Paul Wellstone of Minnesota, who died in a plane accident in the fall of 2002.[21] A year later, the left-wing website BuzzFlash.com warned that Rove might soon be planting weapons of mass destruction in Iraq. "[W]hatever Karl comes up with," the site's lead editorial warned, with mixed metaphors galore, "we are sure that the press will jump onto it like a grasshopper onto stalks of Kansas wheat. Karl knows that he controls the mainstream media like a circus trainer controls his elephants."[22]

Indeed, after pulling the puppet strings at CBS News, Rove then connived with Osama bin Laden to help the Republican Party. That's the story according to the "most trusted man in America," Walter Cronkite. Cronkite put forth his Rovian conspiracy after CNN's Larry King showed him a videotape of bin Laden released in late October 2004 on the al-Jazeera satellite network:

King: OK, Walter. What do you make of this?

Cronkite: Well, I make it out to be initially the reaction that it's a threat to us, that unless we make peace with him, in a sense, we can expect further attacks. He did not say that precisely, but it sounds like that when he says…

King: The warning.

Cronkite: What we just heard. So now the question is basically right now, how will this affect the election? And I have a feeling that it could tilt the election a bit. In fact, I'm a little inclined to think that Karl Rove, the political manager at the White House, who is a very clever man, he probably set up bin Laden to this thing.[23]

Uh, wait a minute. Wasn't the Democrats' rap on Bush that he shouldn't be re-elected because he *hadn't* found bin Laden yet? Maybe they've become part of the Rovian cabal, too! The horror!

Cronkite wasn't the only aging liberal with Rove on the brain. Author/crank Norman Mailer took to doyenne Arianna Huffington's group blog to offer his unsolicited opinion on *Newsweek's* slanderous story about Koran desecration at the Guantanamo Bay detention facility for enemy combatants. After the story prompted fiery riots across the Middle East, the magazine retracted the unsubstantiated allegation.[24]

So whose fault was it? Mailer rattled his Reynolds wrap:

At present, I have a few thoughts I can certainly not prove, but the gaffe over the Michael Isikoff story in Newsweek concerning the Koran and the toilet is redolent with bad odor. Who, indeed, was Isikoff's supposedly reliable Pentagon source? One's counter-espionage hackles rise. If you want to discredit a Dan Rather or a Newsweek crew, just feed them false information from a hitherto reliable source. You learn that in Intelligence 101A.

Counter-espionage often depends on building 'reliable sources.' You construct such reliability item by secret item, all accurate. That is seen by the intelligence artists as a necessary expenditure. It gains the source his credibility. Then, you spring the trap.

As for the riots at the other end, on this occasion, they, too, could have been orchestrated. We do have agents in Pakistan, after all, not to mention Afghanistan.

Obviously, I can offer no proof of any of the above...At the age of eighty-two I do not wish to revive old paranoia, but Lenin did leave us one valuable notion, one, at any rate. It was "Whom?" When you cannot understand a curious matter, ask yourself, "Whom? Whom does this benefit?" Dare I suggest that our Right has just gained a good deal by way of this matter? In every covert Department of Dirty Tricks, whether official, semi-official, or off-the-wall, great pride is best obtained by going real deep into down-and-dirty-land.[25]

"Mainstream" media commentators Keith Olbermann and Craig Crawford wallowed in the same conspiracy theory on MSNBC.

"Something smells funny to me about this *Newsweek* apology, then retraction. Do you sense the same thing? And what the heck are we smelling?" Olbermann bloviated. Crawford indulged Olbermann's paranoia: "This is a pattern we've seen before, Keith. We saw it in the CBS case. As bad as the supposedly fake memorandum that Dan Rather used in the '60 Minutes' report on Bush's National Guard service, bad as that was, they did show it to the administration and ahead of time. It does make you wonder if sometimes they set up the news media."[26]

Such bizarre talk followed in the wake of the first presidential debate in October 2004. Obsessed with wrinkles on the back of President Bush's jacket, the grassy-knoll faction of the Democratic Party spread rumors of Bush being prompted through a hidden earpiece. One Bush-basher started a blog called "Is Bush Wired?" But again, it wasn't just the conspiracy theorists—the prominent left-leaning online journal, Salon.com, actually started investigating "Bush's mystery bulge"[27] and asked "Was President Bush literally channeling Karl Rove in his first debate with John Kerry?"

A follow-up Salon.com article trumpeted the expert opinion of one Dr. Robert M. Nelson, a NASA senior research scientist and "an international authority on image analysis." After spending hours using Photoshop software to enhance the texture in Bush's jacket, Dr. Nelson concluded that the bulge on Bush's back was "consistent with the appearance of an electronic device worn in that manner." A consummate observer of the moon and Mars, Dr. Nelson further explained: "We look at the angle of the light and the length of shadow they leave. In this case, that's clearly a crater that's under the horizontal line—it's clearly a rim of a bulge protruding upward, one due to forces pushing it up from beneath."[28]

The *Washington Post* followed suit with "Bulge under President's Coat in First Debate Stirs Speculation."[29] *Mother Jones* weighed in: "Was Bush wired? Sure looks like it."[30]

Of course, for any rational person, the answer was a lot more obvious. Secret Service sources later confirmed to *The Hill* newspaper that the mystery bulge was, in fact, "a strap holding his bulletproof vest in place."[31]

President Bush handled the off-the-wall charges with good grace and humor. When asked whether he had a "sound system" or "electrical signal" emanating from inside his jacket, Bush said to ABC's Charlie Gibson with bemusement: "[P]lease explain to me how it works so that maybe if I were ever to debate again I could figure it out. I guess the assumption was is that if I were straying off course they would, kind of like a hunting dog, they would punch a buzzer and I would jerk back into, into place. It's just absurd."[32]

Well put. *Too* well put. The dastardly Karl Rove must have transmitted those words into Bush's implanted brain chip from an undisclosed location, with Dan Rather and Osama bin Laden providing covert technical assistance to the White House Department of Dirty Tricks.

Do you Feel a Draft?

Young liberals caught the conspiracy virus, too. In September 2004, college students across the country started receiving alarmist e-mails warning them they might be drafted if President Bush won re-election. Call it "Crock the Vote."

The text of the scare message read as follows:

Mandatory draft for boys and girls (ages 18-26)
Starting June 15, 2005

There is pending legislation in the House and Senate, S89 and HR 163, to reinstate mandatory draft for boys and girls (ages 18-26) starting June 15, 2005. This plan includes women in the draft, eliminates higher education as a shelter, and makes it difficult to cross into Canada.

The Bush administration is quietly trying to get these bills passed now, while the public's attention is on the elections. The Bush administration plans to begin mandatory draft in the spring of 2005, just after the 2004 presidential election.

- The Congress has added $28 million to the 2004 Selective Service System budget to prepare for this military draft that could start as early as June 15, 2005.
- Bush has ordered the Selective Service to report to him by March 31, 2005, on their readiness to implement the draft by June 2005.
- The Pentagon has quietly begun a public campaign to fill all 10,350 draft board positions and 11,070 appeals board slots nationwide.

Please act on this:

- Tell everyone you know—parents, aunts and uncles, grandparents, godparents, friends, teachers
- Call and write to your U.S. Senator and your U.S. Representatives and ask them why they aren't telling their constituents about these bills.[33]

One mother whose daughter received the e-mail at the University of Arizona told me her "daughter said a lot of students are getting the same e-mail and they are believing it and saying they won't vote for Bush because of it."[34] An MTV *Choose or Lose* segment[35] hyped similar rumors and the Rock the Vote youth campaign warned: "A NEW MILITARY DRAFT? It's on everyone's lips. And it directly affects YOU."[36] Democrats Max Cleland (Georgia), Tim

Ryan (Ohio), and Howard Dean (Neptune) exacerbated fears. And on the campaign trail, John Kerry intoned: "With George Bush, the plan for Iraq is more of the same and the great potential of a draft."[37]

Never mind that the chief sponsor of the House bill to restart the draft was Democrat Charlie Rangel; all 14 co-sponsors of his bill were Democrats; the lone sponsor of the Senate version was Democrat Ernest Hollings; and the Pentagon and White House opposed both bills.

Also false: the e-mail's claims about the Selective Service, whose budget was flat and whose staff was scheduled to shrink, not expand. The non-partisan FactCheck.org further noted that the fear-mongering about toughened draft evader rules with Canada was baseless and that the effort to fill draft board positions had been routine and ongoing for years.[38]

But instead of telling the truth and dispelling the big myth of the Bush draft, the mainstream media ignored the facts and stoked the fears. CBS News reporter Richard Schlesinger indulged the conspiracists, featuring a scared mom named Beverly Cocco and her draft-age sons decrying the threat.[39] "I go to bed every night and I pray and I actually get sick to my stomach," Cocco moaned. "I'm very worried; I'm scared. I'm absolutely scared; I'm petrified." The CBS story identified her as a "Republican," but failed to note Cocco's position as Philadelphia-area chapter president of a leftist-dominated, anti-war advocacy group called People Against the Draft. Nor did the story note the factual inaccuracies of the scare-mongering e-mails.

Questioned about the biased use of the e-mails, Schlesinger told investigative blogger Bill Ardolino of INDC Journal (emphasis added): "The fact is, they were going around. I know several people that got them, and it's gotten people all riled up. *Whether or not there's any reality to there being a draft, is almost besides the point.*"[40]

CBS News wasn't the only media outlet hyping the draft conspiracists and failing to disclose the political activism of purportedly ordinary Americans fearful of draft reinstatement. *NBC Nightly News's* Jim Miklaszewski had his own Beverly Cocco in the form of young Jeremy Tor:

Miklaszewski: Twenty-year-old Jeremy Tor, a junior at the University of Arizona, got the scare of his life recently: an e-mail that said if George Bush is re-elected, he will reinstate the military draft.

Jeremy Tor: Well, I thought this is incredible. You know, to suggest that a draft is going to be instituted, you know, harkening back to the days of Vietnam, which is a scary, scary thought.[41]

What *NBC Nightly News* didn't report was that the petrified Mr. Tor had his mind made up about President Bush and the election a long time ago. A December 2003 article in the *Arizona Daily Wildcat*, Tor's campus newspaper, revealed that Tor was a Democrat who supported John Edwards in the primary. His club, Students for Edwards, sprang up on campus at the same time as the Students for Dean group, led by student Jonna Lopez. The article said that Tor's "biggest priority" (after nailing down that Rock the Vote! internship and acing his Peace Studies 101 class, we presume) was removing Bush from the White House.[42]

In spite of President Bush's re-election, the Doomsday date of June 15, 2005, came and went without the apocalyptically predicted draft. Ironically, the same week as that bogus deadline, Democrat Congressman Charlie Rangel vowed to reintroduce his draft bill.[43]

Is he really that unhinged, or is he on a secret GOP payroll? Or both?

Attack of the "Mother Machines"

The loss of the presidential election sent leading Democrats, including Teresa Heinz Kerry, deeper into the paranoia pits. The wife of the defeated presidential candidate openly questioned the validity of the voting results: "Two brothers own 80 percent of the [voting] machines used in the United States," and it is "very easy to hack into the mother machines."[44]

Asked for evidence of her "mother machine"-hacking theory about Diebold Corporation, America's leading vote machine manufacturer, the mouthy ketchup queen refused to elaborate. Instead, she stuck to the kind of cryptic paranoia that always stirs up Democratic anxieties: "I fear for '06."[45]

Bev Harris, a left-wing critic of Diebold who became a media darling with her "black box" theories of master hacking, was all too eager to explain her own suspicions: "There are some who are using election-manipulation techniques to transfer a block of power to their friends. This is a business plan, a form of organized crime."[46] A bumper-crop of voter conspiracy websites sprung up to echo those charges, including Votescam.com, CountTheVote.com, and "Ohio Voter Suppression News." Bush opponents envisioned software "back doors" that would be used by Republican operatives to monkey around with votes. The day before the election, left-wing rumor-mongers warned: "Diebold hacked! New information indicates that hackers may be targeting the central computers counting our votes tomorrow. All county elections officials who use modems to transfer votes from polling places to the central vote-counting server should disconnect the modems now."[47]

After the Kerry/Edwards defeat, the tinfoilers naturally picked up where they had left off before Election Day. "Evidence mounts that the vote may have been hacked," wailed CommonDreams.org. "Fraud took place in the 2004 election through electronic voting machines," asserted BlackBoxVoting.org.

Glitches happen, of course. No technology is fool-proof. Yet unhinged Democrats portrayed occasional errors as a nefarious Vote-Swallowing Grand Master Plan. The mother machine theorists obsessed on Diebold's CEO, a Bush supporter, while conveniently ignoring the company's election-systems division chief, a registered Democrat, and its director of marketing, an exclusive, deep-pocketed Democratic donor and Kerry supporter.[48]

Following on the heels of the internet paranoiacs, three Democrats in Congress—John Conyers Jr. of Michigan, Jerrold Nadler of New York, and Robert Wexler of Florida—sent a letter to the Government Accountability Office demanding an investigation of voting machines. A Democratic House candidate in Florida, Jeff Fisher, claimed to have evidence not only that the Florida election was hacked, but also of who hacked it and how. The political aspirant told CommonDreams.org that "these same people had previously hacked the Democratic primary race in 2002 so that Jeb Bush would not have to run against Janet Reno, who presented a real threat to Jeb, but instead against Bill McBride, who Jeb beat." That scheme was a dress rehearsal for 2004—"practice for a national effort," Fisher reportedly told the website.[49]

Sore losers also cited the discrepancies between exit polls and vote tallies to bolster their suspicions of a stolen election. But as liberal journalist David Corn pointed out, left-wing accusers couldn't even stick to a single conspiracy theory. On the one hand, they accused Diebold and other vendors of "put[ting] in the fix via the paperless touch-screen machines." On the other hand, they claimed that conspirators in Florida rigged "optical-scan voting, not electronic touch-screen voting." Or was it both? A Unified Mother and Father Machine Convergence Conspiracy?

Corn observed that scholars at Cornell, Harvard, and Stanford—those renowned bastions of right-wing conservatism—dismissed recycled Florida fraud allegations as "baseless."[50] The Voting Technology Project, a cooperative effort between the California Institute of Technology and the Massachusetts Institute of Technology, found "no particular patterns" relating to voting systems and the final results.[51] But suspicions of a "stolen" election refused to subside.

Democrats.com spread further hysteria over alleged "widespread election fraud in Cleveland."[52] In Cuyahoga County, Ohio, where Cleveland is located, Kerry defeated Bush by a 220,000-vote margin. Agitated number-crunchers noted that the county's election results web page appeared to show that actual voters exceeded the number of registered voters—and by large numbers in some swing precincts. Diabolical tampering? No. A simple reporting quirk: Turns out that in even-numbered years during congressional elections, the county's results are grouped by the larger contests on the ballot, not by precincts.[53]

Undeterred by the bottom-line fact that John Kerry simply did not have enough votes to win Ohio, even accounting for all the alleged fraud, the Reverend Jesse Jackson accused Ohio Secretary of State Kenneth Blackwell, a black Republican, of fixing votes for the GOP.

Q: So you think Blackwell stole the election for Bush?

Jackson: It was under his domain to have enough machines; the machine calibration, tabulation issue. You could rig the machines. We have reason to believe it was rigged.[54]

Such wild speculation was convincing enough for Democrat Senator Barbara Boxer of California to lead a pointless challenge to Ohio's electoral votes.[55] "Why did, in [the] Columbus area alone, an estimated 5,000 to 10,000 voters leave polling places, out of frustration, without having voted? How many more never bothered to vote after they heard about this?" Boxer asked. Congressman Stephanie Tubbs-Jones of Ohio played Boxer's tag-team partner on the House side. "What happened in Ohio may well have been repeated in counties across this country," Tubbs Jones speculated.

But as former U.S. Civil Rights Commissioner Peter Kirsanow noted, "If there was a conspiracy to disenfranchise Ohio voters, black or white, its execution was profoundly inept. Ohio voter turnout increased from 4.9 million in 2000 to 5.5 million in 2004. Estimated black-voter turnout alone rose by 25 percent."[56] A spokesman for Ohio's secretary of state told the *Washington Post* that census data showed that black turnout reached record levels in 2004, increasing by 84,000 from 2000.[57]

Hoping desperately that something—anything—would stick, unhinged protesters flung charges that the Buckeye State's 160,000 provisional ballots were rife with irregularities and that an election-swaying number had gone diabolically uncounted. The reality was just the opposite, Kirsanow reported: Ohio counted a higher percentage of provisional ballots than any other state in the nation.[58]

Watching the futility of her empty efforts flash before her eyes as Bush's victory was certified, Senator Boxer became unglued on national TV—and actually *cried* (fortunately, Boxer's press aides confiscated the stuffed donkey she was clutching before the cameras went live). Her partners-in-whine disrupted the vote certification in an unprecedented two-hour tantrum during a joint session of Congress. But Congressman Tubbs-Jones' hometown newspaper, the *Cleveland Plain Dealer*, chastised the representative and Reverend Jackson for their obstinacy and paranoia in a scathing editorial titled "Let it go:"

> The 176 Democrats who sit on Ohio's 88 county election boards pondered their jurisdictions' results, accepted their subordinates' good work, and are turning their energies toward the future. Are they all dupes in some Machiavellian Republican scheme? Or do they simply have a firmer grasp of reality than that displayed by the two of you and a handful of unrelenting zealots still ranting in the January rain, eight weeks after the November voting? Yes, long lines built voter frustration. Yes, some electronic machines malfunctioned. Yes, boards rejected more provisional ballots than usual. But such things happen when hundreds of thousands of new voters join the process and new technology debuts under fire. Your doubts notwithstanding, numerous nonpartisan election experts say Ohio did an above-average job. Americans treasure the right to be loudly mistaken—a right you now freely exercise. But for two national figures whose constituencies are among the poorest of the poor, it seems an embarrassing waste of energies sorely needed elsewhere. Fold your mildewed tents, collect your soggy cardboard and focus on the poverty, single-parenthood, and dropout rates that have so impoverished those in whose names you protest too much.[59]

The paper praised Senator John Kerry for having the "good grace and sense" to "go home and resume his life." But over time tinfoil beret-wearer wife Teresa's paranoid pillow-talk apparently took effect. In April 2005, the loser of the 2004 presidential election dredged up allegations of Republican trickery and voter scare tactics in a speech before the left-leaning League of Women Voters: "Last year, too many people were denied their right to vote, too many who tried to vote were intimidated."[60]

The Democrats' 2008 presidential frontrunner, Senator Hillary Clinton of New York, is already singing from the same hysteria-promoting hymn book.

Sarcastically praising the elections in Afghanistan and Iraq, Senator Clinton told Minnesota Democrats: "I believe that the right to vote and the obligation to count all the votes should be promoted not just in the Middle East, but in the Middle West! And in the Northeast! And in the Southeast! And in every. Corner. Of. The. United. States. Of. A-MEH-rica!"[61]

The crowd went wild. Senator Clinton continued: Too many minorities and college students have been "denied an equal right" to vote, she exclaimed. Her "moderate" solution? An election reform bill that allows illegal aliens! And felons! And people without IDs to vote!

Despite such ominous insinuations, the civil rights lawsuit based on election fraud claims in Ohio was dismissed outright, and in June 2005, a study sponsored by the Democratic National Committee (fox, meet henhouse) found no evidence of widespread election fraud in Ohio.[62] DNC chair Howard Dean attempted to spin the results as proof that Republicans conspired to suppress votes in heavily Democratic precincts, but one of the co-authors of the report immediately ditched Dean's diatribe. "Where the partisan bias came from, where it went, we really have no basis for making any assertion about that and I don't believe the report makes any statements about that," said Cornell University professor of government Walter Mebane, Jr.[63]

To the extent that specific incidents of fraud did take place in Ohio, it was left-wing groups behind the wheel, including activist organizations such as the Association of Community Organizations for Reform Now (ACORN), America Coming Together, the American Federation of Labor-Congress of Industrial Organizations (AFL-CIO), and the NAACP National Voter Fund, which were fingered in fraudulent voter registration schemes.

Democratic leaders kept quiet about these and other examples of bona fide voter fraud. And not a peep was heard from the party of peace and tolerance about the far loonier tactics of liberals gone wild—from the drive-by shootings targeting GOP headquarters across the country, to the union mobs who stormed local GOP offices in Florida and the Midwest, to the anti-Bush thugs who burned swastikas into Republican homeowners' lawns, to the Democratic staffers charged with slashing the tires of 20 Republican get-out-the-vote vans on Election Day.

The "NOT ME!" phantoms worked overtime to intimidate, sabotage, and suppress Republican votes. Karl Rove and his all-powerful Republican Dirty

CHAPTER THREE

When Angry Democrats Attack

"We are committed to resolving our differences in a spirit of civility, hope, and mutual respect."

2004 Democratic Party platform [1]

Smashed windows. Slashed tires. Burnt lawns. Bullet holes. Bloody noses.

The 2004 presidential campaign was littered with these remnants of Democratic incivility, destruction, and rage. 'Twas the season of Liberals Behaving Badly. Leftists Gone Wild! But you wouldn't know it from reading the mainstream media's coverage.

As I tracked the nationwide outbreak of election intimidation, harassment, and violence committed by Kerry supporters last year, I wondered: How many hate crime anecdotes does it take before the mainstream media label them a trend? If the victims are politically correct, all it takes is one or two stories. One alleged name-calling. A few alleged acts of vandalism. A suspicious arson here or there.[2] In an instant, an unsubstantiated attack against ethnic, racial, religious, or sexual minorities becomes undisputed evidence of an epidemic of violence. A symbol of rising hate. A national crisis.

But what happens when the targets are the wrong kind of victim? What happens when conservatives and Republicans are on the receiving end of discriminatory threats, harassment, or worse?

Chirp, chirp, chirp. Nothing but the sound of crickets piercing the dead silence in America's newsrooms.

Fortunately, alternative conservative media kept on top of election-related mayhem aimed at Bush/Cheney supporters. While some Democratic apologists downplayed the incidents as run-of-the-mill pranks and engaged in everybody-does-it equivalence, it became clear to rational observers that left-wing activists had escalated their campaign attacks to an unprecedented level.

Simple mischief turned into open-season malice. And although the election campaign came to a close, the physical assaults and threats against conservatives and Republicans have yet to cease.

Liberals like Michael Moore promised to do "whatever it takes" to win the 2004 presidential election.[3] If it had been conservatives spouting that slogan as glass flew and lawns smoked and blood dripped, Karl Rove would have come under federal investigation. Amnesty International would have sent monitors. And the *New York Times* would have called for a National Commission for Reconciliation and Healing.

For too long, the Democrat Party officials and their fellow travelers have claimed moral superiority as the champions of peace, love, and understanding. But with their very own fists of fury and knee-jerk hatred, they have shattered the myth of liberal tolerance. Completely and irreparably. The evidence is overwhelming.

Fight Club

Politics is a rough-and-tumble world. Both major political parties fight hard on the stump and in election-year ads. But time and again in 2004, Democrats crossed the line from verbal sparring to violent brawling. Like mild-mannered Bruce Banners who transmogrified into rampaging Incredible Hulks, granola-munching liberals burst out of their Birkenstocks to show their true, frightening colors. *YEAAARGH!*

In Everett, Washington, a 52-year-old man accosted teenager Perry Valentine at a GOP counter-protest of a John Kerry summer fundraiser. The Bush supporters gathered peacefully across the street from the event. Valentine, 19, held two Bush signs and wore a Kerry sticker on the seat of his pants.[4] Video taken by KING-TV showed the men standing side-by-side on a sidewalk. Then, out of nowhere, the older man suddenly threw a punch at the teenager's face. The boy's head snapped back; the attack knocked the cowboy hat off his head. His Bush signs dropped to the ground. Police intervened and took the unhinged Kerry supporter into custody.[5]

The local newspaper, the *Everett Herald*, covered the attack in an article headlined, "Throng vocal but well-behaved during visit: A Kerry supporter hits a Bush supporter, but the rest of the scuffles are verbal."[6] Well-behaved?

The Republican National Convention attracted mobs of unstable Leftists to New York City. Cops arrested some 1,800 troublemakers (compared to a mere half-dozen arrests[7] of protesters at the Democratic National Convention in Boston). Among those arrested at the GOP event was Jamal Holiday, 21, a supposed "peace" protester who was caught on videotape punching and stomping a police officer until he was unconscious outside the convention site during a march held by the Poor People's Economic Human Rights Campaign.[8] Leftist websites hailed Holiday as a "political prisoner."

The violence continued after the convention and raged right up until Election Day—and it wasn't just hot-headed young punks throwing punches. In Cincinnati, a heckler who interrupted a John Kerry speech with hostile questions about Kerry's war record was thrown to the floor by a Kerry supporter wearing a Sheet Metal Workers union shirt. "He grabbed me and put me in a headlock, twisting it pretty hard," said the heckler, Michael Russell, 48, of Foster, Kentucky "I was trying to get away from him, then I was shoved to the floor and kicked. By that time, I just wanted to get out of there."[9]

Kerry criticized Russell's disruptive behavior—"it's a terrific tactic of the Bush team, they love to disrupt, they love to interrupt"—but said nothing about the assault.[10]

In Gainsville, Florida, a Democrat college instructor named David Philip McCally burst into a Young Republicans club meeting at the local Republican headquarters and walloped a life-size, cardboard cutout of President Bush.[11] But pounding on poor George W. wasn't enough to assuage McCally's pent-up anger. He stormed out of the GOP office and confronted Travis Horn, 32, the chairman of the Alachua County Republican Executive Committee.

McCally bragged about his Ph.D. and called Horn "a stupid Republican" before launching into a string of profanity-laced epithets. Then he punched Horn, knocked him into a wall, busted his lip, and injured his nose. McCally was charged with misdemeanor battery and criminal mischief.

Just a few weeks later, some 60 Democrats in Orlando, Florida, stormed a local GOP headquarters office to wreak havoc as part of a campaign of disruption orchestrated by the AFL-CIO, the country's largest labor union. As the unhinged crew rammed through the entryway, they broke the wrist of one Republican campaign volunteer. One of the union demonstrators reportedly slammed the head of another GOP worker against the office's glass door. The assailant was never caught. The protesters justified their actions by blaming President Bush's "negative campaign."[12]

Union leaders in Florida coordinated similar attacks in Tampa and Miami, where Lenny Alvicar, local spokesman for the Bush-Cheney campaign said about 20 volunteers, including elderly people working phone banks, were at the headquarters when the union workers barged in. "It was pushing, it was intimidation," Alvicar said. "In some cases more than just disruptive but in fact violently intimidating volunteers."[13] Katherine Lambert, a phone bank volunteer for Bush/Cheney in the Orlando suburbs, told me from her office the day after the union thugs struck: "We have all the doors locked and my 23-year-old son told me to sit away from the window today." Her colleagues were so scared that they closed the drapes as well. In response, AFL-CIO spokeswoman Esmeralda Aguilar smugly insisted the coordinated attacks were "peaceful" and that no one was intimidated.[14]

First step: Deflect blame. Second step: Deny, deny, deny. Third step: Blame Bush's "negative" campaign.

The attacks spread to Minnesota, where angry Kerry supporters and members of the Democratic Farm Labor (DFL) Party attempted to raid GOP headquarters in St. Paul. The mob of Democrats shouted into bullhorns and pushed against the office door, startling volunteers and intimidating voters picking up tickets to see President Bush at an upcoming campaign stop. The head of the state GOP, Ron Eibensteiner, pointing to two other recent incidents in which College Republicans were assaulted by Kerry supporters, observed that "the DFL Party and Kerry Campaign can be best described as Anger Incorporated . . . Through their actions, Democrats have shown themselves incapable of governing themselves, much less our nation, during these challenging times."[15]

Wall Street Journal columnist John Fund noted similar attacks by AFL-CIO mobsters in Independence and Kansas City, Missouri, Dearborn, Michigan, and West Allis, Wisconsin.[16] Elsewhere, union steelworkers brawled with Boston College Republicans—taunting them, tearing their signs, and knocking off and smashing one student's glasses.[17] The story was ignored by the *Boston Globe* and national media outlets, but the victims blogged about the incident,[18] which was reported by the conservative-leaning *Boston Herald*,[19] the Drudge Report, and conservative talk radio host Rush Limbaugh.

Violence against Women

For the unhinged, there are no limits of decorum or respect when it comes to political violence—they're always ready to cross the line. Meet Michael Husar, my choice for honorary chairman of Misogynists for Kerry. The 58-year-old male nurse was on a Northwest Airlines flight from New York to Winnepeg, Canada, when he let loose on a female passenger with whom he was discussing politics. Husar was a Kerry supporter; the woman advocated for President Bush in what was initially a friendly debate. When he started losing the argument, Husar lost his marbles. He started getting physically aggressive with his neighbor, so she summoned flight attendants. Husar had been guzzling alcohol from a Snapple bottle; he dumped the remainder on his seat and cursed at the stew-

Democrat Road Rage

Back on land, another madman was on the loose in Sarasota, Florida, targeting Republican Congressman Katherine Harris with his Cadillac. According to an arrest report, Barry Seltzer, 46, intentionally swerved his car onto a sidewalk where Congressman Harris and her supporters were standing and waving at commuters. Seltzer's lawyers denied that he was motivated by partisan bitterness. But a police lieutenant told the *Sarasota Herald-Tribune* that Seltzer, a registered Democrat, had two Kerry-Edwards signs on his lawn and "was eager to discuss his political views when he was interviewed at the station." Harris told police she was "afraid for her life" as the car barreled towards her. Seltzer, charged with aggravated felony assault with a deadly weapon, scoffed that he was just "exercising my political expression."[22]

ardesses. Described as "drunk" and "belligerent," Husar's partisan air rage forced the pilot to dump fuel and make an emergency landing.[20]

Husar, his lawyer said, was "mad as hell."[21] No kidding.

Exercising political expression is precisely what five pro-life college students were doing at a John Kerry rally in Washington, D.C., in April 2004 when they were dragged off by liberal abortion rights' activists. The pro-life women, all from George Washington University, dared to answer NARAL and Planned Parenthood chanters who asked, "What do we want?" by responding "Life!" According to LifeNews.com, that set off the pro-abortion goon squad. "They became angry and began to push and shove the pro-life women," LifeNews reported. One pro-abortion rights' activist told one of the peaceful pro-lifers, Suanne Edmiston, that her mother should have aborted her.[23] "I have never been manhandled like that before—pushed around, shoved and tossed—it was ridiculous," Edmiston said. "So much for 'my body, my choice.'"[24]

A freelance photographer/blogger who witnessed the incident, Bill Ardolino of INDC Journal, noted that uniformed police and Secret Service agents stood on the sidelines and refused to intervene to help the women—one of whom sustained a foot injury when she was dragged across the gravel.[25] Ardolino, who is pro-choice, was himself prevented from taking photos of the brawl by an irate pro-abortion rights' activist.

The video cameras were rolling, however, at the University of Arizona in October 2004 when two scary-looking hoodlums hurled a custard cream pie at conservative author Ann Coulter as she answered questions from students after a speech. Phillip Edgar Smith and William Zachary Wolff, both 24, rushed the stage and ran to the podium where Coulter stood. She gasped audibly as they threw the pie, which brushed her in the face and shoulder. College Republicans in the audience tackled the assailants, who were promptly arrested by campus police. As the pie-throwers were led away in handcuffs, Coulter gave her violent opponents a trademark verbal lashing: "From that far away they can't even hit me?"[26] According to cops, the deranged duo had plotted the assault on Coulter for two days. They sniveled that they were "throwing the pies at her ideas, not at her."[27] Maybe that's why they missed.

Liberal commentators and critics greeted the physical attack with sickening glee. Left-wing *Vanity Fair* writer James Wolcott posted a vulgar exultation on his blog: "The skank can shift ass on a dime."[28] Gawker, another liberal blog, cheered the chance to "listen to Ann Coulter's panicked gasp when the pies start coming."[29] The Democrats.com website gloated: "It would take a lot more than one cream pie to sweeten this miserable sourpuss up! We hear she kills rats with her teeth and eats broken bottles for breakfast!"[30]

Coulter's detractors celebrated again in May 2005 when 19-year-old University of Texas at Austin student Ajai Prasad Raj disrupted her lecture with an obscene rant. According to a campus police affidavit, Raj fumed "What do you think about conservative men that all they do with their wives is fuck them in the ass" and then ran to his seat making vulgar gestures "simulating masturbation." Ick. Raj was arrested and charged with misdemeanor disorderly conduct.

Cops. Children. The elderly. Women. When angry Democrats attack, no person is safe. And neither is our property.

Vandals and Thieves and Slashers, oh my!

Every election has its share of pranksters. But 2004 was the year that unhinged left-wingers drove through the guardrails of civilized political discourse and straight over the cliff. Yes, there were scattered instances of Republican protesters run amok—a Bush supporter shouting rude slogans here, a College Republican getting rowdy there. But the Democrats' path of destruction on the campaign trail was unrivaled. As the coordinated union sieges on GOP headquarters commenced, an astonishing number of campaign offices and private homes were shot at, ransacked, robbed, and targeted in the 10 weeks leading up to the election.

The Bush-Cheney office in Knoxville, Tennessee, had its plate-glass windows shattered by gunfire before volunteers showed up for work. No one was hurt. But Bush-Cheney volunteer campaign coordinator Suzanne Dewar noted that she originally planned to be in the office early the morning of the shooting. "If I had gotten here a couple hours earlier, I'd have been inside," Dewar said. "And we don't turn the lights on until we open, so they wouldn't have known someone was inside."[31]

Knoxville police department spokesman Darrell DeBusk remarked: "You often hear during campaigns, whether it is presidential or local, of signs being stolen or vandalized, but this morning's shooting takes that to a new level."[32] Exactly.

Luckily, no one was seriously hurt when another gunman fired shots into Bush/Cheney campaign offices in Huntington, West Virginia. About 25 Republicans had gathered around the TV to watch President Bush's speech at the Republican National Convention when a bullet shattered the headquarters' glass windows. A glass shard nicked one volunteer's neck. "To think someone would drive by and take a shot is outrageous," said local GOP politician Greg Hoard. "Someone could have been killed."[33]

The Republican Party campaign office in Mankato, Minnesota, also sustained an apparent gunshot that hit a glass pane near the office entrance. Democrats there denied the targeting was politically motivated, falsely claiming that "these activities are unfortunately happening to both sides." [34] Stacie Paxton, a spokeswoman for the Kerry campaign in Minnesota, called it "a sign of desperation" for Republicans to suggest otherwise. [35] But in reality, the only signs of desperation came from Bush-hating vandals with an appetite for destruction.

At the Spokane, Washington, GOP headquarters, vandals smashed a hole in a wall and stole petty cash. In Bellevue, Washington, burglars broke into GOP headquarters and stole computers that contained the Republican get-out-the-vote database. [36] Thieves also broke into the Cincinnati GOP headquarters, smashing windows and stealing money. [37]

In Arizona, someone called in an anonymous bomb threat against Republican headquarters in Lake Havasu City. The next day, the Arizona GOP headquarters in Flagstaff was vandalized. Anonymous thugs smashed the office front door with a section of cinder block, splattered the building walls with eggs, and left anti-Bush flyers at the crime scene. [38]

Meanwhile, the GOP office in Gallatin County, Montana, was vandalized twice in less than a week. First, holes were punched into a sign on the property. Then on the night of President Bush's acceptance speech at the Republican National Convention, the office's outside walls were spray-painted with anti-Bush slogans and, yes, peace signs. A double-paned window was shattered and the front door was coated with eggs. [39]

In Oregon, someone hurled four large rocks through the plate-glass windows of the Multnomah County Republican headquarters, causing up to $2,000 worth of damage. [40] In Lawrence, Kansas, a rock with a burned American flag wrapped around it was thrown through a window at the Douglas County Republican headquarters. [41] The GOP headquarters in Columbus, Ohio, was covered with anti-Bush graffiti. [42]

Republican offices in Canton, Ohio; Fairbanks, Alaska; Edwardsville, Illinois; and Spokane, Washington, were all vandalized. In Mt. Vernon, Illinois, vandals broke into the GOP headquarters and spray-painted the names of Democratic candidates John Kerry and John Edwards on the walls. According to the *Morning Sentinel*, "the glass doors of the building were painted with expletives and 'flip flop this' was written across Bush/Cheney signs."[43]

In Cass County, North Dakota, someone left dog feces at a local GOP headquarters which had posted pro-troop and pro-military signs. Wade Hannon, a spokesman for the area's antiwar activists, denied involvement or knowledge, but made light of the vandalism by remarking: "The policies of the Republican administration tend to be a bit odorous."[44]

In Madison, Wisconsin, someone burned an 8-foot-by-8-foot Nazi swastika into a homeowner's lawn, which had been decorated with Bush-Cheney signs. The vandals used grass killer to spray the hate symbol. (Apparently, Bush-hating trumps environmentalism.) Several other homes nearby were vandalized in the same fashion.[45] Beth Schaeffer, one of the victims, couldn't believe the partisan attacks, which only targeted homeowners who had Bush/Cheney signs in their yards: "I was like, 'Did we do something to [upset] someone?'" she said.[46]

Vandalism of campaign signs is a bipartisan election-year tradition. But in 2004, Kerry supporters took the custom to the extreme. In Vail, Colorado, one crazed Democrat was so upset he/she used a chainsaw—can we get any nuttier than a *chainsaw*?—to destroy two large Bush/Cheney signs on private property.

In Nashville, Tennessee, Andrew Thurman and Frederick Stevenson stole 71 Bush-Cheney signs; when police stopped them, the suspects were found to have three pistols in their car.[47] Elsewhere, Bush/Cheney signs were not merely stolen or trashed, but burned,[48] defaced with swastikas,[49] cut with a power tool, and urinated on.[50] One enraged Bush-hater named Peter Lizon allegedly used a *bayonet* to punch holes in Republican signs, while his wife allegedly acted as the lookout. Cue the *Psycho* soundtrack.

Perhaps the most insidious act of Democrats' vandalism occurred in Milwaukee in the early morning hours of Election Day 2004, when thugs slashed the tires of 20 vans that had been rented by Wisconsin Republicans as part of their get-out-the-vote effort. Can you imagine the mainstream media uproar if Democrats had been victims of such a vicious attempt to intimidate and suppress their votes in one of the most hotly contested states in the nation?

There was, of course, not a peep of outrage from the editorial writers at the *New York Times* or *Washington Post* or from Jesse Jackson or Jimmy Carter after the attack.[51] Then the bombshell dropped: Law enforcement officers arrested Sowande Ajumoke Omokunde, also known as "Supreme Solar Allah," the 25-year-old son of Democrat congresswoman Gwen Moore, in connection with the tire-slashings. Also arrested: Michael Pratt, son of former Milwaukee Mayor Marvin Pratt, a Democrat; Lewis G. Caldwell; Lavelle Mohammad; and Justin Howell. All were paid Democrat Party staffers.[52]

One of the saboteurs reportedly urinated on a wall to distract a security guard who was watching over the parking lot where the GOP vans were located. The rest of the hoodlums then disabled the vehicles. All plead not guilty, and their cases were scheduled to head to trial in mid-summer 2005. "This was not simply a case of vandalism, it was an act of sabotage on our get-out-the-vote effort," said Chris Lato, the Madison-based communications director for the Wisconsin GOP.[53]

Despite the best (or rather, worst) efforts of the left-wing tire-slashers, window-smashers, lawn-burners, drive-by shooters, cop-bashers, sign-destroyers, pie-throwers, violent assailants, and vandals, the nation re-elected George W. Bush on November 2, 2004. The Democratic campaign for the White House was over. But to this day, the vicious assaults against conservatives show no sign of dying down.

Post-election Rage

In the days following the 2004 election, local GOP offices were once again vandalized—this time in Buffalo, New York,[54] and Raleigh, North Carolina.[55] A Chicago GOP office was vandalized three times between November 2 and November 9. In the third incident, three incendiary devices were thrown through the front window.[56] In March 2005, another group of vandals used concrete blocks to smash through the windows of the Clallam County, Washington, GOP headquarters.[57]

Two days after the election, five students at Apple Valley High School near Minneapolis—two Bush supporters and three Kerry supporters—got into an argument about the election. The students reportedly traded insults, with both sides accusing the other of being gay. Later, in a parking lot located near the school, the Kerry supporters accosted the Bush supporters and beat one of them up with a baseball bat. The boy who wielded the bat was charged with second-degree assault, a felony.[58] According to the Dakota County Attorney's Office, two of the three pro-Kerry students were sentenced to "Aggression Replacement Therapy" and/or mental health screening, something that many Kerry supporters apparently could have used. All three were sentenced to community service or work crew service, required to issue letters of apology, and ordered to have no contact with the victims.[59]

Liberals continued to take aim at conservative speakers as well. During a February 2005 debate between Howard Dean and former Pentagon adviser Richard Perle at Pacific University in Portland, a raving protester named Bruce C. Charles threw a shoe at Perle and shouted "Motherfucking liar."[60] After Charles was dragged away, "progressive" and "tolerant" Portland liberals heckled, booed, and interrupted Perle. Not once did Dean, freshly crowned leader of the party of peace, love, and understanding, chastise the audience for its appalling abuse of Perle.[61]

In April 2005, Josh Medlin, a student at Earlham College in Richmond, Indiana, threw an ice cream pie at *Weekly Standard* editor Bill Kristol's face. After the attack, Kristol pulled out his handkerchief, mopped off his face, and joked, "Just let me finish this point." He finished his speech and answered students' questions for 30 minutes. To their credit, the students at the predominantly liberal, antiwar, Quaker college gave Kristol three well-deserved standing ovations for his good humor. Medlin was immediately suspended pending campus judicial hearings. The local county prosecutor initiated an investigation after Medlin issued a public statement claiming credit for throwing the pie.[62] He was charged with misdemeanor battery and faced trial in August 2005.

Two days after the assault on Kristol, a demonstrator hurled a cup of salad dressing at veteran political commentator Pat Buchanan during his speech to students at Western Michigan University. The assailant, a local community college student named Samuel Mesnick, screamed, "Stop the bigotry!" before emptying the dressing onto Buchanan. Buchanan, a former boxer, calmly cut short his appearance, quipping that he doesn't even like ranch dressing. The assailant reportedly cited the Earlham attack as inspiration.[63]

A week later, at Butler University in Indianapolis, Indiana, yet another lunatic tossed a chocolate cream pie at conservative author David Horowitz, hitting him in the face and chest.[64]

The liberal media elite laughed off the attacks on conservative speakers, just as it had done the previous fall when Ann Coulter was attacked. CBS headlined its report on the Buchanan incident, "A Dressing Down For Pat Buchanan."[65] National Public Radio's story on the Kristol assault mused, "What's a little pie in the face?"[66] An essayist at Daily Kos mocked Horowitz as a "sissyboy racist."[67] "Its [sic] just a fucking cream pie," groused a Kos commenter.[68]

Yes, and it was "just" a pie thrown by two unidentified men that caused corneal abrasions and chemical burns—possibly from the fruit filling—to Tim Eyman's right eye in June 2000. Eyman, a leading conservative activist in Washington State, had just left the Secretary of State's office, where he had filed signatures for a road-building initiative; he was subsequently treated and released at Virginia Mason Hospital in Seattle.[69]

And it was "just" two urine-laced pies that were thrown in the face of right-leaning Dutch politician Pim Fortuyn a few weeks before Fortuyn was assassinated. As the *Washington Times* argues, the Dutch media's blasé reaction to the pie-throwing attack may have subtly encouraged further violence: "once violence, however harmless it at first appears, is accepted as an appropriate means of protest, it tends to escalate. The media should highlight these cases not as the jokes they are perhaps intended to be, but as unacceptable perversions of the First Amendment."[70]

Coulter, Perle, Buchanan, Kristol, and Horowitz are public figures, which makes them easy targets. But private citizens are also vulnerable to Democrats' rage. Consider the frightening case of Tampa, Florida, Bush supporter Michelle Fernandez.

The 35-year-old mother was minding her own business, driving her two kids to a baseball game in March 2005. Her green Ford Expedition proudly sported a Bush/Cheney bumper sticker. Next thing Fernandez knew, someone was trying to run her off the road. Here's a partial transcript of Fernandez's frantic call to 911:

> **(Dispatch:)** 911, what's your emergency? **(Fernandez:)** Um, I was just almost run off the road by a man. He just ran me off because I have a Bush bumper sticker in my car. He had some type of—he drove up next to me with—he had a sign on it like hanging from his—from the passenger window that said something about the war in Iraq. I mean, I am shaking like a leaf. Oh, now he's following me. I'm going to get back on Kennedy now. I don't know what to do!

> **(Dispatch:)** Where are you on Kennedy? **(Fernandez:)** Right now I'm on Kennedy and Arrawana. Look, he just pulled over next to me, he's stopping the car, it's ridiculous, this man! Look he's running after my car. Oh my goodness, he's a fanatic, he's in the middle of the street! Now he's following me. He's trying to hurt us. Look at this, what a moron. Look at him! Idiot.

> **(Dispatch:)** Is that him blowing his horn at you? **(Fernandez:)** No, I was blowing my horn at somebody 'cause I'm running stoplights and everything else to get away from him.[71]

The madman behind the wheel was registered Democrat Nathan Alan Winkler. The sign he wielded as he threatened Fernandez and her children's lives read, "Never Forget Bush's Illegal Oil War Murdered Thousands in Iraq." After several harrowing miles, Fernandez pulled into the ball field where her children's game was scheduled and waited for the police. She supplied them with Winkler's license plate number. Later the cops arrested Winkler at his home.

"I respect him for having his beliefs and feeling so strongly," Fernandez said of the man who terrorized her and her children over a harmless bumper sticker, "But here he is protesting the war and lost lives, and he is going to put me and my children in danger? This man has a serious problem."[72]

Winkler's reckless fury at supporters of President Bush and the War on Terror is extreme. But vicious verbal and physical attacks by angry antiwar activists are far more common than you might think. You won't believe just how crazed the pacifists have become.

Top 10 Unhinged Celebrities

10 Singer/actress **CHER**, who claimed that if Bush were re-elected, the government would round up and quarantine homosexual men.

9 Actor **VINCENT D'ONOFRIO**, the crazed Marine in *Full Metal Jacket*, who was hospitalized immediately after the election suffering from "Bush Flu" (doctors found nothing wrong with him).

8 Actor **MARTIN SHEEN**, who marched through Los Angeles with duct tape over his mouth with the word "peace" written on it.

7 Actor **TIM ROBBINS**, who warned journalists ominously that "Every day, the airwaves are filled with warnings, veiled and unveiled threats, spewed invective and hatred directed at any voice of dissent."

6 Singer **CHRISSY HYNDE**, who told concertgoers that Americans "deserve to get bombed" and "I hope the Muslims win."

5 Actress and Air America talk-radio host **JANEANE GAROFALO**, who called the Patriot Act "a conspiracy of the 43rd Reich."

4 Actress **JULIA STILES**, who told radical leftists she was "afraid that Bill O'Reilly would come with a shotgun at my front door and shoot me for being unpatriotic."

3 Actor **SEAN PENN**, who claimed that FOX News host Bill O'Reilly, shock jock Howard Stern, and the U.S. government are greater threats to the American people than Osama bin Laden.

2 **MICHAEL MOORE**, who reportedly couldn't get out of bed for three days after the 2004 election.

1 Actress **CAMERON DIAZ**, who broke down on national TV and implied that the re-election of President Bush would lead to the legalization of rape.

CHAPTER FOUR

They *Don't* Support Our Troops

"I call on those who question the motives of the president and his national security advisors to join with the rest of America in presenting a united front to our enemies abroad. The men and women who are risking their lives in defense of our national and global security deserve nothing less." [1]

> *Democrat Senator Dick Durbin of Illinois, December 17, 1998, defending President Bill Clinton's military action against Iraq.*

"If I read this to you and did not tell you that it was ... describing what Americans had done to prisoners ... you would most certainly believe this must have been done by Nazis, Soviets in their gulags, or some mad regime—Pol Pot or others—that had no concern for human beings. Sadly, that is not the case. This was the action of Americans in the treatment of their prisoners." [2]

> *Democrat Senator Dick Durbin of Illinois, June 15, 2005, comparing U.S. military personnel to totalitarian torturers and genocidal tyrants.*

Senator Durbin is hardly a small-potatoes Democrat. He's his party's Minority Whip—the Number Two Democrat in the U.S. Senate—not some has-been liberal class clown, like say, Jerry "Moonbeam" Brown. Or Al Gore. So when Durbin speaks on national security matters, people listen. And in the summer of 2005, veterans, troops, their families, and other rational Americans did not like what they heard.

Proving that his Clinton-era plea about "presenting a united front to our enemies abroad" was empty partisan rhetoric, Durbin launched a reckless wartime onslaught against the Bush White House—camouflaged clumsily beneath manufactured outrage over the Guantanamo Bay detention facility.

There is perhaps no greater sign of the Left's unhinged nature than its hysteria over Gitmo. Instead of acknowledging the failed law enforcement strategies of the Clinton years and proposing viable alternatives, the civil liberties absolutists have relentlessly attacked the creation, operation, and legal underpinnings for the detention center housing illegal foreign enemy combatants. Amnesty International led the way with its claim that "Guantanamo has become the gulag of our times."[3] Never mind the real gulags that exist today in Cuba, North Korea, China and, until the Bush administration acted, Iraq. Never mind the fact that Guantanamo's holding pen for terrorists is closer to the Holiday Inn than a real gulag.

While our troops served up Baked Tandoori Chicken Breast and broadcast Muslim prayers over a special intercom system for suspected al Qaeda terrorists captured on the battlefield, the Bush-haters howled about the use of loud Christina Aguilera pop music by interrogators[4] and bogus stories of Koran desecration.[5]

Have there been abuses at Gitmo? Yes.[6] But the Democrat Party leadership's military-bashing hyperbole is insanely disproportionate and unquestionably damaging to the war effort.[7] Senator Durbin's comments drew the rightful fury of the Veterans of Foreign Wars: "Our soldiers put the needs of others first, just like generations of Americans before them," said John Furgess, the VFW's commander-in-chief and a retired colonel in the Tennessee Army National Guard. "They answered the call to create our country, to save our Union, and to help free the world from tyranny. And in return, all they ever asked for was to be appreciated for who they are and what they do, and for the country to care for their minds and bodies if broken or care for their families should they die. To link such selflessness to three of world's worst regimes is reprehensible."[8]

The Anti Defamation League also criticized Durbin for his senseless moral equivalence:

> Whatever your views on the treatment of detainees and alleged excesses at the Guantanamo Bay facility, it is inappropriate and insensitive to suggest that actions by American troops in any way resemble actions taken by Nazis in their treatment of prisoners. Suggesting some kind of equivalence between their interrogation tactics demonstrates a profound lack of understanding about the horrors that Hitler and his regime actually perpetrated. [9]

In response to the national uproar over the speech, Durbin first blamed the "right-wing media" for distorting his remarks—and then proceeded to repeat the exact sentiment embedded in his original speech. "This is the kind of thing you expect from repressive regimes but not from the United States," he carped.[10]

Several liberals defended Durbin's remarks. Blogger Steve Gilliard noted that "temeperature (*sic*) control was the Luftwaffe's favored interrogation technique."[11] John Aravosis of AMERICAblog wrote, "The far-right slime machine is going whole hog on Senator Durbin for, oh my, telling the truth about the deplorable things we have done to prisoners in Gitmo."[12] Markos Moulitsas Zúniga of Daily Kos called the controversy a "moronic Right Wing smear attack," said Senator Durbin "had the unmitigated gall to call it like it is." Zuniga proclaimed, "I stand with Durbin. Proudly."[13]

Only after the rational grown-up mayor of Chicago, Richard Daley—a rarity in the Democrat Party—blasted the Senate Minority Whip did Durbin back down. He eventually blubbered disingenuously on the Senate floor about his admittedly "very poor choice of words."[14]

Conservative blogger Ed Morrissey of Captain's Quarters noted the hyperbolic parallels between Durbin's speech and Senator John Kerry's infamous Vietnam War-era testimony before the Fulbright committee, during which he compared American soldiers to Genghis Khan. Wrote Morrissey:

> It seems that the Democrats have, for the past four decades, ever been ready to smear the American military during a time of war—particularly with analogies to Nazis—to bolster their political fortunes at the nation's expense. This hysterical and self-righteous name-calling turned out to be almost completely false in Viet Nam, but we learned that well after we ran out on our erstwhile allies in the South. They are even more ludicrous today, when the Durbins, Kerrys, and others have gotten so desperate for political attention that they now feel the need to toss out genocidal equivalences three at a time for what amounts to nothing more than humiliation techniques, invoking Nazis, Stalinists, and most egregiously the Khmer Rouge that their propaganda allowed to take power in the 1970s.
>
> Durbin doesn't appear to be deranged; he's just following a shameful tradition by radical Democrats of sapping American will to fight and win a war.[15]

These radical Democrats, I needn't remind you, get very upset when you question their patriotism. "I'm sick and tired of people who say that if you debate and disagree with this administration, somehow you're not patriotic. We are Americans. We have the right to participate and debate any administration," shrieked Senator Hillary Clinton at an April 2003 fundraising event.[16] Yet, when asked to respond to Senator Durbin's statement, the perpetually indignant Senator Clinton had no comment.

Neither did fellow Democrat presidential wannabes, Senators John Kerry and Joe Lieberman. Also declining to comment: Senators Charles Schumer, Barbara Mikulski, and Senate Minority Leader Harry Reid. Dead silence.

None of these flag-waving patriots had anything to say in August 2005, either, when supposedly mainstream liberal pundit Eleanor Clift of *Newsweek* magazine derided our troops as a "mercenary Army"—simply because they receive salaries and benefits.[17] Perhaps we should start referring to Clift and her ilk as the "mercenary Media."

The Democrats have long set the tone for bitter, anti-military sentiment; from liberals in city government declaring "nuclear free zones" to liberals banning military recruiters on college campuses and in public schools, to the spiteful yellow ribbon-snatchers in your neighborhood. The effect on the war effort is treacherous. How far is it, really, from demonizing officers at Gitmo as Pol Pot impersonators to embracing signs like the one displayed at an anti-war rally in San Francisco that proclaimed: "We support our troops when they shoot their officers."[18]

Oh, but we shouldn't dare question their patriotism.

The Yellow Ribbon Peril

What could be more innocent and unifying than the symbol of a yellow ribbon?

With roots in America dating back to the Civil War, the yellow ribbon gained popularity as a national emblem of remembrance during the Iranian hostage crisis, surged during the First Persian Gulf War, and reappeared in early 2003 as the war in Iraq progressed. Yellow ribbon magnets with the slogan "Support Our Troops" became as ubiquitous as those "Baby on Board" placards of the 1980s. A North Carolina-based firm, U.S.A. Magnets and More, has sold more than four million magnets since its founding in 2004, according to Vice President Chris Leab, a former corporal in the Marine Corps. "Whether you agree with the war or not shouldn't make a difference on whether you support our boys and girls over there," Leab told the *Saint Paul Pioneer Press*.[19]

Little did this American entrepreneur and his customers know that their harmless magnetic tributes to the troops would soon push unhinged liberals over the edge. Just weeks after the yellow ribbon trend took off, an epidemic of hostile confrontations over the innocent symbol erupted and a wave of yellow magnet thieves menaced parking lots, roads, and drivers.

In Fieldsboro, New Jersey, the all-Democratic town council—led by militant antiwar mayor Edward Tyler—outlawed any display of support for American troops on public property.[20] The ribbon ban was enacted after a resident placed a couple of yellow bows on public property near her liquor store to honor a local Marine, Joshua Carr, in Iraq. "This isn't a swastika or anything bad," the store owner, Diane Johnson, said to the *Philadelphia Inquirer*. "This is to support our troops."[21]

City workers in Thousand Oaks, California, performed a similar Edward Scissorhands routine on yellow ribbons tied by local residents honoring U.S. troops in Iraq. Brenda Freeman, whose young son was a Marine, received an apology from the mayor after Public Works Department employees cut up several hundred feet of ribbon. The scissors-wielding city workers had deemed the symbols "safety hazards."[24]

The Rollerblading Ribbon-Snipper

Apparently, the yellow ribbon concept was intolerable for Lynda Ragsdale of Carpinteria, California. When she saw yellow ribbons displayed around her neighborhood in honor of American soldiers, she grabbed a pair of scissors, strapped on her roller blades, and skated through town chopping off the bows from trees and poles. Witnesses said the pacifist rollerblader brandished the scissors at them. "I'm not for the war," Ragsdale fumed to the Associated Press. "It disturbs me to see other people imposing their thoughts and beliefs."[22] Never mind that the citizens hanging the ribbons had a municipal permit to do so. As she admitted to the *Los Angeles Times*, Ragsdale was "too angry" to discuss the matter rationally.[23] One can only hope that in time, with therapy, she'll realize the danger of rollerblading with sharp objects.

Escalating the war on ribbons, Palo Alto, California, antiwar zealot Seth Yatovitz threatened to sue the nearby city of Burlingame for supporting a city-wide yellow ribbon display.[25] Yatovitz said the decorations represented "violators of international law."[26]

City Administrator Clint Gridley of Cedarburg, Wisconsin, also took up regulatory arms against yellow ribbons on city property.[27] So did local politicians in Camden, Maine, who banned the ribbons from downtown lampposts after the mother of a sailor serving in the Persian Gulf hung them there in honor of her son and his shipmates. The ban came in response to a local resident who complained the ribbons were pro-Bush. But as the mom who hung the ribbons, Bobbie Grant, explained: "It was just a gesture of support for their safe return, that's all it was, although for a few people it was something else."[28]

At the University of Oregon, administrators ordered driver Pete Baker to take down a yellow ribbon magnet he had placed on his state-owned vehicle. Baker displayed the magnet for several months on his truck without hassle until an irate, antiwar employee complained. Baker was initially told the sticker was banned because it was "political" and in violation of neutrality rules—never mind the university's own use of public resources to sponsor antiwar activities, including the performance of an antiwar choral work composed by a University of Oregon music professor, and a formal declaration against the Iraq war by the faculty. But after catching heat for the decision from talk show hosts and military supporters nationwide, the school invoked an obscure state administrative policy that prohibits "unauthorized stickers" on state-owned vehicles.[29]

"The excuse that some people take in events like this to question the patriotism of other Americans is frankly below the belt," University of Oregon president Dave Frohnmayer huffed.[30] Methinks he doth protest too much.

During the past two and a half years, countless unhinged liberals have taken matters into their own hands to eradicate the yellow ribbon peril.

At the Manatee Technical Institute in Bradenton, Florida, a six-foot yellow ribbon crafted out of galvanized steel was yanked from the ground and stolen. Scott Urtel, 17, who spent hours cutting the pieces of metal, told the

Bradenton Herald: "It just made me mad because it was petty, the stupidity of the whole thing."[31]

In Council Bluffs, Iowa, military families experienced repeat thefts of their yellow ribbon magnets. The Associated Press reported that Kim Grosvenor, a mother with two sons in the military, had three of the stickers torn from her truck as she shopped at a local mall. "It made me feel so good to drive around with those," she said. "I didn't think there were people out there who would do something like this."[32]

Thomas and Christine Moen of Winnebago, Illinois, were victimized on September 11, 2004 and recounted the theft in the Lafayette, Indiana, *Journal and Courier*:

> On September 11, we traveled from our home in northwestern Illinois to attend our first parents weekend festivities at Purdue University, where our daughter is a student. We enjoyed the various events, including the football game. Later in the afternoon, we had to go to Tippecanoe Mall to purchase an item for our daughter. When we returned to her car, we discovered that the yellow ribbon magnet inscribed with the message "Support Our Troops" had been stolen from her car. Now, in itself, this is not a tragic situation; however, my daughter had put that ribbon on her car because her brother—our son—reports to Officer Basic Course training at Fort Sill, Okla., on Nov. 16. As a second lieutenant, he will most likely be deployed to Iraq or Afghanistan. So we'd like to say this to the person or persons who took the ribbon: You might have thought it was a joke to take the ribbon and toss it in the garbage or slap it on another person's vehicle. At best, you were acting silly; at worst, you were acting stupid. You are entitled to act silly and stupid—consider it an American freedom. But you're not entitled to act silly and stupid at another person's expense. For the sake of the rest of us, stay indoors and read a book about the sacrifices American soldiers have made over the last century. When you're done, you can come back outside and begin acting like a decent human being.[33]

When *Chicago Sun-Times* columnist Richard Roeper asked readers for stories of yellow ribbon theft, he received more than 100 in less than three weeks.[34]

Douglas Hackney, 18, of Dummerston, Vermont, pushed the boundaries of rage even further. He was arrested a few days after the November 2004 election, not just for stealing magnetic yellow ribbons from vehicles, but also for breaking and entering into a home to steal a yellow ribbon magnet.[35] In Buffalo, New York, police reported a rash of ribbon thefts all over the city. In one case, kids were picked up in South Buffalo for stealing up to 30 magnets off parked cars. South District Officer Anthony LeBron told the *Buffalo News* the thefts were a case of "kids being ignorant."[36]

Clearly, some of the thefts were simple juvenile pranks. But can anyone doubt that many were vengeful acts motivated by anti-military malice and Bush hatred?

Don't take my word for it. Take it from lunatics like Thomas Naughton, a student at the University of Massachusetts and *Massachusetts Daily Collegian* columnist who confessed to tearing yellow ribbon magnets off of cars to indulge his antiwar, anti-Bush views:

> By ripping off these ribbons, we find a way to deal with our guilt, as though with each ribbon swiped we take back a life that was taken by this senseless war started by our senseless president and those who support him.
>
> I will never say, "support the troops." I don't believe in the validity of that statement. People say, "I don't support the war, I support the troops" as though you can actually separate the two. You cannot; the troops are a part of the war, they have become the war and there is no valid dissection of the two.
>
> ... I look into the cars of people with "support the troops" ribbons as I speed past, trying to find some trace of recognition on their face, recognition of their guilt and the fact that they have given up. I usually see nothing; just a mouth moving robotically, singing the pop hits of today or the contemporary country wine of fake cowboys who share a lot with George Bush: no shame.[37]

Jeff McMahan published a similarly angry diatribe against yellow ribbon stickers on the blog Left2Right: "What is it exactly that these decals exhort us to do? How can I, or anyone, support the troops themselves? What can we possibly do for them?" The ribbon decals, McMahan complained, "exploit those young soldiers still stationed in Iraq by invoking their peril to stifle opposition to a war in which they will remain embroiled. The decals don't support our troops but unnecessarily endanger them by seeking to prolong an unjust war."[38]

That's right. Saddam Hussein's goons and Osama bin Laden's suicide bombers aren't the real threat to American soldiers. It's those damned decals!

On National Public Radio, commentator Bob Sommers delivered a seething rant about the ribbons. "I've noticed that these magnets often appear on vehicles that display still-lingering Bush/Cheney stickers. It isn't a big leap to conclude that there's something partisan about them," he griped. "And the sight of all these yellow magnets is starting to bring out the worst in me. Sometimes, I want to roll down my windows and confront the drivers. I want to exclaim: Who doesn't support the troops?!"[39]

Who doesn't support the troops? The smug Sommers is in deep denial about the Left's deep-seated contempt for the military. Let's take a look at some more of the wacky left-wing nuts who mock, disrespect, threaten, and assault American soldiers and veterans.

"Baby killer! Murderer! Liar!"

In Washington state, deep in the deepest blue region of the Pacific Northwest, antiwar agitators and John Kerry campaign supporters showed unbelievable contempt for a disabled veteran.

On Bainbridge Island last year, the Chamber of Commerce held its annual Independence Day parade. Jason Gilson, a 23-year-old Marine who was injured in the line of duty in Iraq, was proud to attend. He pinned on his war medals and brought a sign indicating his support for President Bush—heresy in this liberal bedroom community across from Seattle's Elliott Bay. At the parade, *Seattle Post-Intelligencer* columnist Robert Jamieson reported that "people bearing pro-Kerry signs were cheered and applauded for, among other things, tooling around in an environmentally responsible car."[40]

Well, it does take real courage to be seen in a Prius, if you ask me.

Upon seeing decorated young war veteran Gilson and his pro-Bush sign, the crowd turned ugly:

"Baby killer!"

"Murderer!"

"Boooo!"

Parade-goers also called Gilson a "liar" and made obscene gestures at the wounded Marine. Gilson's mother, who brought her entire family to the parade in support of her son, could not believe the viciousness of her neighbors. She recounted the experience in an e-mail to me:

> The reason for this mob-style degrading was simply because my son had chosen to proudly wear his military awarded medals upon his blazer while holding a small sign that said "Veterans for President Bush." Even one of the announcer[s] in the parade mockingly singled out my son and said in a sarcastic voice over a loud speaker, "And what exactly are you a veteran of?"
>
> How shocked and saddened I was . . . by the total lack of respect and decency I witnessed firsthand at this parade. I have to admit when my family and I were asked to come and march in the parade I felt a surge of pride and was greatly honored to be able to participate in such an event.
>
> I knew that Bainbridge Island has many who do not wish to have our current President re-elected, but never in my wildest dreams did I believe that so many would stoop so low as to degrade mock and cuss at my 8-, 11- and 13-year-old children and call my 23-year old disabled veteran son a murderer and baby killer . . .
>
> . . . My son was 22 when he willingly answered the call to go to war and risk his very life, yet he was treated as a criminal by the very people he has sworn to protect and defend. [T]hat all

changed for him. As he was booed, cursed at and called a murderer and baby killer you could see the pain and total betrayal he felt. I could say nothing to comfort him except that I loved him. His life will be forever changed because of the thoughtless words and actions of many who appear to care nothing for their fellow Americans and even less for those who serve our country. The sad part to all of this is that I have always taught my children that a lesson is repeated until it is learned. I shudder to think that people have not learned the horrible lesson in history by how the Vietnam Veterans were treated when they returned home.

Where have our morals, principals and decency gone? I am heartsick, yet ever and more determined to stand up for what is right.

For who will if we won't?[41]

Who will stand up for what is right? Not any of the area's Democratic politicians (including Seattle's "Baghdad" Jim McDermott), who all remained mum about Gilson's treatment. Nor did Bainbridge Island Mayor Darlene Kordonowy do the right thing and admit her community's anti-military bigotry. Sanctimonious as ever, the mayor called Gilson to "apologize"—but continued to defend her unhinged constituents. "Even though our community may be perceived as left-leaning," Kordonowy told the *Seattle Post-Intelligencer*, "it doesn't mean that we don't listen to all points of view."[42]

Call me nuts, but lambasting a wounded Marine as a "baby killer" on the Fourth of July is a mighty strange way to demonstrate a commitment to tolerance and diversity.

War and "Peace" Thugs

In the fall of 2004, the family of Specialist Chad Drake endured the crazed rantings of supposed pacifists at a candlelight vigil in Dallas. The event was supposed to honor Americans killed in Iraq.

Drake, 23, died on September 7, 2004, when his patrol vehicle was hit by small-arms fire in Baghdad. He was assigned to the 1st Battalion, 82nd Field Artillery, 1st Cavalry Division, Fort Hood, Texas. According to the Associated Press, before Drake was killed, he had been slated to receive a Purple Heart and a Bronze Star for an earlier act of valor: helping rescue two pilots when his Humvee was ambushed. He got out of the vehicle and returned twice to free the driver and hatch gunner. Drake didn't realize that he had been wounded in the leg and neck until later. He thought at the time of the ambush that the cold sensation on his neck was from the cool air of the Humvee.[43]

The Drake family traveled from Garland, Texas, to the vigil at Dallas City Hall Plaza to remember their heroic son, husband, and father. But according to a family friend who alerted the local NBC News Dallas affiliate, vigil attendees verbally assaulted Drake's mother, who was "harassed and yelled at, booed and hissed, told her son died for nothing."[44]

"I want to be clear in issuing an apology to the mother of the recent victim of that war," Lon Burnam, of the Dallas Peace Center, which organized the event, said after the NBC report aired. "I can certainly understand why she would not feel comfortable in that particular venue with that particular group of people."[45]

How compassionate of him. Now, if only he could help us understand how his so-called "Peace Center" could attract members heartless and ruthless enough to shout down a military family in mourning. Specialist Drake left behind a young wife and toddler daughter. He gave his life for his country. His loved ones, only days into the grieving process, suffered an unspeakable insult at the hands of ideological thugs who claim the moral high ground in the name of "pacifism."

The so-called peace movement's disrespect for dead veterans reared its ugly head again in Indianapolis in March 2005, when vandals damaged a beautiful Medal of Honor memorial along the city's canal walk. Two of the monument's giant glass panels, which list the names of Medal of Honor winners, were smashed. Police arrested one of the suspects, Joshua M. Miner, 18, of Danville, Indiana, and charged him with criminal mischief, a felony. Miner claims he accidentally cracked the memorial's glass panels while tossing rocks into the canal, according to court records cited by the *Indianapolis Star*. State Police are skeptical. An engineer for the company that designed the panels said the vandals must have used a heavier object.[46]

On the same night that the glass was smashed, someone sprayed obscene words about President Bush, along with peace and anarchy symbols, all over the canal walls.[47] Was that an accident too?

Oppose the war, support the troops? Bull.

"[Y]ou think you're such a great, goddamn hero"

It's one thing for anonymous cowards to insult the military. But unapologetic troop-bashing by elected Democrats takes liberal lunacy to an entirely different level. Consider the case of Daniel Dow, an Army National Guard sergeant who returned to the U.S. after serving in Kosovo for six months in 2004. Nothing overseas could have prepared him for the verbal assault he suffered at the hands of Washington, D.C.'s most unhinged liberals: Democrat Congressman Pete Stark of California.

What prompted Stark's raving madness? In May 2004, Dow faxed a letter to Congressman Stark expressing displeasure with his vote against a resolution that condemned abuse of Iraqi prisoners[48] while supporting the men and women in uniform. Dow wrote forcefully in defense of the military and argued:

> I urge you to stop your contemptuous display of bitter partisanship and your politicization of this war. Your actions are very divisive and destructive to the morale of our troops and the morale of our nation. I know that a majority of the population of the 13th Congressional District are very strong in their support of our soldiers and in their support of the war in Iraq. Your 'NO' vote today reflects that you are way out of touch with the people of this district.[49]

Congressman Stark responded with an insult-filled voice mail message on Dow's answering machine:

> Dan, this is Congressman Pete Stark and I just got your fax. You don't know what you're talking about. So if you care about enlisted people, you wouldn't have voted for that thing either. But probably somebody put you up to this, and I'm not sure who it was, but I doubt if you could spell half the words in your letter and someone wrote it for you. So I don't pay much attention to it. But I'll call you back later and let you tell me more about why you think you're such a great, goddamn hero, and why you think that this general and the defense department who forced these poor enlisted guys to do what they did shouldn't be held to account— that's the issue. So if you want to stick it to a bunch of enlisted guys, have your way, but if you want to get to the bottom of the people who forced this awful program in Iraq, then you should understand more about it than you obviously do. Thanks.[50]

Can you spell l-o-s-t i-t?

Dow gave Stark's taped diatribe to KSFO-560 AM in San Francisco, which broadcast the minute-long message and sent it to Rush Limbaugh, who discussed it on his program as well. A nationwide firestorm ensued among conservatives, but the 16-term Democrat escaped without so much as a scratch. Instead of issuing a heartfelt apology for mocking Dow's intelligence and engaging in an obscene *ad hominem* attack, Stark released a statement slamming President Bush and exploiting Abu Ghraib. Other than taking the Lord's name in vain, Rep. Stark said, "I would stand by the entire statement that I made" to Dow.[51]

Coming from the same mad dog who called Republican Congressman Scott McInnis of Colorado a "little wimp" and a "fruitcake"[52] and slandered Republican Congressman Nancy Johnson of Connecticut as a "whore" for the insurance industry,[53] Congressman Stark's foul-mouthed attack on an innocent war veteran is no surprise. Neither is the Democrat Party's continued tolerance for such indecent and uncivil behavior toward those with whom they disagree.

"Screw them"

"Screw them." That's how top liberal blogger, Democratic political strategist, and Howard Dean campaign consultant Markos Moulitsas Zúniga reacted to news of the brutal murders of four Americans—all of them retired war veterans—who had been providing security services in Fallujah in April 2004.

Terrorists ambushed the four civilian contractors. Dragged them from their vehicles. Beat them with bricks and killed them. Burned and mutilated their bodies. Then hung two of the charred corpses from a bridge, whacking them with pipes and chanting anti-American slogans in celebration as video cameras rolled. On his widely-read blog[54], Daily Kos, Moulitsas—himself a Gulf War veteran, for shame—ranted:

> Let the people see what war is like. This isn't an Xbox game. There are real repercussions to Bush's folly.
>
> That said, I feel nothing over the death of merceneries [sic]. They aren't in Iraq because of orders, or because they are there trying to help the people make Iraq a better place. They are there to wage war for profit. Screw them.[55]

The "mercenaries" Moulitsas was referring to were Jerry Zovko, a 32-year-old Army veteran and bodyguard; Mike Teague, 38, who served in the Army for 12 years and received the Bronze Star for actions in Afghanistan; Scott Helvenston, 38, who joined the Navy at 17 and served his country with the Navy SEALs for 12 years; and Wesley Batalona, a retired U.S. Army Ranger Sgt. 1st Class who served in elite airborne units and saw action in Panama and Kuwait. Teague, Helvenston, and Batalona all had children. The men worked for Blackwater Security, a North Carolina company that hires former military personnel to provide security training and guard services and which had a contract with the Pentagon to provide security for convoys that delivered food in the Fallujah area.

In an interview with the *Honolulu Advertiser* conducted after the brutal murders, Wesley Batalona's friend and fellow Army ranger Norman Allen noted that the security crews are well-paid, but "it's not just the money. You have this tremendous amount of experience. You want to make an impact... you end up working with people that you worked with for maybe 10 or 15 or 20 years, and that makes the risk acceptable, because you know the background these people have, where they come from."[56] Batalona's daughter, Kristal, said simply of her dad: "He just wanted to help everybody."[57]

Scott Helvenston's fellow Navy man and friend Keith Woulard responded to the mercenary charges. "A lot of people are saying 'Do you think he went over there for the money?' Of course he did," Woulard told the *Los Angeles Times*. "But that wasn't his main goal. It was to go over there and help out and put his knowledge to use."[58]

Mike Teague's friends and family say he grew up poor, was a man of faith, and was passionately committed to defending his country. Just before he left for Iraq, said friend Charlotte Myers, Teague "talked to me a lot about his family and what he wanted to do for his son and his wife. I know Mike was a Christian and he was doing what he loved doing."[59] At his funeral, wife Rhonda told hundreds of loved ones: "He knew the price of being a warrior. He was devoted to duty, honor and country. He loved his son, loved his family."[60]

Jerry Zovko's mom, a proud naturalized American from Croatia, said of her son: "He would just hug me and say, 'Mom, I am needed. I have to go there. I can make a difference. We need to stay united. We need to support our troops. We started something that needs to be done.'"[61]

These are the honorable Americans whom Moulitsas derided as war profiteers. Whose murders he dismissed with the profane "Screw them." When word in the blogosphere spread of Moulitsas's callous comments, he dug in deeper. Instead of offering an apology to the grieving families of the butchered Americans, Moulitsas carped about the media attention they were receiving and repeated his smear of their characters:

They willingly enter a war zone, and do so because of the paycheck. They're not there for humanitarian reasons (I doubt they'd
donate half their paycheck to the Red Cross or whatever). They're
there because the money is DAMN good. They answer to no one
except their CEO.[62]

Several of Moulitsas's blog advertisers withdrew their ads, including
Democrat Congressman Martin Frost of Texas, who commendably condemned Moulitsas's diatribe: "The views expressed by that website in no way
reflect Martin's positions and as stated earlier his advertising has been pulled,"
Frost campaign manager Jess Fassler wrote. "Congressman Frost supported
the President's efforts to remove Saddam Hussein and his murderous regime
and stands 100% behind our troops who are fighting terrorism both abroad
and right here at home. There is no place for these disgusting remarks in this
nation's discussion on foreign policy."[63]

But the outrage was limited and temporary, as conservative blogger Dean
Barnett reported in *The Weekly Standard*: "Political advertisers who had left
were replaced in short order by other office seekers."[64] Unhinged Democrats,
spurred on by the Dean phenomenon, are placing great hope in the internet
as a tool of grassroots communication and mobilization—and Moulitsas has
been a primary beneficiary. A decade into the internet age, the Dems' online
efforts have mostly proven a means for them to lose *faster*—but despite never
having notched a single victory for candidates endorsed by his site (he's cur-
rently 0-16), Moulitsas has accomplished another goal by padding his wallet
along the way.

In the wake of his "Screw them" statement, Moulitsas earned credentials
to cover the Democratic National Convention and now reportedly consults
with staffers from Senate Minority Leader Harry Reid's office almost every
day.[65] His site garnered praise from Senator Barbara Boxer of California[66]—
both she and Senator Ted Kennedy of Massachusetts recently wrote for the
site[67]—and he is now pulling in more than $20,000 a month in ad revenue
from liberal Democratic causes and candidates.[68]

Bashing dead veterans pays.

More Antiwar Antics

In the Seattle area, smearing the troops is a way of life. And the indoctrination starts early. At West Seattle High School, administrators presided over an antiwar spectacle in March 2005 that humiliated three local veterans. The men were invited to speak about the war in Iraq at an assembly that was supposed to present both sides of the debate. Instead, the veterans were forced to confront a theater stage strewn with red-spattered figures costumed as Iraqi men, women and children.[69]

Major Terry Thomas, a Marine who was one of the pro-troop invitees, recounted the scene to local blogger Brian Crouch:

Upon entering the theater at 12:30 PM, approximately 15 minutes prior to the event, I was taken aback by what I witnessed. As I stood there in my Marine Corps Dress Blue uniform, there before me stood numerous kids running around in sloppily dressed and ill-fitted helmets and military fatigues with utter disrespect for the symbols and uniforms of the U.S. military. The walls were covered in camouflaged netting and the stage was covered with approximately twenty white, life-sized cut-out patterns in the shape of dead women and children, all of which were splattered in red-paint to depict human blood. Onstage, children were kneeling and weeping while dressed in ill-fitted Arabic headdress with white-faced masks similarly covered in red paint to depict human blood.

At a podium, children were reading a monologue of how U.S. troops were killing civilians and shooting at women and children. Moreover, several grown adults were standing on stage in bright orange jump-suits, with black bags on and off their heads, some bound and tied, and some banging symbols and gongs in a crude depiction of what I believe were their efforts to depict victims of the Abu Ghraib prisoner abuse episode.

Within the auditorium, numerous adults appeared to have been supervising this behavior and children were literally running amok. What is going on in your classrooms and auditoriums? Who supervised this program? Who are these grown adults dressed as prisoners and performing such the antics on the stage of our public schools? Since when has it become Seattle School Board policy to take an official anti-troops position and declare returning combat veterans from Iraq such as myself as killers of innocent women and children as if this war were some sick sport. As an Iraq war veteran I am outraged by what I witnessed going on at West Seattle High School! [70]

Thomas told me, "It was the classic, Vietnam War-era baby-killer stuff." Outside antiwar groups had free reign on campus. Cowardly school officials initially denied any responsibility for oversight of the antiwar spectacle, claiming the students organized it on their own. But West Seattle High School principal Susan Derse later admitted that the event was coordinated by students "with the guidance of faculty advisors and administrators" and, in fact, that some staff members participated in the skit.[71]

Thomas asked the school officials responsible to apologize to the large military community in the Puget Sound region. The apology never came. The incident, Major Thomas concluded, "shows to what depths the radical antiwar movement will go to invade our public schools and lash out at returning Iraq war veterans like myself."[72]

Some schools lashed back by punishing students attempting to express support for loved ones in the military. The Schenectady, New York, public school district cracked down on 12-year-old Raven Furbert for wearing homemade patriotic jewelry to honor the troops. Raven has four family members serving in uniform, including her uncle, J. Barnes, a member of the Army National Guard's 42nd Rainbow Division who went on active duty in Iraq in January 2005. Raven crafted a red, white, and blue necklace made of beads and wore it to school upon return from Christmas recess. School officials immediately banned her from displaying the pro-military necklace because they feared the colors could be seen as "gang-related." Never mind that the school's own mascot and colors are—guess what?—red, white and blue.[73]

Then the games began. Administrators next told Raven she could wear the beads as long as they were not "displayed." Raven dutifully came to school with the necklace tucked under her clothes. School officials changed their minds and forbade her from wearing the jewelry again. Raven and her mom had enough of being jerked around: They hit back with a freedom-of-expression lawsuit filed at the federal level that is now slowly working its way through the courts.

Another girl who felt the sting of the anti-military mindset in the public schools is 15-year-old Shea Riecke. In March 2005, the freshman student at McKay High School in Salem, Oregon, brought a photo of her Marine brother to share with a teacher. The teacher had a display of graduates in his classroom and gladly agreed to add a photo of Corporal Bill Riecke to his collection. But when the teacher asked his superiors for permission, the request was denied because Riecke—a decorated war veteran on his third tour of duty in Iraq—was holding a gun.[74]

Moreover, the school communications coordinator Simona Boucek reportedly complained to a *Statesman Journal* columnist, "the image of Shea's brother does not necessarily convey military service." Never mind that Riecke was wearing his camouflage uniform with his name prominently stitched on the jacket. "We understand the girl's concerns," Boucek said, "but our policy prohibits any display of weapons. This photo just isn't right for a classroom."[75]

School officials offered to scan the photo into a computer and digitally erase the weapon. But the Riecke family objected to such politically correct whitewashing.

In response to a huge public outcry led by conservative Oregon talk show host Lars Larson, Marine Corps Moms, and other military and conservative bloggers, active-duty troops, and veterans, the school backtracked from its absurd zero-tolerance policy and allowed Shea to bring a different photo of her brother—with his weapon—to display in her teacher's classroom.[76]

Nevertheless, as Shea's mom, Connie, wrote in an open letter when she was informed of the school's initial decision:

"I have raised and educated my children to speak and live the truth, to be proud of their country and themselves. Just how far will our society go to blind themselves from the realization that our country is at war and what that means. Is this a revision of history? As young adults graduate from high school I hoped that their education would provide them with the basic knowledge of our world, especially today as our Marines and soldiers fight every day to secure their freedom and the freedom for others."[77]

Media vs. Military

From the classroom to the newsroom, distorted views of our troops persist. Anti-military bias is rampant at the *New York Times,* where liberal columnists Frank Rich and Paul Krugman likened abuses at Abu Ghraib prison to the My Lai massacre in Vietnam and ran 43 front-page stories in 47 days on the controversy, according to Fox News Channel host Bill O'Reilly's count.[78] It's pervasive at the *Boston Globe*, which recklessly published porn photos passed off by an antiwar city counselor as proof that American G.I.'s were raping Iraqi women.[79] It's in the steady editorial drumbeat of "quagmire, quagmire, quagmire" in Iraq[80] and "abuse, abuse, abuse" at Guantanamo Bay.[81] And it's in the mainstream media's bogus reporting on the military's failure to stop purported "massive" looting of Iraqi antiquities.[82]

It's reflected in the persistent use of euphemisms—"insurgents," "hostage-takers," "activists," "militants," "fighters"—to describe the terrorist head-choppers and suicide bombers plotting to kill American soldiers and civilians alike.[83]

It's demonstrated by the knee-jerk caricature of American generals as intolerant anachronisms;[84] the glorification of military deserters, who bask in the glow of unquestioning—and largely uncorroborated—print and broadcast profiles;[85] and the comparison of female interrogators at Guantanamo Bay to sex workers in New York City.[86]

Reckless disregard for the troops is also apparent in small, but telling, actions such as the fraudulent manipulation of Marine recruits by *Harper's* magazine. In March 2005, the liberal publication plastered a photo of seven recruits at Parris Island, South Carolina, under the headline, "AWOL in America: When Desertion Is the Only Option."[87] None of the recruits was a deserter. When some of the recruits' families expressed outrage over the deception, the magazine initially shrugged. "We are decorating pages," sniffed Giulia Melucci, the magazine's vice president for public relations to the *St. Petersburg Times*.[88] The magazine later issued a "clarification," but no apology, for its deception.[89]

And then there's the propagandistic rumor-mongering about American soldiers deliberately targeting and/or murdering journalists—a baseless slander spread by the likes of former CNN executive Eason Jordan[90] and echoed by Newspaper Guild president Linda Foley.[91] Jordan made the charge at a World Economic Forum gathering in Davos, Switzerland in late January 2005.

According to several eyewitnesses, Jordan asserted that American military personnel had deliberately targeted and killed journalists in Iraq. American businessman Rony Abovitz, who attended the panel Jordan participated in, reported immediately after the forum on a Davos-related blog that "Jordan asserted that he knew of 12 journalists who had not only been killed by U.S. troops in Iraq, but they had in fact been targeted. He repeated the assertion a few times, which seemed to win favor in parts of the audience (the anti-U.S. crowd) and cause great strain on others." Another panel attendee, historian Justin Vaisse, wrote on his blog that Jordan "didn't mince words in declaring that the intentions of journalists in Iraq were never perceived as neutral and were made deliberate targets by 'both sides.'"[92]

Jordan's defenders said he was "misunderstood" and deserved the "benefit of the doubt."[93] But the man's professional record was one of incurable anti-American pandering. He admitted in 2004 that CNN squelched news stories from Baghdad in order to maintain access to Saddam Hussein's regime. Also in 2004, he was quoted telling a Portuguese forum that he believed journalists had been arrested and tortured by American forces. He was in the middle of the infamous Tailwind scandal, in which CNN was forced to retract a Peter Arnett report that the American military used sarin gas against its own troops in Laos. And in 1999, Jordan declared: "We are a global network, and we take global interest[s] first, not U.S. interests first."[94]

Conservative bloggers played a key role in pursuing the story when the mainstream media refused to cover Jordan's remarks; but in this rare instance, it was a centrist and a few sane liberals who ultimately hammered the nails into Jordan's coffin. He resigned in February 2005.[95]

Journalist and presidential adviser David Gergen, the centrist who moderated the panel, confirmed that Jordan had indeed asserted that journalists in Iraq had been targeted by soldiers "on both sides."[96] Panel member and Democrat Congressman Barney Frank of Massachusetts told me that Jordan asserted that there was deliberate targeting of journalists by the U.S. military and that Jordan "left open the question" of whether there were individual cases in which American troops targeted journalists.[97] And panel attendee and Democrat Senator Christopher Dodd of Connecticut issued a statement in response to my inquiry that he "was outraged by [Jordan's] comments. Senator Dodd is tremendously proud of the sacrifice and service of our American military personnel."[98]

Those kind of words are spoken all too infrequently by American journalists predisposed to believe any criticism of our troops, no matter how unsubstantiated or ill-informed. But when it comes to the unhinged left, these words are the exception that proves the rule.

The War on Military Recruiters

As the first free election in Iraq in half a century approached in January 2005, the antiwar movement on college campuses across America reached a boiling point. Desperate to mar President Bush's own election success and distract from the Iraqi people's landmark triumph over tyranny, organized left-wingers took their frustrations out on college military recruiters.

On January 20, 2005, an angry crowd of 500 students descended on Army Sergeant 1st Class Jeff Due at Seattle Central Community College in downtown Seattle.[99] Due and his colleague, Sergeant 1st Class Douglas Washington, were manning a recruitment table on campus when the horde of students—who had ditched classes to protest President Bush's inauguration that day—struck. The antiwar thugs grabbed the recruiters' handouts and tore them apart. Others started throwing water bottles and newspapers at the soldiers. More pounded the walls, shouted profanities, and waved their fists.

"My first instinct was to take a table leg off and start swinging," Due told the *Army Times*. "But I chose to exercise restraint to protect the Army's reputation and my family's reputation. I had to swallow my pride in front of everyone there in order to do the right thing."[100] After a 10-minute standoff, Seattle cops and college security arrived—not to disperse the warring protesters, but to whisk the peaceful soldiers off campus. Wimpy college administrators refused to stand up for the troops. Campus agitators from a group called Students Against War had been lobbying to kick the recruiters out of the school for months. College president Mildred Ollee initially threatened to strip the antiwar group of its affiliation with the college and demanded an apology, but meekly backed off when students outside the antiwar group had also been found to have participated in the melee. Instead of hauling them all up for punishment, Ollee let the entire mob slide.

"I'm not prepared to go on a witch hunt," the college president said. "We did the best we could do in this, and I believe the students have learned something and we're going to move forward."[101] The bratty, brutish kids sure learned something all right: throw a tantrum, threaten soldiers, and you will suffer no consequences. "The administration backed down completely," two of the anti-recruiter protesters crowed in *The Socialist Worker* online.[102]

The 36th District Democrats in Seattle passed a resolution declaring solidarity with the protesters and urging that military recruiters be banned from Seattle Central Community College. Their resolution did not include anything about supporting the troops, but did say that "[m]ilitary recruitment during an illegal war is morally repellent, inasmuch as it aids and abets 'the supreme international crime.'"[103]

Undaunted, the intrepid Due returned to the college without incident a few days after the initial confrontation. But with a new wariness and a need to "watch his back." Committed to doing his duty, Due nonetheless reflected: "I cannot imagine what recruiters faced in the Vietnam era. I wouldn't want to face this on a regular basis."[104]

Unfortunately, recruiters around the nation *have* faced assaults and acts of vandalism on an increasingly regular basis. A little more than a week after the

Seattle Central Community College incident, recruiters in Manhattan reported that a door to their office was beaten in. Anarchist symbols were scrawled in red paint on the building. And on the same day, New York police collared a young Manhattan College junior and charged him with throwing a burning rag into an Army recruiting station and ruining the door locks with super glue. The radical student "was caught carrying a handwritten note declaring that a 'wave of violence' would occur throughout the Northeast on January 31, aimed at the 'military industrial complex' in response to American military actions."[105]

In South Toledo, Ohio, the day after the Manhattan student's arrest, another recruiting center was defaced, one of its windows broken, and manure splattered all over the building. Graffiti with the inventive phrase "War is Shit" was left on the center as well as on another building wall. On the morning of the attack, police discovered the same slogan plastered across the city. An e-mail sent to local television station WTOL-TV by a group calling itself, what else, "War is Shit," claimed responsibility for the property destruction. In its e-mail, the group fumed: "In a nation fueled by murderous lies, we can think of nothing more appropriate than expressing our disgust in this inappropriate fashion."[106]

Mike Gibson, a recruiter at the Toledo center, condemned the faceless weasels who were never caught: "I think they're blaming the people who fought to give them the right to do stuff like that. They should have the courage to stand up and say it rather than doing stuff like that."[107]

Courage was also in short supply just days later in East Orange, New Jersey, where young anti-military protesters shattered the windows of a U.S. Army recruitment center and a neighboring Navy office. Stupidity abounded at City College in New York in March 2005 when a campus secretary who participated in a student demonstration against military recruiters reportedly assaulted a police officer trying to arrest unruly protesters.[108] Carol Lang, 54, was charged with second-degree assault, disorderly conduct, and obstructing governmental administration. Two students, Justin Rodriguez, 23, and Nicholas Bergreen, 22, were also charged with assaulting a public safety officer, resisting arrest and other charges at the same protest.[109]

In February 2005, 20-year-old antiwar goon Brendan Walsh was sentenced to five years in federal prison for hurling a Molotov cocktail through the window of a military recruitment office in Vestal, New York[110] After the sentence was announced, someone posting to IndyMedia's website wrote, "Brendan Walsh is a hero and deserves support. If anyone has or can find an address for him please post it here." [111] Another commenter reportedly wrote, "Brendan, thank you for your inspiring action. If the rest of us worked harder to sabotage the war effort especially by targeting recruiting centers, the Achilles' heel of the army, we might actually be able to affect the bastards. Lets support the folks who get busted taking risks!"[112]

Intimidation and threats to recruiters in New York have been particularly extreme: In the college town of Ithaca, protesters hurled animal blood on the walls of a recruitment station. Twice, the center had its front picture window smashed by Molotov cocktails.[113] At Bronx Community College, noisy protesters shouting anti-military slogans such as ""I'm not going to die for their army" shut down several military recruitment sessions.[114]

On the other side of the country, Bay Area students brought a career fair at San Francisco State University to a standstill over the presence of military recruiters.[115] Congregating at Malcolm X Plaza, the antiwar thugs swarmed booths of the U.S. Army Corps of Engineers and the U.S. Air Force.

In Wisconsin, an Air Force Reserve Officer Training Corps (ROTC) information day was cancelled due to the threat of a protest called by the University of Wisconsin-Madison group Stop the War.[116]

Among the radical groups organizing disruptive counter-recruitment efforts on campus are:

- Code Pink, a far-left feminist outfit of Fidel Castro groupies who instruct their members how to form blockades at military recruitment centers, harass officers, stage "die-ins," and fraudulently pose as military recruits in order to infiltrate meetings.[117]
- The Ruckus Society, the infamous guerilla group involved in the 1999 World Trade Organization riots in Seattle, which is leading

training camps to "give youth the tools we need to stop the military invasion of our schools and our communities."[118]

•➤ And the militant War Resisters League and the Marxist-Leninist-rooted Central Committee for Conscientious Objectors.[119]

The anti-recruitment activists are evidently on the same warped wavelength as left-wing columnist/cartoonist Ted Rall, who argued in one of his columns that "Americans with personal integrity should boycott the volunteer military and discourage everyone they care about to do the same."

Rall, who attacked football player-turned-Army Ranger Pat Tillman as an "idiot" and a "sap" in May 2004 after Tillman was killed in action by friendly fire in Afghanistan,[120] makes no bones about his contempt for the troops:

> Opponents on the U.S. war against Iraq worry that the public may look at them as ideological heirs to those who supposedly used demoralized vets as spittoons. Oppose the war, they say, but support the troops! . . . I'd rather sleep under a bridge, eating trash out of a Dumpster, than murder human beings for Halliburton.[121]

We'd rather you sleep under a bridge, too, Ted. In Havana or Pyongyang.

Look closely at the thanks and support our troops have received from the Left:

- Soldiers stationed at Gitmo slandered.
- "Support Our Troops" ribbons snatched.
- Murdered military veterans mocked.
- Troops cursed at and assaulted.
- Grieving military families berated.
- Pro-military students bullied.
- Military recruiters harassed and harangued.

Need more evidence that liberals have lost it? Enter the unhinged college campus mob.

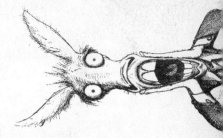

CHAPTER FIVE

Campus Moonbats on Parade

Seasoned observers of the War on Terror have a useful term for the Left's ignorant protesters against progress: "barking moonbats." Perry de Havilland of the libertarian blog Samizdata coined the term, which refers to "someone on the extreme edge of whatever their '-ism' happens to be."[1]

On college campuses across the country, that "-ism" happens to be rabid anti-Americanism. Unhinged academic moonbats nurture their grievances in a hate-infested habitat protected by the padded walls of manufactured victimhood. Observing their interactions, it's clear: They are flailing and flying blind.

The Nuttiest Professor

In the pantheon of unhinged academics, the University of Colorado's Ward Churchill stands above all others. In 2001, Churchill wrote a now-infamous essay smearing the victims of the September 11th terrorist attacks as "little Eichmanns" who deserved to die at the hands of the "combat teams" who made "gallant sacrifices" in their suicide attacks on the Pentagon and World Trade Center.[2] Churchill turned the essay into a little-noticed book crowing over chickens coming home to roost in America.[3] The Amazon.com entry for Churchill's book even boasted a rave from the well-respected *Bloomsbury Review*: "Few are as eloquent or as able to maintain lucidity for the lay reader as is Churchill."[4]

Eloquent? Lucid? Here's an excerpt from Churchill's condemnation of the September 11th victims:

> The [Pentagon] and those inside comprised military targets, pure and simple. As to those in the World Trade Center: Well, really. Let's get a grip here, shall we? True enough, they were civilians of a sort. But innocent? Gimme a break. They formed a technocratic corps at the very heart of America's global financial empire—the 'mighty engine of profit' to which the military dimension of U.S. policy has always been enslaved—and they did so both willingly and knowingly. If there was a better, more effective, or in fact any other way of visiting some penalty befitting their participation upon the little Eichmanns inhabiting the sterile sanctuary of the twin towers, I'd really be interested in hearing about it.

For years, those execrable remarks went largely unnoticed. Churchill became chairman of his ethnic studies department, garnered a six-figure salary, and hit the lecture circuit. Not until late January 2005 did a national furor erupt when student journalist Ian Mandel wrote a front-page story for Hamilton College's student-run *Hamilton Spectator*, which Mandel headed as editor-in-chief, highlighting Churchill's radical views in advance of a speaking engagement there.[5] September 11th family members and students protested Churchill's visit; talk radio and blogs publicized the controversy that the MSM would have otherwise ignored. Hamilton College initially backed Churchill, but relented and cancelled under pressure citing "threats."

Meanwhile, Churchill's own employer was bombarded with complaints about the nutty professor's alleged plagiarism, art fraud, lying about his Native

American heritage to win affirmative action status, bullying, and claims of other unethical conduct. Denver radio talk show hosts Dan Caplis and Craig Silverman obtained audio tapes from August 2003 of a Churchill lecture to admiring Seattle moonbats—in which he advised them how to go about conducting acts of terrorism. Here are excerpts of the question-and-answer session:

Churchill: If you are Arab, for example, you are automatically profiled as a potential terrorist. Period. And you can be asked to leave a plane because some Nordic-looking woman two rows down tells the stewardess she's not comfortable with you being there—her presence makes her uncomfortable—why? Because it was Arabs who flew planes into the Pentagon and the World Trade Center. See. And that fact—she's on an airplane and there's an Arab and somehow psychologically it makes her uncomfortable so it's very understandable that she not be asked to leave since she's made it clear that she's not going to be a very big risk to the flight, but rather the individuals sitting there doing nothing have to leave.

And why by the way did it take Arabs to do what people here should have done a long time ago?

Question from audience: You mentioned a little bit ago, 'Why did it take a bunch of Arabs to do what you all should have done a long time ago,' that's my question. And as a white man standing here in your midst from a fairly liberal/conservative/middle of the road background—and I tell people I'm so far left I'm coming up on the right—and I'd like you to respond to, why shouldn't we do something and how could we move so they don't see us coming?

Churchill: I'm gonna repeat that, tell me if I got that right: Why shouldn't we do something and how do you move so they don't see you coming.

As to the first part, not a reason in the world that I could see. I can't find a single reason that you shouldn't in a principled way—there may be some practical considerations, such as do you know how [laughter from audience]—you know, often these things are processes. It's not just an impulse. And certainly it's not just an event. And the simple answer, although it probably should be more complicated, but I'm not being flip and giving the simple answer, is: You carry the weapon. That's how they don't see it coming.

You're the one... They talk about 'color blind or blind to your color.' You said it yourself. You don't send the Black Liberation Army into Wall Street to conduct an action. You don't send the American Indian Movement into downtown Seattle to conduct an action. Who do you send? You. Your beard shaved, your hair cut close, and wearing a banker's suit.

There's probably a whole lot more to it, you know that. But there's where you start.

Question from the audience: I'm backing up a step to the Twin Towers falling down, um, there's been implications about how... well, the first thing I thought about when it down was 'Oh [expletive], that plays right into what they want to do to us.' Maybe you can follow up on that. [Applause.]

Churchill: Your first thought was, well, yeah, you put it pretty well, I'll accept you at your word, your first thought was 'Oh [expletive], that plays right into what they want to do to us.'

Well, then, welcome to the club! Welcome to the club along with 565,000 Iraqi children who were systemically starved and denied medical attention to death in less than 10 years while Madeleine Albright goes on television on *60 Minutes* no less, receives the number, and says yes, 'I've heard it, we've decided it's worth the cost.'

Welcome to the club with the rest of the world. A little bit. I don't care if it plays into the hands of what they had in mind for you unless you're doing something tangible to make it stop, what's already being done to those people on the receiving end.

Why should you be exempt and immune? So instead of 'Oh [expletive],' right on. Right on.[6]

Near the end of the session, Churchill—barely coherent—offered his fans advice on how to get revenge against cops who issue speeding tickets:

Churchill: And I'm not really comfortable with, since I'm presenting no public hazard ever when I'm ticketed, can attest to that, we can take that further at some point tonight if you'd like to, if you'd like to challenge it, but I'm presenting no public hazard, I'm simply being asked to ante up to pay for my own repression.

Not being comfortable with that, I have a rule of thumb: I smile very politely to the cop, take the ticket, look to see how much the fine is going to be, and before I leave that state, I make sure I cause at least that much property damage in state material before I go, so it's a wash, boys and girls. [Laughter and applause.]

Churchill the peace poseur showed his true colors again when he took a swing at a cameraman for CBS4-Denver. The station dared to challenge him about Indian artwork the professor had copied from others and marketed as his own.[7] As the University of Colorado launched an investigation into Churchill, his notoriety skyrocketed. Left-wing groupies offered Churchill applause at the University of Hawaii, University of California at Berkeley, Reed College, Claremont College, and Cal State Monterey Bay—all of which welcomed Churchill to campus for speaking gigs so he could complain *ad nauseam* about "fascists" stifling his free speech.[8]

At a June 2005 Portland forum on Conscientious Objection and resistance to military recruiters, Churchill seemed to advocate fragging—troops murdering their own on the battlefield—as an effective antiwar tactic (transcript courtesy of the bloggers at Pirate Ballerina):

> For those of you who do, as a matter of principle, oppose war in any form, the idea of supporting a conscientious objector who's already been inducted [and] in his combat service in Iraq might have a certain appeal. But let me ask you this: Would you render the same support to someone who hadn't conscientiously objected, but rather instead rolled a grenade under their line officer in order to neutralize the combat capacity of their unit?...
>
> You cannot maintain a military projection of force in the field when your own troops are taking out the line officers who are directing them in combat. It is as simple as that. Conscientious objection removes a given piece of the cannon fodder from the fray; fragging an officer has a much more impactful effect.[9]

Churchill elaborated later during the Q&A session:

> **Question from the audience:** I think it's important when you're getting into a discussion of violence and appropriate violence and self-defense, of starting to look at what you're trying to build there, what you're trying to create—for example, fragging an officer, which you were talking about before, at the beginning of your talk, the sort of trauma that that inflicts on that officer's family back home is I feel like an important thing to take into account when you try to think about what your action is trying to accomplish in the first place. I really feel like I can[not] articulate [my question] properly, but that's the general direction I'm heading with it.
>
> **Churchill:** How do you feel about Adolf Eichmann's family?[10]

Not content to liken September 11th victims to Eichmann, Churchill couldn't resist smearing military families with the same vulgar comparison.

Who's next? The astronauts who died in the Challenger explosion? The sailors who were killed at Pearl Harbor? The boys who took Point du Hoc on D-Day? So many heroes to malign, so little time.

Tenured Radicals gone Wild!

You can keep your kids away from Churchill's school, but nutty professors abound at nearly every institution of higher learning.

Among Churchill's many like-minded brethren in academia is lecturer Hatem (how appropriate!) Bazian of the University of California at Berkeley, who called for an "intifada" in America with a thinly-veiled incitement to violence:

Are you angry? [Yeah! the crowd responded.]

Are you angry? [Yeah!]

Are you angry? [Yeah!]

Well, we've been watching intifada in Palestine, we've been watching an uprising in Iraq, and the question is that what are we doing? How come we don't have an intifada in this country? Because it seem[s] to me, that we are comfortable in where we are, watching CNN, ABC, NBC, Fox, and all these mainstream . . . giving us a window to the world while the world is being managed from Washington, from New York, from every other place in here in San Francisco: Chevron, Bechtel, [Carlyle] Group, Halliburton; every one of those lying, cheating, stealing, deceiving individuals are in our country and we're sitting here and watching the world pass by people being bombed, and it's about time that we have an intifada in this country that change[s] fundamentally the political dynamics in here. And we know every—They're gonna say some Palestinian being too radical—well, you haven't seen radicalism yet! [11]

An unhinged mob echoed Bazian's militant rhetoric and physically attacked a group of College Republicans at San Francisco State University the day before Election Day 2004. Derek Wray, president of the SFSU College Republicans, said four Palestinian women from the university's General Union of Palestinian Students (GUPS) came to his group's table and launched into a diatribe: "You and the Jews want to kill all the Muslims!" one screamed, according to Wray in the online *Front Page Magazine*. "You and Ariel Sharon want to kill innocent Palestinian babies." A larger crowd of male Arab students also joined in.

Wray reported: "When one of the Republican students asked one of the women that if she hated America so much, why she didn't leave, she screamed at him 'I have some pride. I would strap a bomb on myself and blow myself up as a suicide bomber rather than call myself an American.'" He said the woman also ranted that the Iraqi terrorists were "freedom fighters"—akin to Michael Moore calling the same head-chopping murderers "minutemen." [12] Another one of the Palestinian shriekers began hitting one of the male Republican students, Wray said, and then turned around and accused the victim of attacking her.

Student protesters threw food at their GOP opponents (the new *modus operandi* of unhinged liberals) and dumped drinks on their Republican campaign literature. The police stood by and did nothing except suggest that the Republican students pack up and leave. [13]

Another Berkeley professor, Thomas Laqueur, wrote in the *London Review of Books*: "On the scale of evil the New York bombings are sadly not so extraordinary and our Government has been responsible for many that are probably worse." [14]

M. Shahid Alam, a professor of economics at Northeastern University, who called the mass murder of 3,000 people on American soil "the shot heard 'round the world" and exulted: "On September 11, 2001, nineteen Arab hijackers too demonstrated their willingness to die—and to kill—for their dream. They died so that their people might live, free and in dignity." [15] Alam's terrorist-sympathizing rants earned him the National Lawyers Guild's Free Speech Award.

The Unhinged Gallery

▶ YEARRGH!

▲ Former DNC chairman Terry McAuliffe, leader of the Rovian conspiracy theorists, suggested White House aide Karl Rove might be responsible for the fraudulent National Guard memo highlighted by CBS.

▲ DNC Chairman Howard Dean shares his deep thoughts on America, such as "Not nice...corrupt...braindead...evil...mean... YEARGGHH!"

◀ Al Franken loses it at the 2004 Republican National Convention.

▶ ASSES OF EVIL

◀ Ketchup heiress Teresa Heinz Kerry, wife of failed 2004 Democrat presidential contender John Kerry, passed out "Asses of Evil" buttons, trashed First Lady Laura Bush, and floated far-left conspiracies about rigged "mother machines" to explain her husband's defeat.

David Hume Kennerly/Getty Images

Jeffrey Phelps/Getty Images

▲ America's nuttiest professor, Ward Churchill of the University of Colorado, likened the victims of the 9/11 terrorist attacks to "Little Eichmanns" and suggested support for fragging American troops.

▶ THE LIBERAL LYNCH MOB

www.zombietime.com

zombie at www.zombietime.com

▲ Lynch mobs are no longer a faux pas for the unhinged.

◀ A disgruntled Bush-hater echoes DNC Chairman Howard Dean, who suggested President Bush may have been warned about the 9/11 attacks ahead of time by the Saudis.

▶ STICKS AND STONES

WhenAngryDemocratsAttack.com

◀ In 2004, Kerry supporters took their vandalism to the extreme, attacking poor innocent car windows.

Associated Press

▲ Sgt. 1st Class Jeff Due, right, a U.S. Army recruiter, is hounded off campus by antiwar protesters at Seattle Central Community College.

▶ CELEBRITY BOOBS

Associated Press/Nick Ut

▲ Well, at least we don't have to listen to Martin Sheen's voice.

Scott Gries/Getty Images

▲ Cameron Diaz suggested the re-election of George W. Bush would lead to the legalization of rape, something not mentioned in the GOP platform.

Vince Bucci/Getty Images

▲ Barbra Streisand is easily distracted by shiny objects and nutty conspiracy theories.

Robert Stolpe/NewsCom

▲ Michael Moore stayed in bed for three days after the 2004 election. Let's pray it's three years next time.

▶ YOUR UNHINGED NEIGHBORS

▲ In March 2004, Claremont McKenna College visiting professor of psychology Kerri Dunn falsely claimed she discovered anti-Semitic, anti-black, anti-woman graffiti spray-painted on her 1992 Honda Civic. Dunn was convicted on two felony counts of attempted insurance fraud and one misdemeanor count of filing a false police report.

▲ Nathan Winkler of Tampa, Florida, allegedly chased and terrorized a woman driving her children to a baseball game in March 2005, because she had a Bush-Cheney bumper sticker on her car.

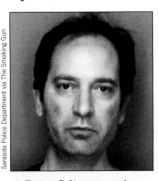

▲ Barry Seltzer, a registered Democrat, was charged with aggravated assault with a deadly weapon after he allegedly tried to run down Republican congresswoman Katherine Harris as she was campaigning in Sarasota, Florida, in October 2004.

▲ Police cited Bruce C. Charles of Portland, for disorderly conduct after Charles threw his shoe at former Pentagon adviser Richard Perle in February 2005.

▶ DON'T QUESTION THEIR PATRIOTISM!

◀ Whose side are they on?

▼ America—Land of the Zionist Nazis.

▲ Bush=Hitler.

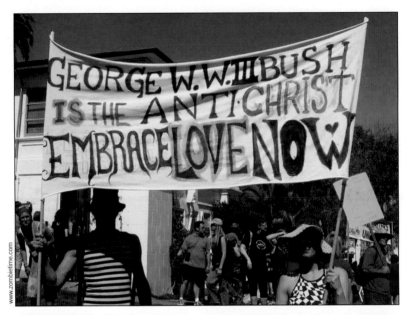

▲ Feel the love.

▲ Dick Cheney—the man behind all that is evil.

◀ The not-so-bright future for the children of the unhinged.

Joining them in the America-bashing pile-on was Robert Jensen, a journalism professor at the University of Texas at Austin. Just three raw days after the September 11th attacks, Jensen asserted that "this act was no more despicable as the massive acts of terrorism—the deliberate killing of civilians for political purposes—that the U.S. government has committed during my lifetime."[16] Naturally, Jensen praised Churchill's chicken-roosting diatribe in *Counterpunch*:[17]

> In the essay he wrote on 9/11, I believe Churchill was facing those harsh and dreadful realities, and I believe that essay was his attempt on that day to take love out of the realm of dreams and make it real in the world, in action. In that action, Churchill is angry. He is harsh. And in the central themes of the 9/11 essay and his life's work, Ward Churchill is right.

So spitting on the graves of the September 11th victims is "love?" This from a man teaching students to be mainstream journalists in wartime. Chilling.

Not to be outdone, University of Pennsylvania professor Francisco Gil-White, a Churchill wannabe and tinfoil hat-wearer in the psychology department, claimed that September 11th was an "inside job" and accused a fellow professor of being a secret agent for the CIA.[18]

Assistant professor of history Assad Pino at Kent State University raged in the pages of the student newspaper: "In a moral universe and university, it would not be Ward Churchill being demonized, but the cocaine cowboy, George W. Bush, who has added an extra 100,000 corpses to the pile of brown colored corpses, collected like Indian heads in the Old West. In an America rapidly descending toward Christian fascism, we need more Ward Churchills."[19]

And don't forget Columbia University's Nicholas De Genova, an assistant anthropology professor who told students at a teach-in that he wished for "a million more Mogadishus"—a reference to the Clinton-era debacle in Somalia where 18 American soldiers were killed—in order to boost antiwar sentiment. De Genova inveighed against the American flag and lectured that "the only true heroes are those who find ways that help defeat the U.S. military."[20] De Genova's Columbia University colleague and Marxist historian, Eric Foner, spewed after the September 11th attacks: "I'm not sure which is more frightening: the horror that engulfed New York City or the apocalyptic rhetoric emanating daily from the White House."[21]

In the Manhattan Institute's *City Journal*, Kay Hymowitz and Harry Stein described more nauseating comments made by tenured radicals at Connecticut's Wesleyan University during an antiwar rally held just nine days after the September 11th attacks:

> The speakers represented the entire spectrum of leftist approaches to the earth-shattering event. Indira Karamcheti, a professor of American studies and English, declared: "We need to understand that the events that happened last Tuesday must be placed within their historical context... There is a long history here we need to understand, not least the long history of resistance to imperialism, in which violence has been seen and often lauded as the most effective means with which to resist. Violence and guerrilla tactics are the tactics of the powerless. It's a system in which ordinary objects can be transformed into weaponry... and it has historical paradigms, not least in the American Revolution, the Black Panthers, the Algerian Revolution."
>
> But the comparison between the homicidal Black Panthers and the Founding Fathers was not the low point of the occasion. Jonathan Cutler of the sociology department began his remarks with the Arabic greeting Salaam Alechem—"in solidarity with Muslims and in defiance of American arrogance and xenophobic jingoism"—but he quickly apologized, noting that as a non-Muslim he hadn't the right to use the phrase, and he had no wish to "mirror the global U.S. arrogance of familiarity in the world, that doesn't notice difference, that doesn't care to notice difference." As a Jew, he added, he had considered instead the Hebrew greeting

Shana Tova—Happy New Year—but "I am not a Zionist, and I am not an American today... If there's a war led by this government, it should not be in my name... Bush said 'hate' before he grieved, he said 'hunt' before he grieved... It is precisely the time for protest against the IMF and the World Bank, and here's why. I think it's wrong to suggest at this point that the attacks on the World Trade Center and the Pentagon were done by terrorists—not because they're not terrorists, but because they're the tip of the iceberg of a very big war; we just didn't know the war was going on until then. I really think we have been missing the anger toward the United States for so long, and operating in a world as if it didn't matter that there is a global movement of resistance to U.S. dominance. Now, I don't like the form of the movement that took down the World Trade towers," he allowed, fastidiously. "I don't like the tactics—I miss the skyline of New York, and I miss the people who died. I also don't like the anti-urban, anti-cosmopolitan nature of much of the resistance to globalization. I love New York. But this much I do know: if there is no justice, there will be no peace."

Then there was Gary Comstock, a sociology professor who is also the university chaplain, still clinging to the make-love-not-war philosophy. As the nation confronted an implacably murderous enemy, he offered these insights: "I think that the inability to love is the central problem, because that inability masks a certain terror, and that terror is the terror of being touched. And if you can't be touched, you can't be changed; and if you can't be changed, you can't be alive." Comstock went on to demonstrate his Ivy bona fides by describing how he had felt moved to turn, in this emergency, to "what I call my elders," including "the late author James Baldwin, a black man who was outspoken before the civil rights movement and a gay man who was 'out' before the gay liberation movement." [22]

Three thousand innocent people are murdered at the hands of Islamists, and this educator/chaplain turns to *James Baldwin* for solace?

At tiny Fort Lewis College in Colorado, a part-time Spanish instructor didn't settle for spouting off a politically correct diatribe. When Maria Spero spotted a student wearing a College Republican t-shirt at an off-campus restaurant, she kicked him. Mark O'Donnell said Spero told him that "she should have kicked me harder and higher."[23] Talk about a knee-jerk liberal. Spero offered a disingenuous apology, noting that she hadn't realized he was a student. (Kicking Republican townies, presumably, is okay in her book.)

In the grand tradition of non-punishment for out-of-control leftists, no charges were filed against Spero for the assault.

Tawana Brawley goes to College

So, what do moonbat professors do when they're not attacking military recruiters, the Bush administration, cameramen, and College Republicans? They manufacture hate crime hoaxes against themselves to gain sympathy, media attention, and political caché. Ever since self-defacing teenager Tawana Brawley smeared feces all over herself, scrawled "KKK" and "nigger" on her skin, climbed into a trash bag, and blamed it on racist cops in New York, warped publicity-seekers have faked hate by any means necessary. Colleges and universities, steeped in race-baiting and America-hating, have become natural hatcheries for the next generation of Tawanas.

In March 2004, Claremont McKenna College visiting professor of psychology Kerri Dunn claimed she discovered anti-Semitic, anti-black, anti-woman epithets ("kike," "nigger lover" and "whore") spray-painted on her 1992 Honda Civic. The car's windows were smashed and the tires slashed. Dunn had been a vocal critic of other alleged racist incidents on campus. After she reported the incident, administrators and students rallied around Dunn; classes were cancelled at all five of the Claremont Colleges; local and federal authorities launched an investigation.

Dunn, however, isn't black or Jewish. She is a white Catholic "considering" converting to Judaism. So how did Dunn's purported assailants know this? She explained that the attack—which she called "a well-planned-out act of terrorism"—must have been committed by her own students, who knew of her plans to convert. More irksome questions arose. How did the assailants know which car on the campus parking lot was hers? The students must have followed her, Dunn said. And what about the $1,700 in property she told police had been stolen, which mysteriously turned up in Dunn's possession? No explanation.

The final blow to Dunn's credibility came when two witnesses told investigators that they saw Dunn drive her car—adorned with the offending graffiti—into a parking lot and smash the car's windows and slash the tires herself. But the perpetrator and her loyal supporters remained in stubborn denial. Dunn, who was involved in past tangles with the law over shoplifting charges, blamed the police for being irresponsible and "irreparably damag[ing] her reputation and emotional health."

Dunn was convicted on two felony counts of attempted insurance fraud and one misdemeanor count of filing a false police report; a judge sentenced her to a year in prison after branding her a "bald-faced liar" who continued to deny responsibility for her actions.

When it comes to smearing America, as Tawana Brawley taught us all so well, the end always justifies artificial means. Indeed, the *Los Angeles Times* reported on more than 20 suspected or confirmed hate crime hoaxes on college campuses since 1997, including:[24]

→ San Francisco State University undergrad Leah Miller, who admitted to scratching "NIGG" on a dorm room door and writing herself a note with the same epithet (she is a black woman). "She apologized to police and said she wanted to be accepted by other students and draw attention to what she regarded as racial issues on campus," according to the *Times*.

→ Jaime Alexander Saide, 19, told cops at Northwestern University that he had discovered the racist phrase "Die Spic" scrawled on the wall near his room and on a paper stuck to his door. Then he told them that someone grabbed him from behind, used the same slur and held a knife to his throat. Saide reveled in his celebrity status as a victim of racism. The campus body rallied in support of Saide and launched a "Stop the Hate" campaign. Saide pontificated about the experience for the student newspaper. But ten days after the alleged attack, Saide admitted to making the whole thing up.

↠ Ed Drago, a junior and a psychology major at the College of New Jersey, informed cops he had received hate messages and death threats because he was gay. After a homemade bomb turned on the outskirts of the campus and classes were canceled, Drago basked in the publicity of media and campus attention. The requisite "teach-in" and condemnations of societal bigotry ensued. And then, the real bombshell: Drago was arrested and plead guilty to charges of harassment and providing false information to authorities. He escaped with a fine and a sentence of one year of probation.

And then there was the boy who cried "Muslim."[25] Just days after the September 11th attacks, Saudi Arabian-born student Ahmad Saad Nasim told Arizona State University campus police he was assaulted and pelted with eggs in a parking lot while assailants screamed "Die, Muslim, die!" Administration officials and classmates earnestly condemned the attack, which received national media coverage. More than 50 Muslim students left the ASU campus as a result of Nasim's claim.

Nasim dramatically described "being slapped and punched on my back." He compared himself to the dead victims of terrorism at the World Trade Center and Pentagon, and he linked himself to recent "hate crime" incidents involving Middle Eastern victims: "A Pakistani man was shot in Texas, a Sikh Indian and an Arab were shot in Mesa, and I was beaten in Tempe . . . I might get shot at some gas station, too! It all depends on fate!"

You can predict the rest of the story. After being interviewed by cops, Nasim confessed to fabricating the assault after another admittedly staged performance. On September 27, 2001, a custodian found Nasim in a library bathroom stall. He had the word "Die" written on his forehead, a plastic bag tied over his head, and a racist note stuffed in his mouth. But, as Lieutenant

John Sutton of the ASU campus police told me, "Something was not right." The bathroom door was locked from the inside, Nasim's hands were free, and he suffered no symptoms of suffocation.

Nasim recently pled guilty to two counts of providing false information to police. His punishment? A measly one year's probation, 50 hours of community service, and an order to seek psychological counseling. "It created a false atmosphere of paranoia and this sort of guilt-ridden atmosphere that leftists thrive in ," ASU student Oubai Shahbander is quoted as telling the *Campus Report*. Not that the truth mattered much to students and faculty convinced that hate was all-pervasive. "What's actually really interesting," Shahbander noted, "is that no student organizations that had been leading the whole anti-hate campaign on campus went out of their way to denounce this individual. In fact, we had two letters to the editor, published by students, actually supporting him."[26]

Even high schoolers are getting in on the act. At Tamalpais High School in liberal Marin County, California, a lesbian student said a bigot pelted her with eggs, vandalized her locker and car, and sent her hate messages. The words "Die Fag" were spraypainted on one of the school's walls. The school's students, teachers, and administrators reacted with the usual outrage, anti-hate vigils, and the like. When the lesbian "victim" later told police she had faked the incidents to garner attention, the school provided students with free counseling to cope with post-traumatic stress.[27]

Unlike Aesop's fable in which the boy who cried "wolf" is spurned, many of today's hate crime fakers suffer little, if any, ostracism. One of Tawana Brawley's patrons, the Reverend Al Sharpton, was a primetime speaker at the 2004 Democratic Convention. As Dan Rather might rationalize: The manufactured hate crimes are "fake, but accurate." The irony is that while professors with persecution complexes and students addled with delusions of victimhood strain to prove how intolerant and bigoted their conservative opponents are, viciously unhinged liberals are themselves guilty of spreading poisonous bigotry about racial, ethnic, and religious minorities that hold dissident views.

Top 10 Unhinged Media Liberals

10   Media critic **ERIC ALTERMAN**, who wished conservative talk-radio host Rush Limbaugh had gone deaf and said the country would be better without Limbaugh and his 20 million listeners.

9   **ELEANOR CLIFT** of *Newsweek* magazine, who derided our soldiers as mercenaries.

8   Air America host **AL FRANKEN**, who loses his composure almost as often as Air America investors lose money.

7   Air America host **RANDI RHODES**, who was investigated by the Secret Service after advocating the assassination of President Bush.

6   Cartoonist **JEFF DANZIGER**, who depicted Secretary of State Condoleezza Rice as the "Prissy" character in *Gone With the Wind*—complete with bare feet, exaggerated lips, and stereotypical dialect ("I knows all about aluminum tubes").

5   **MARKOS MOULITSAS ZÚNIGA**, top liberal blogger and Democrat consultant, who gloated about the murder of American contractors in Fallujah.

4   **BILL MAHER**, comedian and talk-show host, who claimed that religion is a neurological disorder and mocked former Attorney General John Ashcroft's hospitalization for pancreatitis.

3   **EASON JORDAN**, former CNN executive, who accused U.S. troops of murdering journalists in Iraq.

2   Former CBS anchorman **WALTER CRONKITE**, who claimed that Bush advisor Karl Rove and Osama bin Laden are working hand-in-hand to help the Republican Party.

1   Cartoonist/columnist **TED RALL**, for his unrelenting hatred of our troops and racism against minority conservatives.

CHAPTER SIX

"You Are One Sick Gook."

Every minority conservative in public life has stories of being tarred as an "Oreo," "coconut," or "banana" (black/brown/yellow on the outside, white on the inside). Racial and ethnic grievance-mongers accuse us of not being "authentic." Unhinged critics use slave imagery or prostitution metaphors to dismiss our arguments and principles. And they obsess about our skin color in a way that might make even some white supremacists blush.

In October 2003, for example, the national president of the College Democrats derided now-Republican Congressman Bobby Jindal, a staunch conservative of Indian descent, as President Bush's "personal 'Do Boy.'"[1] During Jindal's Louisiana gubernatorial bid, newspaper reporters fixated on his skin color. *New York Times* editorial writer Adam Cohen described him as "the dark-skinned son of immigrants from India."[2] A front-page *Los Angeles Times* article by Scott Gold labeled him "dark-skinned."[3] So did Associated Press reporter-turned-color analyst Adam Nossiter, who described Jindal in one piece as "moderately dark-skinned"[4] and just plain "dark-skinned" in two others.[5] None of the reporters saw fit to describe the skin color of Jindal's opponent.

As a female minority conservative in the public arena for the last 13 years, I've gotten my fair share of racist and misogynist hate mail obsessing about my pigmentation, facial features, and ethnic origins. But none of the past attacks were as vitriolic as the correspondence I received during and after the 2004 presidential campaign. When I shared a sample of these letters on my blog, michellemalkin.com, readers reacted with disbelief.

Here is just a tiny sample of the hate mail—uncensored, unedited, and uncorrected—that arrived at my in-box virtually every day during the past year:

You are one sick gook, get a life wax bean!

• • •

Hi Self hating flat nosed Filipino Bitch! As we used to refer to your kind—little brown Fucking Machines. Looks like this little LBFM learned to whore in a different way to make some pesos. How sweet.

• • •

Surely you are a big put-on. Did some minor Republican operative purchase a mail-order bride and train her to do this?

• • •

Proverbs 69:69 counsels: "Like a whore who infects those she sleeps with, so doth the ultra-republican faux columnist infect her readers with lies." While you are looking in the mirror, cursing the Left because you weren't born blond, think about the above. Amen.

Is is such a shame that you look like a Filipino- because your thinking, writing (if you can call that) is a disgrace to any member of the Asian community. Someday, when you are no longer motivated by greed, and when you are closer to your next life stage, you will realized what a horrible sellout you are.

● ● ●

I just hope that I am still around when the karma catches up to those of you that have spread the lies and attacked the innocent. I hope your fate is somewhat similar to the women of the Phillipines when the Japanese invaded. Then Michelle you can drop the "media" from "media whore" when someone asks your occupation.

● ● ●

You're just a Manilla whore shaking your ass and waiting for the Republican fleet to come in, aren't you? You've even got the lip gloss about right. Maybe if you love sailor long time, he bring you home to big American house? I don't think so. Just like in Manilla, Honey, they'll pass you around 'til they've all shot their load in you, and then they'll try to scrub off the stench so they can sail off in their crisp, white uniforms to the land of W.A.S.P.

● ● ●

Here's a tip. We know you are lyin' pond scum and a whore to your profession . . . and, not a very expensive whore at that. So . . . when we get rid of you neocons; how will you ever pay your rent? You're not good enough to make it as a real writer. fuck you; I hope you get cancer & die a horrible painful death all alone, with your colleges shunning you and the rest of us reading how wrong you are AND WHAT A CRUMMY WRITER YOU ARE.

● ● ●

Malkin, you're a dumb fucking whore. You're a philipino piece of shit who should be wiping my ass. Go back to the massage parlor. Sucky sucky long time. How dare you thing you have any right to express any opinions in this country. You're a joke. Go back to nursing school. Whore.

• • •

Young lady you should be ashamed of yourself. My husband is Filipino and is all I have met have had integrity. However, you have disgraced the Filipino Americans by spreading these awful lies and being a Bush whore. I was going to vote for Bush, but never after these dirty tricks and lies. Just like the old Marcos days' eh. Disgraceful, you family and your community are desparately ashamed of you. How much are they paying you to sell your soul. You have disgraced us all.

• • •

oh, mz. malkin, there are more profitable ways to whore yourself than to do it on television for the likes of the neocons. (they are even quicker to dump their whores when they are finished with them . . .) you would make a discreet fortune on aurora avenue here in seattle, and no one would be the wiser . . .

• • •

Say, how does it feel to be a paid prostitute for the republicans? Go get some more collagen injected in your lips, it makes you look more the part.

• • •

There is some gook out there pandering to the radical right. Rumor has it where Ann Coulter is concerned, she is the Jeff Gannon to Karl Rove. Michelle Malkin you are a disgrace to your parents and to the United States of America. You are a funny pathetic hateful piece of Bushscat.

• • •

my only wish is to be back in nam and have encountered you instead of those syphlis infested whores i settled for

• • •

When will you pose naked for playboy? I think it's time the "Asslickers of the GOP" issue was rolled out and you, with your exotic looks would be a shoo-in. Maybe a centerfold with you blowing Bush's cabinet? After all, it's not that much different from what you do now, hmmmmmm?

• • •

Whore-scum-cunt(just thought i'd drop a line!)

• • •

How much does the GOP pay you to be their propaganda whore?

• • •

First I would like to tell you that your face is asymmetrical. Assuming that you aren't yet old enough to have survived your first stroke (a la Ronald Reagan) this is indicative of a serious psychological disorder (see Katie Couric). That notwithstanding, OH, ME SO HORNY! OH ME SO HORNY! OH, ME SO HORNY! ME LOVE YOU LONG TIME!

• • •

Ms. Malkin (was going to put Mrs. but thought twice . . . as if anyone would actually marry you!! Ha! I just snorted Red Bull all over my keyboard just relishing the thought of some sucker actually being bamboozled into finding you even remotely attractive!!),

Does anyone actually read the drivel you spew out of your anus and all over your website? It is rancid, it is worse than rancid, it is putrid, it is rancid, it has about as much substance as a thinly sliced, piss-and-shit-concocted sheet of putrid, stinking toilet film.

And my god, are you ugly!...You are one hideous-looking and tremendously stupid woman. Keep up the good work!

• • •

Since you can not write a column without calling everyone who has a different opinion than yours some vicious name, I figure I can now call you "that fascist right wing chink broad".

Put your wading boots on. We're just getting started. On the Internet, supposedly "respectable" liberal bloggers allowed their foaming readers to post similarly depraved comments. Duncan Black, who has held teaching and research positions at the London School of Economics, the Université Catholique de Louvain, the University of California, Irvine, and Bryn Mawr College and is a "senior fellow" at David Brock's Media Matters for America, runs a popular blog called "Eschaton." In addition to mocking my Filipino maiden name (Maglalang) because of its ethnic sound, Black's readers posted the following XXX-rated comments on his blog in February 2005:

What I want to really know is whether Malkin has the ability to suck the chrome off of a trailer hitch. I mean, she's gotta have SOME kind of purposeful earthly use walking around on this planet, because she certainly doesn't have one that has anything to do with her intellect or her political views.

• • •

Do you think Malkin's breezer runs horizontally instead of verti-cally? Any opinions on the subject?

• • •

That's Michele Mangalangawanker to you, buddy! Seriously. The more she blogs the stupider she gets. Some people just need edi-tors...or a smack in the head with a pillow case full of weasel shit.

• • •

Do you think there would be a big market for "internment camp porn" starring Michelle Malkin and Chartoff? It could be like "Ernest" movies from the 1980's "hey verne look at the filipina"

. . .

Can I fuck her up the ass?

. . .

You know, if Malkin had been living on the west coast in 1942, I can guarantee that she'd be just another fucking jap as far as the vast majority of the population was concerned.

Maybe what Magalangadingdong is really hoping for is that she'll get tossed in a camp and get to live out her "Comfort Woman" fantasy that she works hard to keep under lock and key at all times.

. . .

Look at how even aggressive educated wogs like this Michelle Malkin serve their white masters at little or no prodding simply because they desire to be white and not what they were born. Malkin's a whore regardless what race she was born. She'd serve any Dark Lord as long as they paid her.

The kindergarten ridicule of my maiden/legal name demonstrates just how nuts the lefties have become. On the one hand, they accuse me of exploiting my ethnicity to get ahead. On the other hand, they attack me for "hiding my ethnic heritage" by taking my husband's name professionally when I got married more than a decade ago. Why can't they get their *ad hominem* attacks straight? They can't make up their minds because they've completely lost them.

Another popular liberal blogger, Kevin Drum, who was hired by the venerable *Washington Monthly* in March 2004, did nothing when I called attention to the following crude remarks posted in his comment section in April 2005:

Michelle Malkin is a cunt.

• • •

Michelle Malkin is a cunt.

Check your talking points, dude. The Official Left-wing Anti-Malkin punch-word is "whore."

• • •

nope. . . . she's a cunt. Coulter is neither cunt nor whore. she's a man. Maggie "Pay for Play" Gallagher is the whore.

• • •

[T]hanks for elevating the discussion.

I prefer to think of Malkin more accurately as profoundly disturbed. And incapable of rational thought. Oh, and racist, oddly enough, even against he own race, which takes a particularly sad strain of self hatred, I guess.

Let's be precise in our criticism, shall we?[6]

Less than two years earlier, Drum issued a seemingly heartfelt plea for more "civility" on his blog. "I don't patrol the comments much, and I don't delete posts. I try to respond now and again, but I don't do it regularly because so many of the threads just get too long too fast," he bleated. "But one thing I'd like, being the idealistic liberal fellow that I am, is a civil discussion that doesn't involve kindergarten levels of invective and personal attacks."[7] When I published his readers' comments on my web site, he wrote me a rather wimpy note: "If you see any outrageous personal insults from my commenters in the future, feel free to email me and I'll remove them."[8] But rather than take personal responsibility for cleaning up the trash on his blog, Drum chose to keep the above-mentioned vulgar comments on his *Washington Monthly*-subsidized site.

There will always be hate-filled lunatics out there mocking prominent public figures' ethnicity, physical appearance, and sex. But we all know that no minority who embraces liberal ideas is ever attacked for being a "race traitor" or "sellout." Those *ad hominem* accusations are leveled only by the Left, and only against minority conservatives. For the unhinged Left, race-baiting has become expedient substitutes for substantive argument.[9]

Hating Condi

Ted Rall is the far-left-wing cartoonist and columnist who reacted to news of President Ronald Reagan's death with infamous glee: "I'm sure he's turning crispy brown right about now."[10] Though his politics are radical, Rall's position in the mainstream media is anything but fringe. Rall's cartoon and column distributor, Universal Press Syndicate, is billed as "the largest independent newspaper syndicate in the world."[11] His work is published in more than 140 publications, including the *Newark Star-Ledger*, *Washington Post*, *Los Angeles Times*, *Las Vegas Review Journal*, *San Jose Mercury-News*, and *Lexington Herald-Leader*. Rall is a Pulitzer Prize finalist and has received several honors from the Society of Professional Journalists and Robert F. Kennedy Journalism Awards.[12]

A month after cackling about President Reagan's death, Rall trained his sights on President Bush's phenomenally accomplished former National Security Advisor and current Secretary of State, Condoleezza Rice.

In a July 2004 syndicated cartoon, Rall fantasized about "appropriate punishments for deposed Bushists"—a crude parody of alleged treatment of Iraqi detainees at the Abu Ghraib prison. Rall included a frame depicting Rice proclaiming herself Bush's "HOUSE NIGGA." Next to her, Rall drew a black man demanding that Rice "HAND OVER HER HAIR STRAIGHTENER." The character's t-shirt sported the phrase: "YOU'RE NOT WHITE, STUPID." The caption below the frame read: "SENT TO INNER-CITY RACIAL RE-EDU-CATION CAMP."[13]

Would liberals stand for a conservative cartoonist mocking any other prominent black woman for having straightened hair? Would a mainstream newspaper editor stand for a right-leaning white columnist labeling a prominent Democrat a "nigga?"

Project 21, a Washington, D.C.-based organization for black conservatives, called for Rall's syndicate to terminate its relationship with him and also asked the NAACP, the National Association of Black Journalists (NABJ) and the Rainbow/PUSH Coalition to make similar demands based on their past involvement in pressuring ESPN to fire radio talk show host Rush Limbaugh in 2003.[14] The calls were ignored.

"Is it OK for Ted Rall to use such vile language because he's using it against a black conservative?" asked Project 21 member Michael King.[15] The silence on the Left spoke volumes.

Rall has gotten away with flinging his pen-and-ink-stained excrement at conservatives because he reflects the closet thinking of mainstream media editors across the country and their mainstream liberal audiences. Just a few months before Rall's cartoon was published, *Doonesbury* creator and Pulitzer Prize winner Garry Trudeau drew a cartoon with President Bush referring to Rice as "Brown Sugar"—a derogatory term with both racist and sexist undertones mocking black women.[16] Another Pulitzer prize winner, Pat Oliphant drew Rice as a thick-lipped, buck-toothed parrot perched on President Bush's shoulder—a racially prejudiced caricature of the minority conservative as a thoughtless mimic of the white man.[17]

Just a few months after Rall's liberal, racist cartoon, Jeff Danziger, a two-time Pulitzer Prize finalist carried by the *New York Times* News Syndicate, depicted Rice as the "Prissy" character in *Gone With the Wind*—complete with bare feet, exaggerated lips, and stereotypical dialect ("I knows all about aluminum tubes.") After *National Review's* Jay Nordlinger[18] and a slew of conservative blogs put the heat on Danziger, the cartoonist issued a form letter in response:

In fact the idea for the cartoon was suggested to me by a friend who is African-American. It wasn't racist. Nor am I. I have been doing this for nearly thirty years, and any review of my work will prove that no racism attaches. Further, I am a decorated Vietnam veteran who voted for Nixon once, GHW Bush twice and even for Bob Dole. So keep your labels. Nothing racist about it at all. Just the standard lies told by a political operative, out of her depth, who happens to be African-American. Whenever this administration is in trouble they send out Condi Rice because the press, which is mostly white and male, gives her a far easier treatment than they would a white male.[19]

Danziger yanked the cartoon from his website and refused a request to reprint it in this book, but it was preserved by countless alert watchdogs on the Internet.[20] Rall, Danziger, and their ilk can run from their inner Klansmen, but they can't hide.

The party of Senator Robert "KKK" Byrd

Remember when Republican Senator Trent Lott of Mississippi lost his Senate Majority Leader post in December 2002 after a boneheaded joke at Strom Thurmond's 100th birthday celebration? "I want to say this about my state: When Strom Thurmond ran for president we voted for him. We're proud of it. And if the rest of the country had of followed our lead we wouldn't have had all these problems over all these years, either."

I needn't remind you of the uproar, first by bloggers and then by the mainstream media, that led to Lott's resignation.[21] Strong condemnations by principled conservatives ensured his downfall for a joke that implied support for Thurmond's Dixiecrat segregationist views.

Now, for a perfect illustration of the bigotry double standards that the self-proclaimed party of tolerance gets away with, contrast the Lott episode with the fate of Democrat Senator Chris Dodd of Connecticut. In an April 2004 speech on the Senate floor commemorating the 17,000th vote of Democrat Senator Robert Byrd of West Virginia, Dodd paid tribute this way:

> "It has often been said that the man and the moment come together. I do not think it is an exaggeration at all to say to my friend from West Virginia that he would have been a great Senator at any moment. Some were right for the time. Robert C. Byrd, in my view, would have been right at any time... I cannot think of a single moment in this Nation's 220-plus year history where he would not have been a valuable asset to this country."[22]

Not "a single moment?"

How could Senator Dodd possibly have forgotten Senator Byrd's role in the Ku Klux Klan in the early 1940s, not merely as a passive participant—but as a "Kleagle" who recruited new members for $10 a head and founded his own local chapter?[23] Senator Byrd said he joined because it "offered excitement" and because the Klan was an "effective force" in "promoting traditional American values."[24]

How about when Senator Byrd filibustered the landmark 1964 Civil Rights Act—supported by a majority of those "mean-spirited" Republicans—for more than 14 hours? Or when Senator Byrd opposed the integration of the armed forces, vowing never to fight "with a Negro by my side. Rather I should die a thousand times, and see Old Glory trampled in the dirt never to rise again, than to see this beloved land of ours become degraded by race mongrels, a throwback to the blackest specimen from the wilds."[25]

And how about March 2001, when Senator Byrd casually used the phrase "white nigger" twice on national TV? *Fox News Sunday* morning talk show host Tony Snow had asked the veteran Democrat about the state of race relations in America. Senator Byrd warned: "There are white niggers. I've seen a lot of white niggers in my time. I'm going to use that word. We just need to work together to make our country a better country, and I'd just as soon quit talking about it so much."

Was Senator Byrd "a valuable asset to this country" then?

Conservatives pressured Senator Dodd to retract his adulatory remarks. But no Democrat leaders or prominent liberals did so. Senator Dodd released a written statement apologizing for "for his poor choice of words" in praise of ex-Klansman Byrd. Civil rights leaders shrugged. Hilary Shelton, the NAACP's chief lobbyist in Washington, told the *New York Times* that Dodd had called him to apologize "but I didn't think it was necessary quite frankly."[26] Ex-Klansman Byrd no doubt agreed.

When a Republican makes a racially insensitive comment, it is splashed all over the front pages and is condemned by both liberals and conservatives. When a Democrat does the same thing, it barely gets noticed.

Remember when Senator Hillary Clinton cracked a stereotypical joke about Indians and gas stations? At a fundraiser in January 2004, she mocked renowned peace activist and religious leader Mahatma Gandhi by saying he "ran a gas station down in St. Louis." While Gandhi scholars and some Indian community leaders were appalled, the mainstream media and liberal apologists shrugged off Senator Clinton's remarks. David Robertson, a University of Missouri-St. Louis political science professor, demurred that "there's no reason to think she doesn't admire Gandhi, like so many people do. After all, Gandhi was influential to Martin Luther King Jr., and I know she respects King."[27]

One wonders if Robertson would have been so forgiving if Senator Clinton had mocked Dr. King by saying he ran a fried-chicken restaurant down in Birmingham.

Few paid attention when former Senate Majority Leader Tom Daschle mixed up the two black reporters who regularly cover Congress. Daschle referred to PBS reporter Linda Scott as "Evelyn"—evidently a reference to CBS News producer Evelyn Thomas. "It's Linda," Scott angrily shot back, "and I know we don't look alike." As blogger Dave Wissing pointed out, "You can be sure that if a Republican had made this mistake, CNN would have devoted hours of coverage to it claiming how the entire Republican Party are a bunch of racists still living in the 1960's. But since it was a Democrat, not even a mention."[28]

The national media devoted even less coverage to Pennsylvania state Senator Vincent Fumo's use of an anti-gay slur in October 2004. The powerful Democrat from Philadelphia repeatedly screamed "faggot" at his Republican opponents on the Senate floor.[29] According to several people who were in the chamber at the time, Fumo was shouting at the top of his lungs. "The use of the word came with such force and invective behind it that it almost sounded like someone yelling at a football stadium," said Ray Smith, a reporter for the Radio Pennsylvania Network.[30]

Republican State Senator Jeffrey Piccola of Pennsylvania, who was just feet from Fumo at the time, told the *Aberdeen News* that the look in Fumo's eyes was "almost as frightening as the comments."

What Liberal Racism?

Astonishingly, Democrat Congressman Corrine Brown of Florida proclaimed during a congressional briefing that Hispanics and whites "all look alike to me." Jennifer Lopez. Hillary Clinton. Laura Bush. Barbara Bush. She can't tell 'em apart! It's a wonder how this woman can function in Washington, let alone in her district. Is there an eye doctor in the house who can advise Congressman Brown on whether Lasik could fix her strange condition? Prior to this comment, the congresswoman, who is black, claimed Republican leaders were "racist" in their policies toward Haiti, and called the White House's representatives "a bunch of white men." At the time, she was sitting across from Assistant Secretary of State Roger Noriega, a Mexican-American. The incident was reported by Fox News and the Associated Press, but was completely ignored by ABC, CBS, NBC, CNN, MSNBC, *Time*, *Newsweek*, *U.S. News and World Report*, the *New York Times*, *Washington Post*, and *USA Today*.

"He was a man possessed and on the verge of getting out of control," Piccola said.[31]

Fumo later apologized for his remarks, sort of. "I should have called them 'girlie men,'" he explained. "They have no integrity, no guts, and no class."[32]

That was good enough for Mark Segal, publisher of the *Philadelphia Gay News*. "Vince is the kind of guy, when he gets angry colorful things come out of his mouth," Segal rationalized. "But he is also the No. 1 supporter of gay and lesbian issues in the Pennsylvania Senate . . . and deeds speak louder than words."[33]

Just ignore the filth that comes out of their mouths, in other words, because liberals can't be prejudiced.

Democrat Congressman Pete Stark of California got a similar pass in the summer of 2003 when he hurled homophobic slurs at Republicans during a mark-up session on pension funds legislation of all things. "You little fruitcake. You little fruitcake," ranted Stark to Scott McInnis, a Republican Congressman from Colorado. "I said you are a fruitcake."[34]

According to Fox News Channel—citing witnesses—Stark then called Republican House Ways and Means Committee Chairman Bill Thomas of California a "cocksucker." Stark's press office refused to answer my questions on the record about these remarks.[35]

Gay rights groups, whose fax machines and phone lines would have been on fire had the comments been made by any prominent conservative, shrugged at Stark's remarks. "I think he meant nothing by it," Human Rights Campaign official Winnie Stachelberg told Fox News.[36]

Only the self-anointed preachers of tolerance and civility on the Left can have their fruitcake and eat it, too.

Of course, liberals' civility toward gays only goes so far. When openly gay Republican political operative Arthur Finkelstein launched a "Stop Her Now" effort against Senator Hillary Clinton, former President Bill Clinton responded that Finkelstein might be "self-loathing"[37]—a comment that had nothing to do with Finkelstein's political advocacy and everything to do with his sexual orientation. Can you imagine the outcry if President Bush made the same remark about a gay Democrat?

Conservative women have long been subjected to similar attacks.[38] Despite the feminist demand that women be judged on the contents of their character rather than the appearance of their skin, liberal women seem to have no misgivings whatsoever about laughing at their conservative counterparts' looks.

New York Times columnist Maureen Dowd was among those who likened Republican Congressman Katherine Harris of Florida to Cruella de Ville, the dog-killer in "101 Dalmatians."[39] Shortly after the 2000 election, the *Washington Post* published an entire article ridiculing Harris's appearance:

> One of the reasons Harris is so easy to mock is because she, to be honest, seems to have applied her makeup with a trowel. At this moment that so desperately needs diplomacy, understatement and calm, one wonders how this Republican woman, who can't even use restraint when she's wielding a mascara wand, will manage to use it and make sound decisions in this game of partisan one-upmanship. Besides, she looks bad—not by the hand of God but by her own. She took fashion—which speaks in riddles, hyperbole and half-truths—at its word, imbibing all of those references to the '70s and '80s, taking styling cues from Versace ads in which models are made up as if by a mortician's assistant, believing the magazines when they said that blue eye shadow was back. She failed to think for herself. Why should anyone trust her?[40]

After readers complained, the *Post's* ombudsman, Michael Getler, conceded that the piece went too far. "Mocking someone's appearance is not something that newspapers should do," he admitted.[41]

Mocking a woman's decision to give up work and raise children at home is not something that a presidential candidate's wife should do either. But "cheeky" Teresa Heinz Kerry seemed not to care about ridiculing millions of stay-at-home moms. Following in the footsteps of Hillary "I suppose I could have stayed home and baked cookies and had teas" Clinton, the cranky ketchup heiress told *USA Today* that First Lady Laura Bush—a former librarian, schoolteacher, and stay-at-home mom—had never held down "a real job."[42]

As any librarian, schoolteacher or stay-at-home mom can attest, that is truly nuts.

Bashing "Jesusland"

Another favorite target of liberal bigots: evangelical Christians.

The day after the 2004 election, sore Kerry losers concocted maps of the North American continent divided into the blue region of "The United States of Canada" and the red region of "Jesusland" or "Redneckistan." The graphics spread like a virus across the Web.[43] The *Washington Times* reported: "The Internet has exploded with talk of a blue-state confederacy, including one screed circulating by e-mail that features a map of a new country called 'American Coastopia' and proposes lopping off the Northeast, the West Coast and the upper Midwest to form a new country, away from the 'rednecks in Oklahoma' and the 'homophobic knuckle-draggers in Wyoming.'"[44]

Los Angeles-based blogger Ken Layne published a bitter, bigoted diatribe that summed up the unhinged Left's rage:

> Rove's re-election strategy was elegantly simple: Scare the bejesus out of Jesusland. F@ggots are headed your way! Satanic Muslims are hiding everywhere! That's all it took to get Jesusland to do the job. Intellectual conservatives like the National Review staff are flattering themselves if they honestly believe Jesusland cares about conservative thought. The "reality-based" folks are learning that Jesusland doesn't even care about jobs or the economy. In Jesusland, it's all the will of Jesus. No job? No money? Daughter got her clit pierced? Jesus is just f*cking with you again, testing your faith. Got the cancer? Oh well. Soon you'll be with Jesus. Reality is no match for a mystical world in which an all-powerful god is constantly toying with every detail of your mundane life, just to see what you'll do about it. Keep praying and always keep your

eye out for homosexuals and terrorists, and you will eventually be rewarded . . . all you have to do is die, and then it's SuperJesus-Land, where you will be a ghost floating in a magic cloud with all the other ghosts from Jesusland, with Jesus Himself presiding over an Eternal Church Service.[45]

Hysteria immediately set in among the media elite as Associated Press and network news exit polls purportedly showed that moral values above all else propelled President Bush to victory.[46] (The exit polls were later judged to have suffered from poor wording, Andrew Kohut of the Pew Research Center noted no disproportionate surge in the evangelical vote or self-identified pro-life voters.[47]) Gary Wills fumed in the *New York Times* about "moral zealots" taking over in an alarmist op-ed titled "The Day the Enlightenment Went Out."[48] Maureen Dowd carped about Bush's "devoted flock of evangelicals" and warned of a return to the Dark Ages.[49] Bob Herbert commiserated by insulting Bush voters' intelligence. He concluded that values voters were too stupid to know what they were doing and urged more Democrat teach-ins to solve the problem: "Anything that shrinks the ranks of the clueless would be helpful."[50]

Novelist Jane Smiley lambasted Southern people of faith in a commentary for Slate.com. The election results, she wrote, "reflect the decision of the right wing to cultivate and exploit ignorance in the citizenry."[51] Red-staters, she sneered, "do not want to be told what to do—they prefer to be ignorant. As a result, they are virtually unteachable."

In a speech at the University of Chicago and on his National Public Radio show, left-wing "humorist" Garrison Keillor called for barring born-again Christians from voting. The *Chicago Maroon*, the university student newspaper quoted Keillor's remarks:[52]

"I'm trying to organize support for a constitutional amendment to deny voting rights to born-again Christians," Keillor smirked. "I feel if your citizenship is in Heaven—like a born again Christian's is—you should give up your citizenship. Sorry, but this is my new cause. If born again Christians are allowed to vote in this country, then why not Canadians?"

MSNBC senior political analyst Lawrence O'Donnell went even further, raising the prospect of John Kerry-supporting blue states seceding from the U.S.[53] Veteran Democratic activist Bob Beckel also voiced pro-secessionist sentiments on Fox News: "I think now that slavery is taken care of, I'm for letting the South form its own nation. Really, I think they ought to have their own confederacy." And by February 2005, Democrat Congressman Charles Rangel of New York felt comfortable mocking his fellow Democrat, former President Bill Clinton, as a "redneck" and expanding the smear to include all people "from Arkansas."[54]

The Anti-Life Brigade

Next on the unhinged target list: ordinary, peaceful, pro-life protesters who traveled to Florida in support of Terri Schiavo, the disabled woman starved to death by her husband and the courts after a protracted legal battle in March 2005. Here's how writer Michelle Cottle of *The New Republic* expressed contempt for Schiavo's religious supporters on CNN's *Reliable Sources* with Howard Kurtz:

Kurtz: Michelle Cottle, has the press ridiculed, or maybe I should say marginalized, religious people who believed the Terri Schiavo must be kept alive as a matter of Christian morality?

Cottle: Well, it's not that they get out there and make fun of them. It's just you come with a ready-made kind of visual here. *You have people on the streets praying.* They're, you have very dramatic and even melodramatic protests and things like this.

These people are very easy to kind of just poke fun at without even saying anything. You just kind of show these people. And the majority of Americans who don't get out there and do this kind of, you know, really dramatic displays feel a little bit uncomfortable on that level. [Emphasis added.]

If Cottle was willing to be this honest on national TV about her discomfort with people praying on the street, can you imagine what her colleagues in newsrooms and control rooms across the country say about "these people?" A *Washington Post* story published the day after Cottle's remarks underscored her point. Highlighting a pro-Terri evangelical protester who carried around a giant spoon with a message asking Florida Governor Jeb Bush to "Please Feed Terri," *Post* reporter Dana Milbank's piece reeked of barely-concealed contempt for those crazy Christians.[55]

The religion-bashing rhetoric kept on raging after Schiavo's death. *New York Times* columnist Paul Krugman hysterically suggested that "religious extremists" on the right might be on the verge of assassinating liberal politicians. Actually, it was the Left that daydreamed not only about assassinating President Bush, but about the death of Pope John Paul II.[56] The *New York Press* even published a cover story listing "The 52 Funniest Things About the Upcoming Death of the Pope," including the following:

52. Pope pisses himself just before the end; gets all over nurse.

49. After beating for the last time, Pope's heart sits there like a piece of hamburger.

47. Upon death, Pope's face frozen in sickening smile, eyes wide open and teeth exposed, like a baboon.

31. Dead Pope, still with baboon face, wheeled through corridors of Gemelli Polyclinic in Rome, learns answer to Great Mystery.

17. In his last days, the Pope was in tremendous pain.

2. This is what happens when weird old men in dresses communicate with the world with doors and chimneys.

1. Throw a marble at the dead Pope's head. Bonk![57]

Church-bashers proceeded to savage John Paul II's successor, Cardinal Ratzinger (who had been compelled to join the Hitler Youth as a boy growing up in Bavaria, but was the son of an outspoken anti-Nazi activist and later deserted the German army[58]) as a "Nazi Pope." The smear didn't just surface in the far-left fever swamps of the Internet. It was also featured prominently on the *New York Times* website, which headlined a hysterical letter to the editor: "Nazi pope a clear and present danger to the civilized world."[59] The Anti-Defamation League expressed outrage at the *Times'* journalistic recklessness. "We reject that outright," ADL spokeswoman Mryna Shinebaum told United Press International. The group's director, Abraham H. Foxman, had welcomed Ratzinger's election: "Cardinal Ratzinger has great sensitivity to Jewish history and the Holocaust. He has shown this sensitivity countless times."[60]

Not that the *Times* would let the truth get in the way of a good anti-religious swipe.

The religion-haters called Cardinal Ratzinger everything but the Anti-christ. That epithet was saved for the conservative Christian group, Focus on the Family. The rhetorical bomb was thrown by Democrat Senator Ken Salazar of Colorado, who joined the ranks of unhinged liberals with this doozy in April 2005: "'From my point of view, they are the Anti-christ of the world."[61] The *Anti-christ*? Of the *world*?

What exactly was Focus on the Family's act of evil that warranted Senator Salazar's attack? The group had voiced its support for an up-or-down vote on President Bush's judicial nominees.

Senator Salazar retreated from his overheated remarks after Christians across the country objected, but he did so only grudgingly. "I spoke about Jim Dobson and his efforts and used the term 'the anti-Christ,'" Salazar said in a written statement from his office, according to the *Denver Post*. "I regret having used that term. I meant to say this approach was un-Christian, meaning self-serving and selfish."[62]

Oops. Curdled with hate for Christian conservatives in the political arena, Senator Salazar overlooked the insult to non-Christians inadvertently (or maybe not?) implied in his blundering so-called apology. At least he made the pretense of apologizing, which is more than people of faith could ever expect to receive from comedian Bill Maher. "I think religion is a neurological disorder," Maher told MSNBC's Joe Scarborough.

Professing to love America, Maher fumed that he was "embarrassed that it has been taken over by people like evangelicals, by people who do not believe in science and rationality." A model of tolerance and modesty, Maher fumed further that he was disgusted by religion "because it is arrogance parading as humility."[63]

Maher's bigotry was just one shining example of Hollywood intolerance parading as liberal idealism. Since George W. Bush took office, celebrities have become far more unhinged, outspoken, and profane about their hatred for mainstream America than ever before.

CHAPTER SEVEN

The Hollywood Walk of Hate

Once upon a time, there were people in Hollywood who loved America. And when America came under attack from enemies abroad, these actors, producers, screenwriters and directors put aside their partisan differences and created movies that made all moviegoers proud to be Americans.

During World War II, Tinseltown roused the country's fighting spirit instead of trying to stifle it.

Hollywood celebrities of the past didn't just play soldiers in front of the cameras. They volunteered to put their lives on the line for America. Clark Gable joined the Army Air Corps at 41, became a B-17 air gunner, and earned the Air Medal and Distinguished Flying Cross. Jimmy Stewart led B-24 bombing raids over Germany. They both appeared in pro-America documentaries, produced by the military-operated First Motion Picture Unit, when not in combat. Director Frank Capra made films for the U.S. government, including the seven-part *Why We Fight* (1942-44).

Those who stayed behind during World War II starred in countless films—*Bataan*, *The Battle of Midway*, *Flying Tigers*, *So Proudly We Hail!*, *Wake Island*, and *Yankee Doodle Dandy*, to name just a few—which rallied Americans through the long, dark days of the war to support the Allied cause. The movies depicted good and evil in stark terms. And there was no politically correct revisionism about who our enemies were.

The president of the Motion Picture Association, independent movie mogul and World War I pilot and intelligence officer Walter Wanger, went out of his way to use the Academy Awards to support the war effort. Wanger invited President Roosevelt to address the crowd. In an unprecedented radio speech simulcast on all three major networks, FDR praised Hollywood for its wartime fundraising efforts and thanked filmmakers for "sanctifying the American way of life."

Can you imagine Hollywood extending such an invitation to President Bush today? Can you imagine CBS, ABC and NBC agreeing to simulcast such an event? And can you imagine the howling from the American Civil Liberties Union, ethnic groups, Barbra Streisand and Sean Penn if President Bush were allowed to appear at the Academy Awards to speak in support of "sanctifying the American way of life?"

The greatest generation had the dashing Gable and the earnest Stewart. We got Michael Moore, who wrote on the day after the September 11th terrorist attacks: "Many families have been devastated tonight. This is just not right. They did not deserve to die. If someone did this to get back at Bush, then they did so by killing thousands of people who DID NOT VOTE for him. Boston, New York, D.C., and the planes' destination of California—these were the places that voted AGAINST Bush." In other words: right reason, wrong target.

The greatest generation had big-band leader Glenn Miller, who led the U.S. Army Air Force band in Europe and died for our country when his plane went down over the English Channel. We got "Moby" (real name: Richard Melville Hall), an "electronic musician," whose idea of supporting America in 2004 was to encourage Democrats to engage in fraud and dirty campaign tricks. "For example," he told the *New York Daily News*, "you can go on all the pro-life chat rooms and say you're an outraged right-wing voter and that you know that George Bush drove an ex-girlfriend to an abortion clinic and paid for her to get an abortion."[1]

It is not news that modern-day Hollywood is liberal. What has changed since the Bush administration took office is that left-leaning celebrities in the entertainment industry have, to put it bluntly, gone completely bonkers. Like rock stars and supermodels on made-for-tabloid rampages, Hollywood liberals are on an unstoppable tear: trashing the White House; trashing conservatives; trashing the American way of life at home and abroad; and all with absolutely no recognition of the appalling propaganda value to America's enemies of constantly cursing this nation and its leadership during wartime.

Dr. Ergun Mehmet Caner, a Persian Turkish immigrant who became a proud American in 1982, describes this phenomenon—fueled by the likes of far-left crockumentarian Michael Moore—as "Hate-riotism."[2] In a critical piece on Moore's *Fahrenheit 9/11*, Caner wrote:

> The irony is, for all of their false bravado behind the First Amendment and their right to "free speech," the hatriots are exercising this right because American men and women shed their blood to afford them this right against those who would seek to oppress it. I would invite Michael Moore to my homeland to make a movie criticizing Turkish oppression and see what happens. The freedom he enjoys now was purchased with a dear price.

Celebrities' unhinged assaults on the defenders of freedom surely must have Hollywood's lost patriots turning in their graves.

Foaming at the Mouth

If the Motion Picture Association of America gave out ratings for Hollywood political fund-raisers, it would have to award them the most restrictive mark: NC-17. No one under 17 admitted due to explicit sexual content and extreme profanity.

In December 2003, Democrat presidential candidate Howard Dean attended a fund-raiser in Chelsea, New York, courtesy of C-list stand-up comedians who wallowed in the gutter. As Deborah Orin of the *New York Post* reported, comic Judy Gold attacked President Bush as "this piece of living, breathing shit" and Janeane Garofalo mocked the massive Medicare prescription-drug bill that Bush had just signed as the "You can go fuck yourself, Grandma" bill.[3] Others took to savaging Vice President Dick Cheney's family—referring to Cheney's wife, Lynne, as horror movie star Lon Chaney and Cheney's daughter Mary, who is a lesbian, as a "a big lezzie."[4]

Dean, to his credit, distanced himself from some of the jokes that night. But he gladly took all of the foul-mouthed fundraisers' money and ran. The media and political establishments shrugged. Why? "It's like an Upper West Side Manhattan left-wing Ku Klux Klan mentality," explained Republican Congressman Peter King of New York. "If some Southern redneck talked like this about a liberal, everyone would denounce it. But because it's Upper West Side humor, somehow it's supposed to be chic."[5]

Not to be outdone, B-list celebrities pulled out all the stops for Democrat presidential nominee John Kerry in July 2004 at the famous Radio City Music Hall. Hollywood has-been Whoopi Goldberg performed as if she were playing the seediest strip joint in Las Vegas. Scraping the bottom of the humor barrel, Goldberg was vulgar, barely coherent, and (worse in the Hollywood crowd's eyes, no doubt) embarrassingly unfunny. A sample of her performance:

> You have to meet the King and Queen of Kupeepee and you know you're going to look dumb if you don't know where Kupeepee is because everybody else pretends they know where it is. And when you get the menu for the State Dinner, you know that you have bears balls' and frog lips as a delicacy and you cannot say, "Hell No!" ...[T]hat's why I'm here tonight. Because I love bush. But someone's giving bush a bad name. Someone has tarnished the name of 'bush.' Someone has waged war, someone has deliberately misled the country, someone has attempted to amend the constitution, all in the name of bush. The bush I know and cherish

would never do such things. My bush is smarter than that. And if my bush is smarter than that, you can understand just how dumb I think that other bush is. And anyone who would wave to Stevie Wonder is not fully there. I will do whatever it takes to restore bush to its rightful place and that ain't in the White House. Vote your heart and mind and keep bush where it belongs. [6]

Goldberg was joined by fellow Bush-basher John Mellencamp, who warbled a country tune calling the president a "Texas Bandito" who is "just another cheap thug that sacrifices our young." Academy Award-winning actress Meryl Streep sneered at the president's religious beliefs: "I wondered to myself during 'Shock and Awe,' I wondered which of the megaton bombs Jesus, our president's personal savior, would have personally dropped on the sleeping families of Baghdad?"[7] And Hispanic actor John Leguizamo said the idea of Hispanic Republicans was an "oxymoron" because "Latins for Republicans—it's like roaches for Raid."[8]

Here's a real oxymoron, Mr. Leguizamo: Tolerant liberals. Thank you for the in-living-color demonstration.

How did Democrat presidential nominee John Kerry and his running mate John Edwards respond to this uncensored filth and unbridled hatred? Edwards said it was "a great honor" and promised that the campaign would "be a celebration of real American values." Kerry thanked all the attendees and organizers for "an extraordinary evening" and claimed "every single performer" represented "the heart and soul of our country." Kerry and Edwards raked in $7.5 million from their foul-mouthed friends.

Among the celebrities who couldn't keep their obscene thoughts to themselves was actress Jennifer Aniston, named one of *People* magazine's "Most Beautiful People." She told *Rolling Stone* magazine in September 2004 that "Bush is a fucking idiot." The reporter described her as flipping the president "a double-bird" while cursing.[9] A lovely sight for sore liberal eyes, no doubt.

At a MoveOn gala in January 2003 to honor Bush-bashing ads, the aforementioned "Moby" ranted from the stage about his "contempt and loathing for George Bush, who's a big, fat, fucking liar."[10] Angry comedian Margaret

Cho (who, by the way, named her dog after an infamous terrorist leader of the German Baader-Meinhof Gang) inveighed:

> Despite all of this stupid bullshit that the Republican National Committee, or whatever the fuck they call them, that they were saying that they're all angry about how two of these ads were comparing Bush to Hitler? I mean, out of thousands of submissions, they find two. They're like fucking looking for Hitler in a haystack.[11]

The self-parody of all liberal Hollywood parodies during the campaign season was the Einstein of the entertainment biz, Chevy Chase. The star of National Lampoon's *Vacation* movies disparaged the president as dumb as "an egg-timer" and said John Edwards would make Vice President Dick Cheney look "as bright as a bundt cake" during their debates. A month after Cheney cleaned Edwards' clock and President Bush was re-elected, Chase was back in the rhetorical sewer. At the hallowed Kennedy Center in Washington, D.C., of all places, he called the vice president a "dumb fuck" as outgoing Senate Minority Leader Tom Daschle and a crowd of political heavyweights sat in the audience.[12] Attacking President Bush, Chase ranted: "This guy in office is an uneducated, real lying schmuck." Contrasting himself with Bush, he continued: "I'm no fucking clown either... This guy started a jihad."[13]

Land of the Lost

As plans to invade Iraq moved closer to fruition, actors became increasingly agitated about what they described as an effort by the White House and its supporters to silence President Bush's critics.

Actress Julia Stiles reportedly told MoveOn activists she "was afraid that [Fox News Channel host] Bill O'Reilly would come with a shotgun at my front door and shoot me for being unpatriotic."[14]

When actor Danny Glover signed a statement calling the Iraq war an unprovoked, unjustified invasion, some conservatives called for a boycott of telecommunications giant MCI, which had hired Glover as a spokesman.

Tim Robbins: Somehow Still Alive

"A chill wind is blowing in this nation," left-wing actor Tim Robbins warned ominously at a National Press Club luncheon. "A message is being sent through the White House and its allies in talk radio and Clear Channel and Cooperstown. If you oppose this administration, there can and will be ramifications. Every day, the air waves are filled with warnings, veiled and unveiled threats, spewed invective and hatred directed at any voice of dissent."[15]

Glover had never fretted about First Amendment rights when left-wing activists orchestrated boycotts targeting conservatives, such as talk show hosts Rush Limbaugh, Michael Savage and Dr. Laura Schlessinger. But this boycott was different. He called his critics a "dark and very sinister" threat to freedom of speech. "It's basically this rabid nationalism that has its own kind of potential of being maniacal," he told the Associated Press. "The whole idea is to crush any kind of dissent."[16]

No one was claiming that Stiles, Robbins, or Glover should be denied the right to express their opinions. Yet the ridiculous notion that the Bush Administration and its conservative supporters were mounting an all-out assault on the First Amendment quickly became accepted as conventional wisdom among the Hollywood elite.

At a Los Angeles antiwar march, actor Martin Sheen marched with duct tape over his mouth—not a bad idea, and something conservatives could cheer—with the word "peace" on it.[17] Singer Rickie Lee Jones said, "You know, people in America are afraid to say anything; they are afraid of George Bush, afraid of the police, afraid of being fined, afraid of being accused."[18] Nearly a year later, British pop singer Elton John told *Interview* magazine that U.S. stars were still scared to speak out because of "the current administration's bullying tactics."[19]

Yet somehow, celebrities kept finding the courage—and dodging Bush's Homeland Security Gestapo—to speak out. A lot. Over, and over, and over again.

Among those who refused to be silenced was rocker Chrissie Hynde of The Pretenders. "We fuckin' deserve to get bombed," she declared at one of her concerts, "Let's get rid of all the economic shit this country represents! Bring it on, I hope the Muslims win."[20]

When a crowd member responded negatively to that truly loony statement, Hynde shrieked, "Shut your face!"

Another star who continued to speak out was actor Sean Penn, who claimed that Bill O'Reilly and shock jock Howard Stern have caused more harm to the world than Osama bin Laden. "I'd like to trade O'Reilly for Bin Laden," he said.[21] I wonder who we could trade Sean Penn for? Maybe to China for another panda?

O'Reilly responded to Penn's desire to trade him by repeatedly praising Penn's Oscar-winning performance in the movie *Mystic River*.[22]

When Penn was asked whether the Iraqi people were better off without Saddam Hussein in power, he could have backtracked from his earlier remark. Instead, he again pooh-poohed the threat posed by al Qaeda. The bigger threat, of course, was posed by George W. Bush. "We have a dictatorship in this country [the U.S.]," Penn said. "Our government is presently the greatest threat to our people."[23]

Madonna took a break from her Kabbalah classes and faux-English accent to underline her ex-husband's kooky meme in an e-mail to her fans: "Our greatest risk is not terrorism and it's not Iraq or the 'Axis of Evil.' Our greatest risk is a lack of leadership, a lack of honesty and a complete lack of consciousness." Leaving no doubt as to where exactly she thought this lack of leadership, honesty, and consciousness resided, she went on to blast the Bush administration.[24]

Comic Sandra Bernhard went even farther, telling washingtonpost.com readers that "the real terrorist threats are George W. Bush and his band of brown-shirted thugs."[25]

As Bernhard's comment demonstrates, no historical allusion was too hyperbolic for Hollywood's Bush critics.

Rocker Ozzy Osbourne, for example, opened at least one concert with the song "War Pigs," featuring a video montage comparing Bush to Hitler along with the caption: "Same shit, different asshole."[26]

Actress and Air America talk radio host Janeane Garofalo lamented the Bush administration's support for the Patriot Act by charging: "It is in fact a conspiracy of the 43rd Reich."[27] The conspiracy behind the Patriot Act included virtually every Democrat in the U.S. Senate, which approved the Act 98-1.[28]

A few celebrities asserted that the comparison between Bush and Hitler was unfair—to Hitler, that is. "George Bush is not Hitler," said Margaret Cho. "He would be if he fucking applied himself."[29] David Clennon, star of *The Agency*, told talk show host Sean Hannity that the only difference between Bush and Hitler is that Hitler was smarter.[30]

Hollywood liberals used Nazi references to smear not just President Bush, but ordinary flag-waving Americans. "I worry that some people are entertained by the idea of this war [against Iraq]," said singer Linda Ronstadt. "They don't know anything about the Iraqis, but they're angry and frustrated in their own lives. It's like Germany, before Hitler took over. The economy was bad and people felt kicked around. They looked for a scapegoat. Now we've got a new bunch of Hitlers."[31]

Singer Rickie Lee Jones told the *Guardian*. "My skin crawls when I think of the first week after 9/11. I was looking out of the window and there were people marching down the street carrying flags. It reminded me of spontaneous, angry Nazis and I thought, 'Oh, man, we are in a lot of trouble.' There's a whole bunch of people who have flags hanging from their cars and who are mistaking fascism for patriotism."[32]

Yes, you heard right: flags hanging from cars. It's Kristallnacht, all over again!

And for unhinged liberals, another apparent difference between Hitler and Bush is that Hitler was at least elected honestly. Disgruntled Hollywood stars continued to hyperventilate about President Bush's election: "[Bush] stole the presidency through family ties, arrogance and intimidation, employing Republican operatives to exercise the tactics of voter fraud by disenfranchising thousands of blacks, elderly Jews and other minorities" (Barbra

Streisand);[33] "[w]hat happened in the [2000] election was completely corrupt (Sandra Bernhard);[34] "what happened in 2000 did as much damage to the pillars of democracy as terrorists did to the pillars of commerce in New York City" (Alec Baldwin);[35] and "we've got a president we didn't elect...we need a little shift on over toward the left" ("It Takes Time," by the Beastie Boys).[36] Never mind that if Al Gore had gotten the manual recounts he requested in Florida, Bush still would have won.[37]

Rappers be Hatin'

The Beastie Boys were more tolerable when they were fighting for their right to party. But they're hardly alone. The recording artist known as Jadakiss earned big bucks and bling-bling with a summer 2004 hit single called "Why?" The song accuses President Bush of involvement in the September 11, 2001 terrorist attacks, with the lyric "Why did Bush knock down the Towers?"[38]

The album on which "Why?" appeared sold more than 246,000 copies in its first week, according to Nielsen SoundScan, debuting at No. 1 on the Billboard 200.[39]

MTV and some radio stations edited out the controversial line in "Why?" but Jadakiss said his fans insisted that they be allowed to hear the original version. "A lot of my people felt that [Bush] had something to do with [the events of September 11]," the rapper explained to Billboard.com.[40]

"My people" apparently includes The Coup, two rappers who had the good taste to release an album, *Party Music*, less than three months after the September 11th attacks showing themselves partying in front of the flaming World Trade Center towers. One of the rappers, self-described communist Boots Riley, posed in the foreground with a guitar tuner being used as a bomb detonator. His sidekick, "Pam the Funkstress," stood defiantly with a conductor's baton in each hand while fireballs engulf the buildings.[41]

Riley explained that he wanted to spread the message that "the blood that happened on [September 11] is on the hands of the U.S. government."[42]

The *Washington Post*'s staff writer David Segal called "Party Music" the best album of 2001. He praised the album's "jarring ingenuity, soul and wit."

Since Segal liked *Party Music* so much, he must have loved "What Would You Do" by rapper Paris, which includes this stanza:

Now ask yourself who's the one with the most to gain (Bush) 'Fore
911 motherfuckas couldn't stand his name (Bush)[43]

Given an opportunity to elaborate, Paris reportedly said that "higher ups in the government conspired to self-induce terrorism on the United States so that they could go about achieving more government control; so that they could go about initiating a way by which to increase defense spending and to profit from the horrible events that took place [on September 11]."[44]

Rapping duo M1 and Stickman of "dead prez" expressed similar views in their song, "Know Your Enemy:"

Know your enemy, know yourself, that's the politic/George Bush
is way worse than Bin Laden is/Know your enemy, know yourself,
that's the politic/FBI, CIA, the real terrorists.[45]

During the middle of a packed concert in Chicago, the rappers said, "If you're feeling this, put a middle finger up to George Bush." According to a music reviewer for the *Chicago Tribune*, nearly everyone in the audience did so.[46]

Immoral Technique (or "Tech") provided further insights about what really happened on September 11th. In his album "Rev. 2," which reportedly sold more than 35,000 copies, he states:

I was watchin' the towers/and though I wasn't the closest/I saw
them crumble to the earth/like they were full of explosives[47]

When freelance journalist Michael Kane asked what inspired that line, Tech said, "The line about the explosives comes from actual interviews and comments from firemen about the way they saw the buildings collapse—some saying they heard 'loud explosions' when the buildings were collapsing. Some people have speculated that it was simply each floor caving in, but that would sound different. These are professionals saying this."[48]

Later in the song, Tech clarified his views:

> And just so conservatives don't take it to heart/I don't think Bush did it, cause he isn't that smart/He's just a stupid puppet taking orders on his cell phone/From the same people that sabotaged Senator Wellstone.[49]

In other words, Bush was not the mastermind of the September 11th attacks, but merely the hitman. At least he's that smart.

Given such conspiracy-mongering, is it any wonder that the world's most popular rapper, Eminem, felt comfortable not only singing, "Fuck Bush,"[50] and telling *Rolling Stone* that Bush has "fucked up so bad," but also openly wishing for our president's death with lyrics that prompted a Secret Service investigation:[51]

> Fuck money, I don't rhyme for dead presidents/I'd rather see the president dead.[52]

Eminem's mother and ex-wife, previous primary targets of the rapper's lyrical death wishes, welcomed the diversion of his attention.

Chicken Little Chic

Clearly, when it comes to Bush and September 11th, some rappers are operating with a screw loose. But they are models of rationality compared to singer/actress Cher and actress Cameron Diaz.

Cher warned shortly before the 2004 election that if Bush were re-elected, the government would round up and quarantine homosexual men:

> All the gay guys, all my friends, all my gay friends, you guys you have got to vote, alright? Because...the people, like, in the very

right wing of this party...if they get any more power, you guys are going to be living in some state by yourselves. So, I hate scare tactics, but I really believe that that's true. I think that...if Bush gets elected, he will put in new Superior Court judges [sic], and these guys are not going to want to see gay pride week.[53]

An interesting thought—but as a matter of political strategy, do Republicans really want to gentrify, say, Idaho?

On Oprah Winfrey's show, Cameron Diaz ignored the issue of the possible herding of gays into their own state, but claimed that a Bush re-election would lead to the legalization of rape:

> **Diaz:** We have a voice now, and we're not using it, and women have so much to lose. I mean, we could lose the right to our bodies. We could...if you think that rape should be legal, then don't vote. But if you think that you have a right to your body, and you have a right to say what happens to you and fight off that danger of losing that, then you should vote, and those are the ...
>
> **Winfrey:** It's your voice.
>
> **Diaz:** It's your voice. It's your voice, that's your right.[54]

Diaz's beautiful blue eyes then welled up on cue. Oprah milked the melodrama. Outside of La-la-land, we call this pulling your leg. On Oprah's stage, it's called "having a moment:"

> **Winfrey:** Cameron is having a moment. What is this about?
>
> **Diaz:** Well, I'm so proud of my friend [Drew Barrymore]. She took a whole year out of her busy schedule. She's a producer, she's an actor...she did this to take the time to educate people about it. And then I started listening to people saying, 'Oh, I don't vote

because it just doesn't affect me. And I just got overwhelmed, because I think this is the best country in the world. And it just scares me that we're just going to squander it all away. That we're going to lay down and let people take it away from us.

Winfrey: I am very, very afraid.

Diaz: I'm really scared. I don't know if you guys know this about our country. . . but people—we're all alone right now. And, where we used to be the strongest in the world, we're alone. So, that's the beginning of something terrible, and so it's very important to go out there.

Winfrey: I know. You're afraid of what's going to happen if people do not vote.[55]

Millions of people didn't vote on November 2. The sky didn't fall. Gay men weren't quarantined. Oh, and rape remains illegal.

Attacks from Abroad

It's bad enough when unhinged artists and entertainers make wild attacks against our president on American TV. It's worse when they issue Bush-hating and America-hating edicts to overseas media outlets.

"The war against terrorism is terrorism," actor Woody Harrelson told Britain's *Mirror* newspaper, implicitly equating U.S. soldiers with the al Qaeda hijackers responsible for incinerating 3,000 innocent men, women, and children. "The whole thing is just bullshit."[56]

"I hate Bush," said actress Jessica Lange at a film festival in Spain. "I despise him and his entire administration." Lange also said that she was embarrassed to be an American and thanked the festival organizers for giving her the opportunity to get out of America for a few days.[57]

Less than a month before the invasion of Iraq, George Clooney showed his support for U.S. troops by asserting on German TV that "We [America] can't beat anyone anymore."[58] Also in Germany, aging actor Larry Hagman called Bush a "sad figure: not too well educated, who doesn't get out of America much. He's leading the country towards fascism."[59] (One hopes that Germans who are old enough to remember real fascism appreciated the lunacy of Hagman's allegation.)

One week after President Bush visited Bangkok, rock legend Carlos Santana told 10,000 cheering Thai concert-goers that Bush must change his "evil ways."[60] One month earlier, Thailand's Prime Minister Thaksin Shinawatra had, at the United States' request, sent 420 Thai soldiers to help our troops in Iraq.

That same week, Michael Moore informed the London Daily Mirror that Americans "are possibly the dumbest people on the planet."[61] He offered no comment on whether his own popularity is an example of that.

Gwyneth Paltrow later told Britain's Glamour magazine that the "over-patriotic atmosphere" in America is "weird."[62] But for really weird, you need to turn to Paltrow's husband, British rock star Chris Martin of ColdPlay, who declared at a British music awards show that "We're all going to die if George Bush has his way."[63] Strike a blow for immortality: defeat George W. Bush!

Post-election Trauma

But, of course, the celebriliberals failed to defeat the President. So how did the denizens of Hollywood handle George W. Bush's re-election?

Not well.

West Wing screenwriter Lawrence O'Donnell—last seen having a rhetorical seizure on MSNBC in an appalling appearance with Swift Boat Veteran John O'Neill—sobbed on the shoulder of the New York Times. "There's a mournfulness going on—people are talking about secession, and they're not completely joking," he said. "The intensity of disappointment is so enormous. I haven't experienced or witnessed anything like it since 1972," when Richard Nixon defeated George McGovern.[64]

The loss left many Kerry supporters "reaching for their Prozac vials," noted the *Washington Times*. "Mine is already empty," joked a high-level publicist who counts A-list celebrities as his clients. At least the reporter thought the publicist was joking. "There's a lot of disappointment out here. A lot of apprehension," added Robert Dowling, editor-in-chief of the *Hollywood Reporter*. "People are comatose."[65] So maybe their Prozac vials *had* been drained.

Others questioned the legitimacy of the election, as they had done four years earlier. Said Barbra Streisand: "Diebold's chief executive declared that he was 'committed to helping Ohio deliver its electoral votes to the president,' just as his company was bidding to supply voting machines to the state... [I]f we continue to have elections run by private companies that are immersed in conspiracy and fraud, more and more voters will become cynical and decide to stay home on Election Day. Ultimately that only helps deliver the Republican's [sic] another victory."[66]

At least one Hollyweirdo coped by creating her own alternative universe. At a folk concert a few days after the election, aging hippie singer Joan Baez transformed herself into a black minstrel stereotype that the KKK would love. Journalist Ronald Bailey was there. After moping about President Bush's victory and going through the motions of singing some tunes, Baez stopped singing and announced that she had "multiple personalities:"

> One of her multiple personalities is that of a fifteen year old poor black girl named Alice from Turkey Scratch, Arkansas. Baez decided to share with us Alice's views on the election. Amazed and horrified I watched a rich, famous, extremely white folksinger perform what can only be described as bit of minstrelsy—only the painted on blackface was missing. Alice, the black teenager from Arkansas Baez was pretending to be, spoke in a dialect so broad and thick that it would put Uncle Remus and Amos and Andy to shame. Baez' monologue was filled with phrases like, "I'se g'win ta" to do this that or the other and dropping all final "g's." Baez as Alice made statements like, "de prezident, he be a racist," and "de

prezident, he got a bug fer killin'." Finally, since Bush won the election with 58.7 million votes to Kerry's 55.1 million, Alice observed, "Seems lak haf' de country be plumb crazy..."

Once Joan finished her minstrelsy riff, the audience, in which I did not see a single black person, went wild with applause and hoots and hollers. I have never felt so embarrassed for a bunch of "liberals" in my life.[67]

Michael Moore was so upset after the election that he couldn't get out of bed for three days, according to *New York Post* gossip columnist Liz Smith.[68] (It normally takes him two days.)

Actor Vincent D'Onofrio, famed for his portrayal of a Marine gone crazy in *Full Metal Jacket*, fainted several times after the election and was hospitalized—though doctors found nothing wrong with him. Colleagues said D'Onofrio, a strong Kerry supporter who reportedly had placed anti-Bush posters on the set of his TV show, suffered from "Bush Flu."[69]

But such celebrity sickness was mild compared to the malignant hatred that turned average Bush-bashers into thoroughly unstable Bedlamites obsessed with fantasies of murdering the president.

Top 10 Unhinged Politicians

10 Congressman **JIM McDERMOTT**, who claimed that the capture of Saddam Hussein had been staged by GOP operatives to help the Bush re-election campaign.

9 Pennsylvania State Senator **VINCENT FUMO**, who repeatedly screamed "faggot" at the top of his lungs at his Republican opponents on the Senate floor.

8 Senator **BARBARA BOXER**, who bawled at a press conference protesting the certification of President Bush's election.

7 Fieldsboro, New Jersey, mayor **EDWARD TYLER**, who outlawed any display of support for American troops on public property.

6 Congresswoman **CYNTHIA MCKINNEY**, who peddled wild-eyed "Bush knew" theories about 9/11.

5 Congressman **PETE STARK**, who hurled homophobic slurs at Republicans and left an insult-filled harangue on the answering machine of a war veteran.

4 Congressman **MAURICE HINCHEY**, who blamed CBS News's "Rathergate" debacle on Bush senior advisor Karl Rove.

3 **DICK DURBIN**, the #2 Democrat in the U.S. Senate, who invoked Pol Pot, Nazis, and Soviet gulag operators when discussing American troops at Guantanamo Bay.

2 **TERESA HEINZ KERRY**, wife of failed presidential candidate John Kerry, who said that the 2004 election results were manipulated by GOP operatives who hacked into the "mother machines" that tally the vote.

1 DNC chairman **HOWARD DEAN**, who suggested that Saudi Arabia may have given President Bush advance knowledge of the 9/11 terrorist attacks.

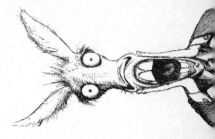

CHAPTER EIGHT

Assassination Fascination

"Quirky." "Oddball." "Funky." "Morbidly funny." "Charmingly obsessed." "Macabre and patriotic." "A fun read."

These are descriptions the mainstream media would never, ever think of using to describe a gruesome book about political assassinations written by a disgruntled conservative. But Sarah Vowell, author of the *New York Times* non-fiction best-seller *Assassination Vacation*, is a Bush-hating, antiwar liberal. And so instead of being criticized as an emotionally unstable ideologue, she has received lavish praise for her hate-fueled work, which can only honestly be described in one word:

Creepy.

Vowell's book, published in the spring of 2005, is a disjointed and incoherent (or as liberal reviewers admiringly describe it, "rambling" and "discursive") history of the assassinations of three Republican presidents (Lincoln, Garfield, and McKinley). She embarked on the travelogue project as Operation Iraqi Freedom kicked off—"right around the time my resentment of the current president cranked up into contempt."[1] Vowell admits she is so crippled by her contempt for President Bush that she can't stand to refer to him by name.

While Vowell grudgingly provides the requisite disclaimer that she does not want "the current president" killed—threatening the president is, of course, a federal crime[2]—she confesses that "my simmering rage against the current president scares me." You and me both, sister. Empathizing with her murder-minded subjects, Vowell muses that

> "if I can summon this much bitterness toward a presidential human being, I can sort of, kind of see how this amount of bile or more, teaming up with disappointment, unemployment, delusions of grandeur and mental illness, could prompt a crazier narcissistic creep to buy one of this country's widely available handguns. Not that I, I repeat, condone that."[3]

Uh-huh. It would take an even crazier, narcissistic creep to do that.

Vowell recounts telling a friend before the Republican National Convention opened last summer that she was worried about the president's safety. Not because of any compassion she has for her fellow man, mind you, but because "I don't think I can stomach watching that man get turned into a martyr if he were killed."[4]

As Vowell recounts her trips across the country to ogle President Lincoln's skull parts, President McKinley's blood-stained pajamas and the various remnants of their assassins, she reveals just how obsessive she has become. During social get-togethers she sits "silently chiding myself, Don't bring up McKinley. Don't bring up McKinley." She has extra shelves installed in her apartment to accommodate all her books on the murder of Republican presidents—"I like to call that corner of the hallway 'the assassination nook.'" One of Vowell's friends observes: "No matter what we're talking about, you will always bring the conversation back to a president getting shot."

Vowell is no fringe figure. She is a much-praised commentator on National Public Radio. She gained fame as the voice of teenage superhero Violet Parr in the hit movie, *The Incredibles*. She wrote a twice-a-week column for the *New York Times* during the summer of 2005 when regular op-ed columnist Maureen Dowd was on leave. Reviewers of her book called her "smart" and "sassy." And in her twisted, Bush-hating obsession with political murder, she is not alone. In the left-wing entertainment industry, media, and Democratic party base, assassination chic is all the rage.

The Art of the Death Wish

In the preface to her book, Vowell recounts a trip to the Berkshire Theater Festival to see a Steven Sondheim musical called, you guessed it, *Assassins*. The musical, like Vowell's book, explores the lives of the men and women behind successful and attempted assassination plots against American presidents. In the opening scene, a character runs a carnival game inviting players to "Shoot the President, Win a Prize." The assassins in the cast sing:

> Hey, pal–feelin' blue? Don't know what to do?/Hey, pal—I mean you—yeah. C'mere and kill a president./No job? Cupboard bare?/One room, no one there?/Hey, pal, don't despair—You wanna shoot a president?/C'mon and shoot a president ... [5]

Other memorable songs include a duet featuring John Hinckley, President Reagan's would-be assassin, and Squeaky Fromme, President Ford's attempted assassin; a cheerful ballad sung by Charles Guiteau, President Garfield's assassin; and "The Gun Song," with President Lincoln's assassin, John Wilkes Booth chiming in:

> And all you have to do/Is move your little finger, Move your little finger and/You can change the world. Why should you be blue ... Prove how just a little finger/Can change the world. [6]

Written during President George H.W. Bush's tenure, *Assassins* had been slated to open on Broadway before the first Persian Gulf War broke out and was rescheduled to debut there in 2001. It was postponed again after the September 11th attacks. The musical's 2004 Broadway production ended up winning five Tony Awards. In the revealing program notes for the Berkshire Theater Festival production of the musical, director Timothy Douglas discussed his own anti-Bush feelings and empathy for presidential assassins: "Proportionate to my own mounting frustrations at feeling increasingly excluded from the best interests of the current administration's control in these extraordinary times helps me toward a visceral understanding of the motivation of one who would perpetrate a violent act upon the leader of the free world."[7]

Translation: I hate Bush and I can feel a presidential assassin's pain. Like Vowell, Douglas gives a routine disclaimer that he's "completely against violence"—and yet, he confesses that he has "no idea how far away I am from the 'invisible line' that separates me from a similar or identical purpose."

Michael Feingold, a theater critic for the *Village* Voice, demonstrated that the musical's embedded political message resonated loud and clear with left-wing audiences: "Today the Republican Party is nothing but a worthless collection of Dylan Klebolds, and some good therapist should take them in hand before it's too late for the rest of us here at Columbine High. Their temporary dominance clarifies both *Assassins*' current success and its perturbing hollowness: The real convocation of America-killers will not be at a shooting gallery, but this coming August when the GOP meets in Madison Square Garden."[8] So Republicans are assassins of America. No wonder even anti-violence liberals can understand why Republican presidents deserve to be assassinated.

Just as the GOP convention kicked off, another assassination-themed, off-Broadway production opened titled, "I'm Gonna Kill the President." According to a Salon.com writer who attended the play:

At one point, when the actors apparently prank-call the White House on an audience member's cellphone, the audience is led in shouts of, "I'M GOING TO KILL THE PRESIDENT," and there's a tastelessly joyous sense of release in screaming out those six criminal words. [9]

"Tastelessly joyous" is one way to describe it. "Fantasizing about murder" is another.

Meanwhile, left-wing audiences embraced "dissident" American comedian Rich Hall, who performed his hate anthem, "Let's get together and kill George Bush."[10] He was just kidding, of course.

Yet another assassination-obsessed work was released in the summer of 2004: popular fiction author Nicholson Baker's political novel, *Checkpoint*. An avowed antiwar Bush-hater, Baker didn't waste any of his creative energies using past history to disguise his hang-ups. The 115-page book, published by Knopf, is a dialogue between two characters mulling over whether and how to kill President George W. Bush in the here and now.

"Jay," the main character plotting the murder, is a demented bum who intersperses his antiwar rants with delusions about "radio-controlled flying saws" and "homing bullets." The other character, "Ben," is the saner anti-Bush gent who persuades Jay to put off his plans. Like Sarah Vowell, Jay is compelled by his Bush hatred to get in touch with his inner assassin by visiting a historical monument to presidential murder—in his case, the Texas School Book Depository in Dallas, where Lee Harvey Oswald fired the shots that killed President John F. Kennedy. He explains to Ben why he took the trip: ". . . that creep, that fucking Texas punk, who can't even talk, whit [sic] his drugged-out eyes, he brought us to this point, to this war, and for nothing, for not one red fucking thing. And I thought, I want to see what it feels like to be in the last place where a president was shot deat [sic]. Where somebody had moved from the fantasy stage over to the reality stage, shall we say."[11]

A generous reading would give Baker credit for satirizing the unhinged Left. But as *Newsweek* reported in an interview with Baker, the book grew out of his "own fury, grief and helplessness over Iraq." He *wept* as he typed the manuscript, he told the magazine: "[I]t was as if I was mourning the war, the stupidity and the wastefulness of what we did. There was no other way to deal with this than to take on the most extreme and the most horrifying response, and see why somebody would consider that, and, ultimately, why it's wrong."[12] In a separate statement, Baker said: "I wrote 'Checkpoint' because a lot of people felt a kind of powerless, seething fury when President Bush took the country to war. I wanted to capture the specificity of that rage."[13]

At one point in the book, Jay rips President Bush as "this unelected fucking drunken oilman"[14]—and it isn't hard to imagine Baker himself muttering the phrase as he bawled and raged at his writing desk. Ted Anthony of the Associated Press praised the book as a "timely and tense screed." Deirdre Donahue raved in *USA Today*: "It is less a novel and more of a passionate cry from the heart about American foreign policy that Baker clearly opposes." The *Village Voice's* Benjamin Strong exulted: "If one of our supreme chroniclers of mild manners can be roused to such patriotic indignation, democracy yet has a fighting chance."[15]

Therapeutic? Perhaps for the dangerously unhinged. But also poisonously exploitative. As Timothy Noah of the left-leaning *Slate* magazine put it: "What makes *Checkpoint* a work of pornography isn't that its characters debate killing George W. Bush. What makes it pornography is the shameless way it panders to its readers' crudest beliefs. Jay and Ben's debate about something that's plainly wrong serves to disguise their complete agreement about every facet of the Bush administration and the Iraq war. It isn't a debate at all."[16] Conservative radio giant Rush Limbaugh excoriated apathetic liberals in a monologue about the book: "How far does the Bush hatred have to go before every fair-minded American says, 'Enough!' At what point do you people on the left not get it?"[17]

They still don't get it. In the spring of 2005, Columbia College violated the boundaries of artistic responsibility even further. As part of an exhibit titled "Axis of Evil, the Secret History of Sin," the college's Glass Curtain Gallery displayed a piece titled "Patriot Act," showing President Bush on a mock 37-cent stamp with a revolver pointed at his head:

When the Secret Service did its duty and investigated the gallery, the curator of the show, Michael Hernandez de Luna said he was frightened by the investigation "because it starts questioning all rights, not only my rights or the artists' rights in this room, but questioning the rights of any artist who creates—any writer, any visual artist, any performance artist. It seems like we're being watched."[18] Don't artists *want* to be watched?

In De Luna's case, there's a good reason, and it's not artistic merit. De Luna had previously come under federal scrutiny for creating fake anthrax stamps—in "orange, lemon-lime and grape flavors"—and sending them through the mail after the September 11th terrorist attacks and at the height of the still-unsolved anthrax postal scare.[19] He's just another liberal who can understand why someone would want to assassinate the president and kill Americans with anthrax. Call it "art."

Reading Between the Lines

But assassination fantasies aren't confined to liberals in the art world. In April 2004, the St. Petersburg Democratic Club took out an advertisement in a local newspaper urging the assassination of Secretary of Defense Donald Rumsfeld. The ad—a fund-raising appeal for John Kerry's presidential campaign—included this passage:

And then there's Rumsfeld who said of Iraq, "We have our good days and our bad days,... We should put this S.O.B. up against the wall and say 'This is one of our bad days,' and pull the trigger."[20]

The club's Vice President, Edna McCall, told The Drudge Report that the ad was not meant as a call for actual injury to Rumsfeld. "'Pull the trigger' means let Rumsfeld know where we stand, not shoot him," she said. "We are getting raped, and they are planning to steal the election again."[21]

Just weeks before the 2004 presidential election, columnist Charlie Booker at the far-left British newspaper, the *Guardian*, fumed:

> Throughout the debate, John Kerry, for his part, looks and sounds a bit like a haunted tree. But at least he's not a lying, sniggering, drink-driving, selfish, reckless, ignorant, dangerous, backward, drooling, twitching, blinking, mouse-faced little cheat. And besides, in a fight between a tree and a bush, I know who I'd favour.
>
> On November 2, the entire civilised world will be praying, praying Bush loses. And Sod's law dictates he'll probably win, thereby disproving the existence of God once and for all. The world will endure four more years of idiocy, arrogance and unwarranted bloodshed, with no benevolent deity to watch over and save us. John Wilkes Booth, Lee Harvey Oswald, John Hinckley Jr.—where are you now that we need you?

Where? Why, they were dancing on Stephen Sondheim's stage and in Sarah Vowell's head and on the edge of Nicholson Baker's subconscious!

Charlie Booker's murder-approving invocation sparked outrage in red state America. Grudgingly, the *Guardian* (which also tried to meddle in our election by calling on its readers to write antiwar, anti-Bush letters to undecided voters in Ohio[22]) pulled the article from its website. But instead of admitting its appalling lack of editorial judgment, the paper pooh-poohed Booker's unhinged screed "as an ironic joke, not as a call to action—an intention he believed regular readers of his humorous column would understand. He deplores violence of any kind."[23]

Same old disingenuous disclaimer from the assassination-friendly Left. Of course, if a conservative journalist had written this tripe, no one would let him get away with the "ironic joke" alibi. He'd be figuratively hanged instead for a hate crime. Booker skated free.

The weekend after President Bush's re-election, assassination chic seeped onto the pages of the *New York Times*. Under the headline "Can History Save the Democrats?," reporter Dean Murphy pondered ways in which a "nation-shaking event" could alter the political landscape" and save the country from the Bush agenda.[24] The piece opens with a reference to President Lincoln before he was assassinated, mentions the assassination of President McKinley, and ends with a lament from liberal Princeton University professor Sean Wilentz and a dark editorial comment from Murphy:

> "The Republicans are basically unchecked," Professor Wilentz said. "There is no check in the federal government and no check in the world. They have an unfettered playing field." Until the next act of God, that is.

When outraged readers took Murphy to task for his bloody obvious insinuation, the reporter protested too much. "No disrespect for, or ill will toward, the president was intended, and I don't believe any was conveyed," Murphy wrote in a form letter. "As the article states near the beginning, "an act of God" during the Bush presidency could range from "a national calamity, a deep schism in the ruling party, the implosion of a social movement under the excesses of its own agenda or the emergence of an extraordinary political figure. While assassination would certainly qualify as a national calamity, many other events would as well. Certainly, the article never advocated any of them."[25]

Of course, Murphy never "advocated" assassination. He merely mentioned it in the introduction, middle, and end of his piece. Why, an "act of God" could mean anything. Say, a lightning bolt or a flash flood or a giant meteor. Wherever did we get the idea that he was suggesting assassination?

Bush in the Crosshairs

Gatas Parlament, a Norwegian rap group (who knew there was such a thing?), threw subtlety to the wind with the creation of a video and website titled "Kill him now." The band called for donations in order to pay anyone who succeeded in murdering President Bush before the November 2004 election. When the Secret Service launched an investigation, the rappers claimed they didn't mean the call to be taken seriously.[26]

On Air America, ultra-liberal talk show host Randi Rhodes also invoked the "just kidding" card. In May 2004, during one of her usual anti-Bush rants, she compared the president and his family to the Corleones of *Godfather* fame and griped: "Like Fredo, somebody ought to take him out fishing and phuw." Rhodes then imitated the sound of a gunshot. (In *Godfather II*, Fredo Corleone is executed on orders from brother Michael at the end of the film.)

The *Washington Post* followed up in a lengthy, sympathetic profile of Rhodes that fawns:[27]

> [O]nce on the air, the seasoned pro takes over, and Rhodes sounds quite at ease trashing the president and his administration and declaring that the Bush dynasty is much like the Corleones of "The Godfather," with George W. as Fredo. Equipment malfunctions, callers vanish, blunders abound, and she doesn't lose her cool.

Not even a mention of Rhodes' assassination insinuation, but plenty of praise for Rhodes' purported level-headedness. Less than a year later, the "seasoned pro" took almost literal aim at Bush again. In April 2005, her show featured the following skit:[28]

> **Announcer:** "A spoiled child is telling us our Social Security isn't safe anymore, so he is going to fix it for us. Well, here's your answer, you ungrateful whelp: [audio sound of 4 gunshots being fired.] Just try it, you little bastard. [audio of gun being cocked]."

"What is with all the killing?" Rhodes said, laughing, after the clip aired. After the Drudge Report called attention to the appalling broadcast, Air America was forced to apologize. The radio network's president of programming and co-Chief Operating Officer Jon Sinton said in a release: "We regret that a produced comedy bit that was in bad taste slipped through our normal vetting process. We do acknowledge that it was an internal error and internal discipline will be enforced." Rhodes deflected blame: "It was bad. I apologize a thousand times," she grumbled before complaining, "I'm not in charge of the bits." The "bits" didn't laugh at the sound of gunshots. Rhodes, the "seasoned pro," did. Even liberal talk personality Lynn Samuels, who herself was the subject of a Secret Service probe for an out-of-bounds joke about former Vice President Dan Quayle, condemned Rhodes' conduct: "There are very few things that you absolutely, positively cannot do on the radio, and pretending to shoot the president is right up there at the top."[29]

Common-sense expectations of decorum didn't stop hate-mongers from putting Bush in the crosshairs on street signs around Kerry-loving New York City. In April 2005, blogger/documentarian Evan Coyne Maloney reported on the appearance of George W. Bush shooting targets—"complete with simulated bullet holes penetrating various parts of the body"—around the Big Apple. "Despite the cartoonish look, it is a bit eerie that these posters, which implicitly advocate the assassination of a sitting U.S. president, could remain unmolested in the nation's largest city for days on end." Maloney observed. It's "a graphic monument to the mentality of today's left."[30]

Indeed.

Perhaps the darkest, starkest sign of Bush hatred surfaced on a popular Internet store called CafePress, which offers products designed by a wide variety of small-scale vendors and individuals.[31] Included in a line of "Kill Bush" products for sale was a 10-pack of magnets depicting the president holding a gun to his head with the caption "End Terrorism Now:"

To cheer up liberals with post-election stress disorder, the violent product line also offered this handy "Kill Bush" messenger bag with a macho pic of John Kerry on a motorcycle:

And to spell out the Democratic death wish unambiguously, liberals could choose this bright yellow "Kill Bush" t-shirt in bold font and splattered with blood:[32]

There's tasteless political paraphernalia on both sides of the aisle, but no "Kill Kerry" products, blood-spattered or otherwise, were being sold at Cafe-Press at the time the "Kill Bush" line was available. "Oh, but it's all in good fun," the libs will shrug. "Where's your sense of humor?" the libs will ask.

Where's their decency? Their sanity? For all the left's fear and loathing of the "religious right," religion and patriotism are powerful conservative incentives to decency—perhaps the absence of liberal decency is explained by their lack of both. As for their sanity, who knows?

As eminent historian Victor Davis Hanson observed in response to unhinged Democrats before the November 2004 election: "The radical Left is courting disaster and threatens to destroy the credibility of liberals who are apparently fearful of condemning the madness in their midst."[33]

Mission accomplished. Credibility shredded into pieces tinier than the Lincoln bone fragments Sarah Vowell obsessed over.

From highbrow art galleries and the Broadway stage to bookstore shelves, radio airwaves, newspaper op-ed pages and city streets, the mainstreaming of presidential assassination chic reveals much about the Left's mental state. At a time of war, with Islamist extremists gunning for the President, our troops, and civilians at home and abroad, America-loathing liberals continue to find warped comfort in murderous plot lines and homicidal images of our president. They feel more kinship with dead presidential assassins than with fellow Americans butchered by Islamists. They share with Al Qaeda's cold-blooded killers the same dreams of murdering President George W. Bush. By the Bush-haters' own admission, they are "simmering" and "seething" and gathering in theaters to share "a tastelessly joyous sense of release" while screaming out the words, "I'M GOING TO KILL THE PRESIDENT."

With the Democratic Party leadership handed over to a screaming Howard Dean, with rank-and-file Democrat activists on the couch with post-election disorder, and with the Left's antiwar movement full of spokesmen who think President Bush is a terrorist, it's no wonder the party of perpetual whimper can't stop fantasizing about ending the source of its collective misery with a bang.

AFTERWORD

The Road to Recovery

I spoke to President Bush and I offered him and Laura our congratulations on their victory. We had a good conversation, and we talked about the danger of division in our country and the need—the desperate need for unity, for finding the common ground, coming together.

Today I hope that we can begin the healing.[1]

John Kerry, November 3, 2004

You cannot cure a problem until you acknowledge that you have one. And you cannot start the "healing" process until you stop blaming everyone else for your self-inflicted wounds.

Democrats are baffled by the American people's rejection of their party: how could this country be against the destruction of marriage, the abandonment of the unborn, high taxes, unrestricted immigration, and appeasement of terrorists? They sincerely do not understand. They are, they think, self-evidently right—and how could anyone think otherwise? Convinced they are the party of rightness, in reality they've become the party of New Coke.

Freudian projection specialist Paul Krugman of the *New York Times* provides one of the best exhibits of the unhinged Left's stubborn refusal to deal with reality. In a March 2005 column, Professor Krugman decried right-wing extremism and warned that *conservative Christians* might soon assassinate liberals if "moderates" didn't intervene:

> America isn't yet a place where liberal politicians, and even conservatives who aren't sufficiently hard-line, fear assassination. But unless moderates take a stand against the growing power of domestic extremists, it can happen here.[2]

The column was titled "What's Going On?"—and it's clear that Krugman doesn't know or care about what's really going on around him.

As Krugman and his ilk in the mainstream media constantly remind us, fringe right-wingers do indeed exist. But it's not Republicans taking chainsaws to Democrat campaign signs and running down political opponents with their cars. It's not conservatives burning Democrats in effigy, defacing war memorials, and supporting the fragging of American troops. And it's not conservatives producing a bullet-riddled bumper crop of assassination-themed musicals, books and collectible stamps.

It's not a Republican who invoked Pol Pot and Nazis and Soviet gulag operators when discussing American troops at Guantanamo Bay. That was Democrat Senator Dick Durbin of Illinois, who kept his Senate Minority Whip position and who continues to blame an "orchestrated right-wing attack" for what came out of his mouth.[3]

It's not Republicans who suggested that President Bush had advance knowledge of the September 11th attacks or that Osama bin Laden has already been captured. Those notions were advanced by former Secretary of State Madeline Albright and current Democratic National Committee chairman Howard Dean.

And it wasn't a Republican who asserted that the war Iraq was "just as bad as six million Jews being killed." That was Democrat Rep. Charlie Rangel, who has refused to apologize and whom no Democrat leader has denounced.[4]

As I've shown throughout the book, the views of unhinged liberals are no longer relegated to the private remarks of a few Democrat politicians or the bloviations of a few fringe figures on the far Left. The syndrome is far more pervasive, intense, and sanctimoniously self-delusional than anything on the Right.

And while conservatives zealously police their own ranks to exclude extremists and conspiracy theories, extremism and conspiracy theories have become the driving force of the Democrat Party.

This unhinged disease has infected the entire party leadership—from the 2004 Democratic presidential candidate and his wife, to the Democratic National Committee chairman, to the U.S. Senate Minority Whip, to the U.S. Senate Minority Leader, Harry Reid, who just couldn't restrain himself in May 2005, when he lambasted the president of the United States as a "loser" in front of a bunch of high school kids.[5]

It has infected the anti-war movement—from crazed "counter-recruiters" to profanity-spewing protesters to feces-hurling vandals.

It has infected academia—from terrorist-sympathizing historians to enraged multiculturalists to hate crime-hoaxing students.

It has infected Hollywood and the literary elite—from conspiracy-obsessed rappers to Christian-bashing comedians to Bush-hating starlets, writers, and musicians.

It has infected grass-roots activists and party operatives—from yellow ribbon-stealing pranksters to office-storming union goons to desperate campaign saboteurs.

And it has infected the mainstream media—from cable TV bullies to sneering news executives to bigoted newspaper cartoonists to talk radio assassination fantasizers.

I've documented a few outbreaks of liberal sanity: Elizabeth Edwards chastising ill-wishers at the Democratic Underground; Chicago Mayor

Richard Daley lambasting Senator Dick Durbin over his Gitmo hyperbole; Congressman Barney Frank and Senator Chris Dodd standing up to anti-American slander at Davos; and former Congressman Martin Frost refusing to advertise on Daily Kos, the most highly trafficked leftist blog, after its founder, Markos Zuniga wrote "Screw them" in response to the brutal murder of American civilian contractors in Fallujah. But these are exceptions to the left-wing rule of madness.

In July 2005, as my book deadline neared, the 7/7 terrorist bombings in London killed more than 50 innocent people and prompted unhinged liberals to engage in a whole new round of paranoia indulgence,[6] violence,[7] and Bush-bashing.[8] Moonbats at home and abroad blamed Karl Rove, President Bush and Prime Minister Tony Blair for the attacks. "Was it the CIA? It's one way to prop up your poll numbers, and wouldn't be the first time the CIA has killed many innocents to promote U.S. foreign policy," a Daily Kos reader opined.[9] Radical leftists in San Francisco protesting the G-8 conference in Scotland, which had kicked off concurrently with the bombings, attacked a police officer who sustained serious head injuries and was hospitalized with brain swelling and a blood clot. Moulitsas of The Daily Kos himself finally clamped down and performed an unprecedented "mass banning of people perpetuating a series of bizarre, off-the-wall, unsupported and frankly embarrassing [sic] conspiracy theories:"

> I have a high tolerance level for material I deem appropriate for this site, but one thing I REFUSE to allow is bullshit conspiracy theories. You know the ones—Bush and Blair conspired to bomb London in order to take the heat off their respective political problems. I can't imagine what fucking world these people live in, but it sure ain't the Reality Based Community.
>
> So I banned these people, and those that have been recommending diaries like it. And I will continue to do so until the purge is complete, and make no mistake—this is a purge.
>
> This is a reality-based community. Those who wish to live outside it should find a new home. This isn't it.[10]

The "purge," however was short-lived. Within hours after his loyal readers started complaining, Moulitsas reinstated their accounts. He explained further:

> It's telling that I have NEVER done something like this before. Because this has been an extreme situation. This isn't about disagreeing with what people are saying. If that was the case, everyone would've been banned by now. The myth of the "echo chamber" is just that. A myth.
>
> But as for warnings, well, this has been my warning. I wanted it clear that I was serious, and I think that has come through. I am reinstating those who ask to be reinstated. But the message has been sent.

The message, apparently, was that conspiracy theorists diligent enough to ask to be reinstated to the site would be. That's pretty tough—just like the Democrats' foreign policy.

Coincidentally, a prominent MoveOn.org activist named Charles Fazio sent a similar message to his colleagues the same weekend as the Kos "purge," warning them to tone down their anti-Bush psychosis for a *Washington Post* team planning to attend one of his activism parties. Internet sleuth Matt Drudge reported that Fazio had disseminated an e-mail memo admonishing the moonbats in advance of the newspaper's arrival:[11]

> Its [sic] very important that if you talk to the reporter, you stay on message. Remember, it is quite possible that our event will be the one the POST uses to represent the entire MoveOnPac effort this weekend. The momentum is finally shifting away from extremism. We will not accept a extremist nominee. This is not about conservatism vs liberalism or Republicans vs Democrats, this is all about extremism vs moderation and we're on the side of moderation. We don't want to come across as leftist, liberal activists. We want to come across as we are—regular folks who are finally

saying enough is enough to the extremists; that we're not falling for their extremist rhetoric anymore and we're finally going to expend the effort necessary to get our country back. Please stay on message and just know that ANYTHING you say can be taken out of context and used against the effort. Oh, because a photographer will be here, might I suggest we put away our 'Bush is a Liar' t-shirts. Let's look like they do.

"They," of course, means you and me. Normal people who don't spend our free time holding up "FUCK BUSH" signs at anti-war rallies and sulking obsessively about the 2000 and 2004 elections. Normal people who don't blame every natural or political catastrophe on Karl Rove. Normal people who don't look like dangerous escapees from Edward Munch's artistic nightmares.

This glimmer of self-awareness, however fleeting, is a step in the right direction. But the road to recovery will take more than combed hair and clean underwear. As the next presidential election approaches -and with it the return of the Clintons and their cadre, with Bill in his new role as First Man, it's unlikely that the unhinged left will lose its grip on the Democratic Party.

Witness the political aftermath of Hurricane Katrina in late August 2005. Immediately after landfall, unhinged Democrats went into Category 5 Bush-bashing mode. They attacked the administration's stance on global warming, Republican racism, and Halliburton profiteers, while letting hapless local and state Democrat officials, self-serving black leaders and attention-grabbing celebrities off the hook.

Robert F. Kennedy, Jr., blamed Republicans for engineering "climate chaos." Jesse Jackson invoked "slave ships" to criticize evacuation efforts. Democrat Louisiana Senator Mary Landrieu threatened to punch anyone, including President Bush, who questioned the local law enforcement response. And anti-war moonbat Cindy Sheehan called for President Bush to "pull our troops out of occupied New Orleans."

The Basket Case Party has serious issues that threaten a healthy republic. We can help by holding up a mirror. But first, unhinged liberals must open their eyes.

Acknowledgements

First, thanks to all of my left-wing hate mail correspondents and critics. This book, especially the back cover, would not have been possible without you. Now, go seek help.

Many thanks to Lisa De Pasquale of the Clare Booth Luce Institute and Floyd Resnick of the New York Close Protection Services for their incredible research assistance and encouragement. And for watching my back.

A special note of thanks to David Limbaugh, for his always wise counsel and support of this project.

Deepest thanks to caricaturist/illustrator/cartoonist/superhuman Roman Genn, a kindred spirit, for the perfect cover illustration. More at www.rgenn.com.

Thanks to Bill Walsh and the Republican Party of Minnesota (www.whenangrydemocratsattack.com), Bill Ardolino of INDC Journal (www.INDCjournal.com), and zombie (www.zombietime.com) for permission to use their excellent photos of moonbats in action.

I'm grateful to bloggers Ed Morrissey of Captain's Quarters (http://www.captainsquartersblog.com/mt/) and John Hawkins of Right Wing News (http://www.rightwingnews.com/) for taking the time to read the manuscript. Thanks also to E.F. for his sharp, non-political junkie's eyes. And as ever, bottomless thanks to my dear friend Mike Fumento, who managed to digest the manuscript with only a fraction of a colon.

Thanks to Mark Jaquith for technical assistance with my blog, www.michellemalkin.com, where monitoring of the unhinged continues.

Thanks to everyone at Eagle Publishing and Regnery, especially Marji Ross, Jeff Carneal, Harry Crocker, Ben Domenech, and Amanda Larsen.

As always, incalculable thanks to Jesse—for understanding, appreciating, sacrificing, loving, laughing, and keeping me on the rails.

Lastly, to my munchkins: Let's dance!

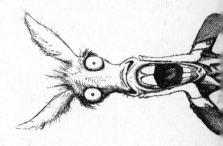

Introduction

1. John T. Jost, et al., "Political Conservatism as Motivated Social Cognition," *Psychological Bulletin*, 2003, Vol. 129, No. 3, 339–375; available online at www.wam.umd.edu/~hannahk/bulletin.pdf [accessed August 29, 2005].
2. Michelle Malkin, "Ambush journalism . . . or my evening with caveman Chris Matthews," michellemalkin.com, August 20, 2004; available online at http://michellemalkin.com/archives/000418.htm [accessed August 29, 2005].
3. Matt Drudge, "Helen Thomas angry after 'kill self' over Cheney comments published," drudgereport.com, July 31, 2005; available online at http://www.drudgereport.com/flash3ht.htm [accessed August 29, 2005].
4. Melissa Healy, "Dejected voters find themselves in an even bluer state; feelings of grief can be severe for those who backed the defeated candidate," *Los Angeles Times*, November 8, 2004 , p. F1.
5. Ibid.
6. Sean Salai, "Dozens more Kerry supporters flock to Florida therapists," *Boca News* (Florida), November 10, 2004; available online at: http://www.bocanews.com/index.php?src=news&prid=10147&category=Local%20News [accessed May 29, 2005].

7. Jan Jarvis, "Election defeat has some in a blue funk," *Fort Worth Star Telegram*, November 6, 2004, p. 1A.

8. Deborah, "Post Election Selection Trauma," News Hounds, November 21, 2004; available online at: http://www.newshounds.us/2004/11/21/post_election_selection_trauma.php [accessed May 28, 2005].

9. Associated Press, "Many Americans suffering post-election blues; Kerry supporters struggle with disappointment and frustration," November 5, 2004; available online at: http://www.msnbc.msn.com/id/6417285/ [accessed May 28, 2005].

10. Ibid.

11. Samara Kalk, "Blue state of mind; area therapists are flooded with post-election depression," *Capital Times* (Madison, Wisconsin), November 13, 2004, p. 1A.

12. Jennifer Dukes Lee, "Many feel post-election gloom; while some Iowans were pleased as punch by the results, others are downright depressed," *Des Moines Register*, November 12, 2004, p. 1B.

13. Ibid.

14. Frank Cerabino, "Post-election 'victims' need (get-)real relief," *Palm Beach Post* (Florida), December 10, 2004, p. 1B.:

15. Sean Salai, "Dozens Kerry supporters seek therapy in South Florida; Boca Raton trauma specialist has treated 15 patients," *Boca News*, November 9, 2004; available online at:
http://www.bocanews.com/index.php?src=news&prid=10127&category=Local%20News [accessed May 29, 2005].

16. Ibid.

17. Pat Nason, "Coping with PEST," United Press International, December 8, 2004.

18. Rob Borsellino, "Borsellino: Writer says Vilsack could be anti-depressant," *Des Moines Register*, December 3, 2004; available online at:
http://www.dmregister.com/apps/pbcs.dll/article?AID=/20041203/OPINION01/412030377/1035/archive [accessed July 17, 2005].

19. Gene Stone, *The Bush Survival Bible: 250 Ways to Make it Through the Next Four Years Without Misunderestimating the Dangers Ahead, and Other Subliminable Stategeries* (New York: Villard), 2004.

20. Dahlia Lithwick and Alex Lithwick, "Moving to Canada, Eh? Let Slate help you decide if it's really for you," Slate.com, November 5, 2004; available online at: http://slate.com/id/2109300 [accessed May 28, 2005].

21. Bryant Urstadt, "Electing to Leave; a reader's guide to expatriating on November 3," *Harper's*, November 3, 2004; available online at:
http://www.harpers.org/ElectingToLeave.html [accessed May 28, 2005].

22. Gregory Boyd Bell, "Go Canada!; Northern lights look bright to 'Dubya dodgers,'"*Newsday,* November 10, 2004, p. A41.

23. Julia Levy, "It's a Dismal Day for Bush-Haters," *New York Sun*, November 4, 2004, p. 1

24. David Stoltzfus, "Market incident reported," *Sunday News* (Lancaster, Pa.), November 28, 2004, p. P-3.

25. John M. Spidaliere, "Flap erupts over photos of Bush at market stand; Democratic City Councilman Nelson Polite says the photos are inappropriate in a public place. Others rally behind standholder," *Lancaster New Era* (Lancaster, Pa.), December 3, 2004, p. B1.

26. John M. Spidaliere, "Polite defended in wake of 'hateful' calls, e-mails; After week of ridicule over photo at market stand, councilman gets support from friends, colleagues," *Lancaster New Era* (Lancaster, Pa.), December 15, 2004, p. B1.

27. Colette Bancroft, "We're sorry, world ... or maybe not," *St. Petersburg Times*, November 20, 2004; available online at: http://www.sptimes.com/2004/11/20/Floridian/We_re_sorry__world__o.shtml [accessed May 29, 2005].

28. Available online at: http://www.sorryeverybody.com/gallery/single/se30519.jpeg/ [accessed May 29, 2005].

29. Available online at: http://www.sorryeverybody.com/gallery/single/se31012.jpeg/ [accessed May 29, 2005].

30. Available online at: http://www.sorryeverybody.com/gallery/single/se30703.jpeg/ [accessed May 29, 2005].

31. Available online at: http://www.sorryeverybody.com/gallery/single/se31023.jpeg// [accessed May 29, 2005].

32. "Judgment Malfunction," *New York Times*, August 25, 2005, p. A22.

33. Cindy Sheehan, "A lie of historic proportions," commondreams.org, June 6, 2005;; available online at http://www.commondreams.org/views05/0606-29.htm [accessed August 29, 2005].

34. Duncan Black, "The worst America," atrios.blogspot.com, August 10, 2005; available online at http://atrios.blogspot.com/2005_08_07_atrios_archive.html [accessed August 29, 2005].

35. Clara Frenk, "Why Michelle Malkin must be destroyed," DC Media Girl.com, August 15, 2005; available online at http://dcmediagirl.com/index.php?entry=entry20050815-182839&comments=y&id=819 [accessed August 29, 2005].

36. "In Defense of Michelle Malkin," The Talent Show.com, August 17, 2005; available online at http://www.thetalentshow.org/archives/001993.html [accessed August 29, 2005].

Chapter One: Stark Raving Lunatics

1. Greg Beato, "F'dom is on the March in America," Wonkette, June 6, 2005; available online at: http://www.wonkette.com/politics/white-house/fdom-is-on-the-march-in-america-106585.php [accessed July 3, 2005].

2. Paul Sand, "State revokes controversial anti-Bush license plate," *The News Tribune*, June 10, 2005.

3. John Wilkens, "Clean plates: DMV censors won't grant license to offend," *San Diego Union-Tribune*, March 6, 2005; available online at: http://www.signonsandiego.com/uniontrib/20050306/news_mz1c6plates.html [accessed July 3, 2005]. See also: mhking, "Help get rid of "F DUBYA" license plate," Ramblings' Journal, September 29, 2004; available online at: http://mhking.mu.nu/archives/047949.php [accessed July 3, 2005].

4. John McCaslin, "Inside the Beltway," *Washington Times*, April 11, 2005, p. A07.

5. Bill Maher, "Grouchy Old Party needs to chill out," *Los Angeles Times*, April 29, 2005, p. B13.

6. Jonathan Chait, "Mad about you," *The New Republic*, September 29, 2003, p. 20.

7. Jonathan Chait, "Mad about me," *The New Republic*, December 13, 2004, p. 50.

8. Al Franken, letter to the editor, *Time* magazine, December 6, 2004, p. 10.

9. Robert Cox, "Franken Explodes in SwiftVet Fueled Rage on Michael Medved Show," The National Debate, February 18, 2005; available online at: http://www.thenationaldebate.com/blog/archives/2005/02/franken_explode_1.html [accessed July 27, 2005].

10. Brian M., "Post-Election Map," undated; available online at: http://politicalhumor.about.com/library/images/blpic-mapdumbfuckistan.htm [accessed July 3, 2005].

11. Celeste Katz, "Call it the Teresa factor: Kerry's quirky, outspoken spouse a wild card in race," *New York Daily News*, July 24, 2004; available online at: http://www.nydailynews.com/news/politics/story/215497p-185540c.html [accessed July 3, 2005].

12. Brian Faler, "A Scathing Chairman Dean Finds Republians 'Evil,' 'Corrupt' and 'Brain Dead,'" *Washington Post*, April 25, 2005, p. A6; Jill Lawrence, "Dean launches an anti-GOP 'missile,'" *USA Today*, June 3, 2005, p. 10A; *Hotline*, "Democrats: vote for us, we're nicer than GOPers," April 5, 2005; Carla Marinucci, "The mouth that won't stop roaring," *San Francisco Chronicle*, June 8, 2005, P. A1; FDCH Political Transcripts, "Howard Dean delivers remarks to the campaign for America's future," June 2, 2005.

13. Quoted in Brian Carnell, "Eric Alterman: Hey, I'm No More Insensitive Than Rush Limbaugh!," Leftwatch.com, February 13, 2003; available online at:

http://www.leftwatch.com/archives/years/2003/000002.html [accessed July 4, 2005].

14. Ibid.

15. Bernard Goldberg, "Today's 'Liberals': Close-Minded, Nasty and Fringe," Newsmax.com, October 16, 2003; available online at: http://www.newsmax.com/archives/articles/2003/10/15/124248.shtml [accessed July 4, 2005].

16. Michelle Malkin, "America, land of the Ashcroft-haters," March 10, 2004; available online at: http://www.townhall.com/columnists/michellemalkin/printmm20040310.shtml [accessed July 4, 2005].

17. "NN Breaking - Ashcroft hospitalized..," Democratic Underground, March 5, 2004; available online at: http://www.democraticunderground.com/discuss/duboard.php?az=view_all&address=102x400872 [accessed July 5, 2005]; "Ashcroft in hospital," Democratic Underground, March 5, 2004; available online at: http://www.democraticunderground.com/discuss/duboard.php?az=view_all&address=104x1197069 [accessed July 4, 2005]; Michelle Malkin, "America, land of the Ashcroft-haters," March 10, 2004; available online at: http://www.townhall.com/columnists/michellemalkin/printmm20040310.shtml [accessed July 4, 2005].

18. If because of his Alzheimer's," Democratic Underground, June 6, 2004; available online at:
http://www.democraticunderground.com/discuss/duboard.php?az=show_mesg&forum=104&topic_id=1726149&mesg_id=1731149 [accessed July 4, 2005].

19. Ibid.

20. Ibid.

21. Ted Rall, "How Sad...," Search and Destroy, June 6, 2004; available online at: http://www.rall.com/2004_06_01_archive.html#108653231413264149 [accessed July 4, 2005].

22. "Laura Ingraham has breast cancer" Democratic Underground, April 26, 2005; available online at:
http://www.democraticunderground.com/discuss/duboard.php?az=view_all&address=104x3545777 [accessed July 4, 2005].

23. Ibid.

24. Michelle Malkin, "Elizabeth Edwards counsels the moonbats," michellemalkin.com, April 27, 2005; available online at: http://michellemalkin.com/archives/002242.htm [accessed July 4, 2005]; John Hawkins, "The Democratic Underground vs. Laura Ingraham: The Elizabeth Edwards Edition," Right Wing News, April 27, 2005; available online at: http://www.rightwingnews.com/category.php?ent=3781 [accessed July 4, 2005].

25. Michelle Malkin, "Moonbat watch: Wishing Cheney ill," michellemalkin.com, June 24, 2005; available online at: http://michellemalkin.com/archives/ 002846.htm [accessed July 4, 2005].

26. "Elizabeth Edwards Has Breast Cancer ," Free Republic, November 4, 2004; available online at: http://www.freerepublic.com/focus/f-news/1270669/posts [accessed July 4, 2005]; "Edwards' Wife Has Breast Cancer ," Free Republic, November 4, 2004; available online at: http://www.freerepublic.com/focus/f-news/1270681/posts [accessed July 4, 2005]; "Mrs Edwards has breast cancer," Free Republic, November 4, 2004; available online at: http://www.freerepublic. com/focus/f-news/1270563/posts [accessed July 4, 2005]; "BREAKING: John Edwards' wife diagnosed with breast cancer- Fox News," Free Republic, November 4, 2004; available online at: http://www.freerepublic.com/focus/f-news/1270508/posts [accessed July 4, 2005]; "[Bill] Clinton to have quadruple bypass surgery," Free Republic, September 3, 2004; available online at: http://www.freerepublic.com/focus/f-news/1206587/posts [accessed July 4, 2005]; "Bill Clinton to get quadruple bypass surgery today," Free Republic, September 3, 2004; available online at: http://www.freerepublic.com/focus/f-news/1206585/posts?q=1&&page=1#1 [accessed July 4, 2005].

27. "Paul Wellstone's plane crashes [8 on board, no survivors, Wellstone, wife, daughter deceased]," Free Republic, October 25, 2002; available online at: http://www.freerepublic.com/focus/f-news/775853/posts?q=1&&page=101 [accessed July 4, 2005].

28. E-mail correspondence with the author, June 25, 2005.

29. Richard Roeper, "News piles up as country takes a long weekend," *Chicago Sun-Times*, September 7, 2004, p. 11.

30. Cox News Service, "Rises beyond the grave; some using their obituaries to target President Bush," *Charleston Daily Mail* (West Virginia), February 21, 2004, p. 9A.

31. Anemona Hartocollis, "Coping; Partisan Words to Remember Them By," *New York Times*, February 1, 2004, sec. 14, p. 1.

32. "Paid Notice: Deaths; Tully, Mary Jean," *New York Times*, January 1, 2004, p. B9.

33. "Shanahan, Virginia R.," *Chicago Tribune*, October 6, 2004, p. C14; Gina Kim, "In lieu of flowers, please donate a vote," *Chicago Tribune*, October 25, 2004, p. 1.

34. "Obituaries," Tucson.com Classified, undated; available online at: http://www.tucson.com/classified/index.php?action=view_obit&ticket_id=0003 881983-01802 [accessed July 4, 2005].

Chapter Two: The Party of Paranoia

1. Richard Hofstadter, "The Paranoid Style in American Politics," *Harper's*, November 1964, pp. 77-?86; available online at: http://karws.gso.uri.edu/JFK/conspiracy_theory/the_paranoid_mentality/The_paranoid_style.html [accessed June 27, 2005].

2. Dana Milbank, "Democrats Play House To Rally Against the War," *Washington Post*, June 17, 2005, p. A06; available online at: http://www.washingtonpost.com/wp-dyn/content/article/2005/06/16/AR2005061601570_pf.html [accessed June 27, 2005].

3. James Lakely, "Albright's 'Joke' Joins Growing List of Bush Theories," *Washington Times*, December 18, 2003, p. A1.

4. Fox Special Report with Brit Hume transcript for December 17, 2003.

5. Matthew Daly, "McDermott in Hot Water for Saddam Quip," Associated Press, December 15, 2003.

6. The Diane Rehm Show, National Public Radio, December 1, 2003.

7. Fox News Sunday transcript for December 7, 2003.

8. Charles Krauthammer, "The Delusional Dean," *Washington Post*, December 5, 2003, p. A31.

9. Markos Moulitsas Zuniga, "Establishment lining up behind Dean," Daily Kos, December 6, 2005; available online at: http://www.dailykos.com/story/2003/12/6/6237/86925 [accessed July 12, 2005].

10. FoxNews.com, "Gore Endorses Dean for President," December 9, 2003; available online at: http://www.foxnews.com/story/0,2933,105230,00.html [accessed June 27, 2005].

11. CNN.com, "Kennedy's 'Texas' remark stirs GOP reaction," September 18, 2003; available online at: http://www.cnn.com/2003/ALLPOLITICS/09/18/kennedy.iraq/ [accessed June 27, 2005].

12. Matthew Continetti, "Cynthia McKinney (D-Conspiracy)," Weekly Standard, January 3-10, 2003; reprinted online at: http://frontpagemag.com/Articles/ReadArticle.asp?ID=16502 [accessed June 27, 2005].

13. Bob Kemper, "McKinney reopens 9/11: Conspiracy theories implicating president aired at 8-hour hearing," Atlanta Journal Constitution, July 23, 2005.

14. See, for example, "The sixty-first minute," Power Line, http://www.powerlineblog.com/archives/007760.php and "9/11/2004: One More CBS Document Example," Little Green Footballs, http://www.littlegreenfootballs.com/weblog/?entry=12551

15. http://www.cbsnews.com/stories/2004/09/20/politics/main644539.shtml

16. Stephen Dinan, "McAuliffe denies involvement in memos flap," *Washington Times*, September 10, 2004; available online at:

http://washingtontimes.com/national/20040910-011417-2610r.htm [accessed June 27, 2005].

17. Dick Thornburgh and Louis Boccardi, Report of the Independent Review Panel on the September 8, 2004 60 Minutes WednesdaySegment "For the Record" Concerning President Bush's Texas Air National Guard Service, January 5, 2005; available online at: http://wwwimage.cbsnews.com/htdocs/pdf/complete_report/CBS_Report.pdf [accessed July 20, 2005].

18. Ibid.

19. Charles Johnson, "Congressman Says Rove Planted CBS Memos," Little Green Footballs, February 20, 2005; available online at: http://www.littlegreenfootballs.com/weblog/?entry=14781_Congressman_Says_Rove_Planted_CBS_Memos&only=yes [accessed Jnue 27, 2005].

20. Hannity & Colmes, "A Congressman Alleges that Karl Rove was Behind CBS' 'Memogate' Scandal," February 24, 2005; available online at: http://www.foxnews.com/story/0,2933,148611,00.html [accessed June 27, 2005]. (Note; Fox News edited the transcript for clarity.)

21. Kevin Diaz, "Conspiracy theories thrive after Wellstone plane crash," Minneapolis Star-Tribune, June 3, 2003; available online at: http://www.realnews247.com/conspiracy_theories_thrive_after_wellstone_plane_crash.htm [acccessed June 27, 2005].

22. BuzzFlash, "Planting Weapons of Mass Destruction, Karl Rove, And "Sympathy for the Devil," July 9, 2003; available online at: http://www.buzzflash.com/editorial/03/06/09.html [accessed June 27, 2005].

23. CNN Larry King Live transcript, "Bin Laden Releases New Videotape," October 29, 2004; available online at: http://transcripts.cnn.com/TRANSCRIPTS/0410/29/lkl.01.html [accessed June 27, 2005].

24. Evan Thomas, "How a Fire Broke Out; the story of a sensitive Newsweek report about alleged abuses at Guantánamo Bay and a surge of deadly unrest in the Islamic world," Newsweek, May 23, 2005; available online at: http://msnbc.msn.com/id/7857407/site/newsweek/ [accessed June 27, 2005].

25. Norman Mailer, Intelligence 101A, Huffington Post, May 17, 2005; available online at: http://www.huffingtonpost.com/theblog/archive/norman-mailer/intelligence-101a_1142.html [accessed June 27, 2005].

26. Countdown with Keith Olbermann transcript for May 16," May 17, 2005; available online at: http://www.msnbc.msn.com/id/7886443/ [accessed June 27, 2005].

27. Dave Lindorff, "Bush's mystery bulge; The rumor is flying around the globe. Was the president wired during the first debate?" Salon.com, October 8, 2004; cached version available online at: http://64.233.179.104/search?q=cache:nms9-ErtB-QJ:www.salon.com/news/fea-

ture/2004/10/08/bulge/ 1 1 Dave 1 Lindorff 1 bush%27s 1 mystery 1 bulge&hl
=en&start=1&client=firefox-a [accessed June 29, 2005].

28. Kevin Berger, "NASA photo analyst: Bush wore a device during debate; Physicist says imaging techniques prove the president's bulge was not caused by wrinkled clothing," Salon.com, October 29, 2004; available online at: http://www.salon.com/news/feature/2004/10/29/bulge/ [accessed June 27, 2005].

29. Mike Allen, "Bulge Under President's Coat in First Debate Stirs Speculation," *Washington Post*, October 9, 2004, p. A16; available online at: http://www.washingtonpost.com/wp-dyn/articles/A18734-2004Oct8.html [accessed June 27, 2005].

30. Dave Lindorff, "Was Bush Wired? Sure Looks Like It," *Mother Jones*, October 30, 2004; available online at: http://www.motherjones.com/news/update/2004/11/10_407.html [accessed June 27, 2005].

31. Albert Eisele and Jeff Dufour, "Under the Dome," *The Hill*, November 4, 2004; available online at: http://hillnews.com/under_dome/110404.aspx [accessed July 23, 2005].

32. ABC News Transcripts, Good Morning America, October 26, 2004.

33. http://www.factcheck.org/article200.html

34. Michelle Malkin, "Scaring up Demo votes," michellemalkin.com, September 21, 2004; available online at: http://michellemalkin.com/archives/000561.htm [accessed June 27, 2005].

35. http://www.mtv.com/chooseorlose/headlines/news.jhtml?id=1486574

36. http://www.rockthevote.com/rtv_draft.php

37. Jim VandeHei and Dan Balz, "Kerry Says President May Bring Back Draft; Bush Campaign Dismisses Charge," *Washington Post*, October 16, 2004, p. A06; available online at: http://www.washingtonpost.com/wp-dyn/articles/A35517-2004Oct15.html [accessed June 27, 2005].

38. FactCheck.org, "Draft Fears Fueled by Inaccurate E-mails; a scare story spreads electronically, but it gets facts wrong," June 15, 2004 [modified September 29, 2004]; available online at: http://www.factcheck.org/article.aspx?docID=200 [accessed June 27, 2005].

39. CBSNews.com, "The Issues: Reviving The Draft," September 28, 2004; available online at: http://www.cbsnews.com/stories/2004/09/28/eveningnews/main646055.shtml [accessed June 27, 2005].

40. Bill Ardolino, "INDC Interviews the CBS Evening News," INDC Journal, September 30, 2004; available online at: http://www.indcjournal.com/archives/001032.php [accessed June 27, 2005].

41. NBC Nightly News transcript for September 29, 2004.

42. Greg Holt, "New clubs form to handle election," *Arizona Daily Wildcat*, December 3, 2003; available online at: http://wildcat.arizona.edu/papers/97/69/01_3.html [accessed July 19, 2005].

43. Joseph L. Galloway, "Army lowers standards, ups bonuses; recruiters falling short of goals in face of Iraq war," *Lexington Herald Leader* (Kentucky), June 14, 2005, p. A1.

44. Joel Connelly, "Teresa Heinz Kerry hasn't lost her outspoken way," *Seattle Post-Intelligencer*, March 7, 2005, p. A2.

45. Ibid.

46. George Rowland Jr., "Black box backlash," *Seattle Weekly*, March 10, 2004, p. 26.

47. Cory Doctorow, "Diebold Hacked!," TomPaine.com, November 2, 2004; available online at: http://www.tompaine.com/articles/diebold_hacked.php [accessed June 27, 2005].

48. Julie Carr Smyth, "Diebold Executive to Keep Lower Profile," *Plain Dealer* (Cleveland), September 16, 2003; reprinted online at: http://www.diebold.com/whatsnews/inthenews/executive.htm [accessed June 27, 2005].

49. Thom Hartmann, "Evidence Mounts That The Vote May Have Been Hacked," CommonDreams.org, November 6, 2004; available online at: http://www.commondreams.org/views04/1106-30.htm [accessed July 20, 2005].

50. David Corn, "A Stolen Election?," *The Nation*, November 29, 2004; available online at: http://www.thenation.com/doc.mhtml?i=20041129&s=corn [accessed July 20, 2005].

51. The Voting Technology Project, Voting Machines and the Underestimate of the Bush Vote, November 11, 2004; available online at: http://www.vote.caltech.edu/media/documents/VotingMachines3.pdf [accessed July 20, 2005].

52. Bob Fertik, "Widespread Election Fraud in Cleveland?," Democrats.com, November 22, 2004; available online at: http://blog.democrats.com/node/812 [accessed June 27, 2005].

53. Wyatt Buchanan, "If it's too bad to be true, it may not be voter fraud; most statistical enigmas in recent election have logical explanations, despite Web rants," *San Francisco Chronicle*, November 11, 2004; available online at: http://sfgate.com/cgi-bin/article.cgi?file=/c/a/2004/11/11/MNG2P9PJ5M1.DTL [accessed June 27, 2005].

54. Susannah Meadows, "'We Will Not Faint,'" *Newsweek*, December 30, 2004, p. 0.

55. Brian Knowlton, "Democrats Force Debate on Ohio Election Problems," *New York Times*, January 6, 2005; available online at: http://www.nytimes.com/2005/01/06/politics/06cnd-

elec.html?ex=1120017600&en=eb39ef3c672df606&ei=5070 [accessed June 27, 2005].

56. Peter Kirsanow, "The Florida Myth Spreads," National Review Online, January 10, 2005; available online at: http://www.nationalreview.com/comment/kirsanow200501100742.asp [accessed July 7, 2005].

57. Dan Balz, "Democrats Say 2004 Election System Failed in Ohio; Party Concedes No Evidence of Fraud; Republican Decries 'Political Fiction,'" *Washington Post*, June 23, 2005, p. A10; available online at: http://www.washingtonpost.com/wp-dyn/content/article/2005/06/22/AR2005062202273.html?nav=rss_politics [accessed June 27, 2005].

58. Peter Kirsanow, "The Florida Myth Spreads," National Review Online, January 10, 2005; available online at: http://www.nationalreview.com/comment/kirsanow200501100742.asp [accessed July 7, 2005].

59. "Let it go," *Plain Dealer* (Cleveland), January 4, 2005, p. B8.

60. Michael Kunzelman, "Kerry: Trickery kept voters from polls," Associated Press, April 10, 2005; available online at: http://abcnews.go.com/Politics/wireStory?id=658420 [accessed July 20, 2005].

61. Friends of Hillary, "Senator Clinton's Remarks at the Minnesota DFL Hubert Humphrey Dinner," April 9, 2005; available online at: http://www.friendsofhillary.com/speeches/20050409_Minnesotaphp [accessed July 7, 2005].

62. James Dao, "In Ohio Vote, Woes, Yes, Fraud, No," New York Times, June 23, 2005.

63. FOXNews.com, "Dean Charges Black Vote Suppressed in Ohio," available online at: http://www.foxnews.com/story/0,2933,160404,00.html [accessed June 27, 2005].

Chapter Three: When Angry Democrats Attack

1. Democratic Party Platform 2004, p. 39, available online at: http://a9.g.akamai.net/7/9/8082/v002/www.democrats.org/pdfs/2004platform.pdf [accessed April 30, 2005].

2. See, e.g., Mike Fumento, "The Great Black Church-burning Hoax," available online at: http://www.fumento.com/column8.html [accessed April 30, 2005]

3. Michael Moore, for example, urged his supporters to "Offer a six-pack to anyone in the office who votes (make sure you're not working in cubicles full of Republicans!). Promise to have sex with a nonvoter - whatever it takes!) " [emphasis added]. See Michael Moore, "Mike's Pledge," undated; cached page available online at: http://64.233.179.104/search?q=cache:kUlG4AeXdT4J: www.michaelmoore.com/takeaction/vote/pledge.php 1 %22Promise 1 to 1 have

1 sex 1 with 1 a 1 nonvoter 1 - 1 whatever 1 it 1 takes!%22&hl=en&start=5 [accessed June 23, 2005].

4. Bill Sheets, "Throng vocal but well-behaved during visit: A Kerry supporter hits a Bush supporter, but the rest of the scuffles are verbal," *Everett Herald*, August 28, 2004.

5. Daily Recycler, "The Buck Stops: With Kerry's Little People," Auugst 28, 2004, available online at: http://www.dailyrecycler.com/blog/2004/08/buck-stops-with-kerrys-little-people.html

6. Bill Sheets, "Throng vocal but well-behaved during visit: A Kerry supporter hits a Bush supporter, but the rest of the scuffles are verbal," *Everett Herald*, August 28, 2004

7. Casey Ross and Laurel J. Sweet, "Police take bow for safe DNC, citywide drop in violent crime," *Boston Herald*, July 31, 2004, p. 010.

8. Laura Italiano, "Cop Stompers' 'Angry' Defense," *New York Post*, September 30, 2004, p. 32.

9. Associated Press, "Heckler From Ky. Thrown To Floor After Interrupting Kerry's Speech," September 8, 2004; available online at: http://www.wave3.com/Global/story.asp?S=2275114&nav=0RZFQhUk [accessed July 9, 2005].

10. Ibid.

11. Associated Press, "Democrat scuffles with Republican, Bush cutout in Gainesville," September 18, 2004.

12. Mike Schneider, "Florida GOP workers claim intimidation by labor protesters," Associated Press, October 5, 2004.

13. Ibid.

14. Personal e-mail correspondence with the author, October 6, 2004

15. Republican Party of Minnesota press release, "Anger Inc.," October 5, 2004; available online at http://www.whenangrydemocratsattack.com/angerinc.pdf.

16. John Fund, "Getting Physical: Union thugs target Republicans," Opinion Journal, October 11, 2004; available online at: http://www.opinionjournal.com/diary/?id=110005741

17. Matt Margolis, "The Margolis Incident," March 27, 2004; available online at: http://www.mattmargolis.com/blog/index.php?p=356.

18. Ibid.

19. Steve Marantz, "Tensions run high as visit ignites clashes," Boston Herald, March 26, 2004, p. 007.

20. Mike Mcintyre, "U.S. politics sparks air rage: Discussion on Bush, Kerry campaign ends with male nurse tossed off flight," *Winnipeg Free Press*, September 14, 2004, p. C1.

21. Alfonso A. Castillo, "LI man arrested in air rage case; Huntington retiree who'd 'had a few' lands in Canadian jail after political debate gets too heated," *Newsday* (New York), September 16, 2004, p. A02.

22. Mike Saewitz, "LI man arrested in air rage case; Huntington retiree who'd 'had a few' lands in Canadian jail after political debate gets too heated," *Sarasota Herald-Tribune* (Florida), October 28, 2004, p. A1.

23. Steven Ertelt, "Pro-Life Women Forcibly Dragged From John Kerry Abortion Rally," LifeNews.com, April 27, 2004 ;available online at: http://www.lifenews.com/nat483.html [accessed April 29, 2005].

24. Ibid.

25. Steven Ertelt, "Photographers Discuss Manhandling of Women at John Kerry Abortion Event," LifeNews.com, April 28, 2004; available online at: http://66.195.16.55/nat485.html [accessed April 30, 2005]. See also "INDC Journal Rally: Into the Gates of Mordor and John Kerry's Pro-Choice Party," available online at: http://www.deanesmay.com/archives/007096.html [accessed April 30, 2005].

26. Jennifer Amsler, "Coulter avoids pie in face," *Arizona Daily Wildcat*, October 22, 2004.

27. Smoking Gun, "'Al Pieda' Targets Ann Coulter," available online at: http://www.thesmokinggun.com/archive/1022042coulter1.html [accessed April 30, 2005].

28. James Wolcott, "Feets, Do Ya Stuff ," October 22, 2004; available online at: http://jameswolcott.com/archives/2004/10/feets_do_ya_stu.php [accessed April 30, 2005].

29. Gawker, "The Ann Coulter Pie Video," available online at: http://www.gawker.com/topic/the-ann-coulter-pie-video-024061.php [accessed April 30, 2005].

30. Democratic Underground, "Ann Coulter Gets 'Pied' During Hatespeech," available online at: http://archive.democrats.com/preview.cfm?term=Ann%20Coulter.

31. WBIR-TV (Knoxville, Tennessee),"New photos: Shots fired into Knox Bush/Cheney headquarters," available online at: http://www.wbir.com/news/news.aspx?storyid=20241 [accessed April 30, 2005].

32. Associated Press, "Shots fired at Knoxville Bush-Cheney office; no one hurt," USA Today, October 5, 2004; available online at: http://www.usatoday.com/news/politicselections/nation/president/2004-10-05-gop-office-attack_x.htm [accessed July 22, 2005].

33. Eric Fossell , "No leads in shooting at GOP headquarters," *Herald-Dispatch*, October 4, 2004.

34. My searches of the Nexis database did not turn up any incidents in which someone shot at a Democratic campaign office during the 2004 election campaign.

35. Terry Collins, "Apparent shot hits near GOP office in Mankato," *Star Tribune* (Minneapolis, Minnesota), October 30, 2004, p. 3B.

36. David Postman, "Bush's campaign office in Spokane burglarized, vandalized," *Seattle Times*, October 11, 2004; available online at: http://seattletimes.nwsource.com/html/localnews/2002059735_webbushoffice11.html [accessed April 30, 2005].

37. 9News (Cincinnati), "No Suspects In Local Bush/Cheney Headquarters Breakin," October 22, 2004; available online at: http://www.wcpo.com/news/2004/local/10/22/breakin.html [accessed April 30, 2005].

38. Seth Muller, "Flag GOP office vandalized," *Arizona Daily Sun*, October 23, 2004.

39. Walt Williams, "Bozeman see also GOP headquarters vandalized in political protest," *Bozeman Daily Chronicle*, September 4, 2004; available online at: http://www.bozemandailychronicle.com/articles/2004/09/04/news/02smashed.txt [accessed April 30, 2005].

40. Stephanie Ryan, "Republican headquarters vandalized," *The Portland State University Daily Vanguard*, October 22, 2004; available online at: http://www.dailyvanguard.com/vnews/display.v/ART/2004/10/22/4178b87987338 [accessed April 30, 2004].

41. Janet Reid, "Republican headquarters vandalized," 6News, October 28, 2004; available online at: http://www.6newslawrence.com/stories/2004/oct/28/flag/ [accessed April 30, 2005].

42. Stu Nicholson, "GOP Headquarters Vandalized," Statehouse News Bureau, March 24, 2004.

43. Tesa Culli, "Republican blames 'cowards' for office vandalism," *Morning Sentinel*, October 13, 2004; available online at: http://www.morningsentinel.com/ news/2004/1013/Region_Cent/026.html [accessed April 30, 2005].

44. Dave Forster, "Cass GOP headquarters vandalized with dog feces," Fargo-Grand Forks (North Dakota), April 3, 2003; available online at: http://www.inforum.com/specials/iraq/index.cfm?page=article&id=30908 [accessed April 30, 2005].

45. Nathan Leaf, "vandals swapping political signs for swastikas," *Wisconsin State Journal* (Madison, Wisconsin), October 2, 2004, p. B1.

46. Ibid.

47. Associated Press, "Nashville teen, angry over brother's deployment, steals 71 Bush signs," September 29, 2004.

48. Larry Carson, "Man found guilty of destroying signs supporting Bush," *Baltimore Sun*, February 18, 2005, p. 4B.

49. Mark Stodghill, "Teens confess to vandalizing campaign signs," *Duluth News Tribune*, September 16, 2004; available online at: http://www.duluthsuperior. com/mld/duluthtribune/9674817.htm [accessed June 2, 2005]; Matt Dees, "Yard signs lure vandals; 'As fast as we can put them up, they get taken down again,' a resident says of election signs," News & Observer (Raleigh, North Carolina), October 24, 2004, p. B3.

50. Ibid.

51. Search of Nexis database, 11/3/2004 to 11/6/2004: (wisconsin or milwaukee) and (tire! or van!) and (slash! or cut!) and (new york times or washington post or jimmy carter or jesse jackson)

52. David Doege, "Two more arrested in slashing of tires on GOP vehicles," Milwaukee Journal Sentinel (Wisconsin), November 7, 2004, p. B3; Derrick Nunnally, "DA drags feet on tire case, GOP complains; Republican party news release criticizes 'lack of action' in car vandalism," Milwaukee Journal Sentinel (Wisconsin), January 13, 2005, p. B1; "Dems charged in slashing GOP tires on Election Day, Associated Press/The Capital Times (Madison, Wisconsin), January 25, 2005.

53. Veronika Oleksyn, "Rep. Moore's Court Date With Her Son," *Congressional Quarterly Weekly*, January 29, 2005.

54. WIVB , "Vandals Target Two Locations," November 4, 2004; available online at: http://auto_sol.tao.ca/node/view/997 [accessed April 30, 2005].

55. Mandy Locke, "Search for vandals continues," *The News & Observer* (Raleigh, North Carolina), Novembrer 8 ,200, p. B1.

56. "Vandals repeatedly target 43rd Ward GOP headquarters," *Chicago Sun-Times*, November 10, 2004, p. 8.

57. Brian Gawley, "GOP headquarters in Port Angeles vandalized," *Peninsula Daily News* (Washington), March 20, 2005; available online at: http://www.peninsuladailynews.com/sited/story/html/201840 [accessed April 30, 2005].

58. John Hinderaker, "The violence Continues," Power Line, November 10, 2004; available online at: http://powerlineblog.com/archives/008578.php [acccessed July 9, 2005].

59. E-mail correspondence to the author from Monica Jensen, Dakota County Attorney's Office, July 18, 2005.

60. Doasfu, "Dean vs. Perle—Framing, Flying Shoes, and More," Daily Kos, February 17, 2005; available online at: http://www.dailykos.com/story/2005/2/18/2535/72934 [accessed July 22, 2005].

61. Rukmini Callimachi, "Protester throws shoe at Richard Perle," Associated Press, February 18, 2005.

62. Associated Press, "Earlham student hits pundit with pie during speech," March 30, 2005.

63. Associated Press Online, "Pat Buchanan doused with salad dressing," April 1, 2005.

64. Kevin O'Neal, "Activist hit by pie at Butler lecture," *Indianapolis Star*, April 7, 2005, p. 2B.

65. CBSNews.com, "A dressing down for Pat Buchanan," April 1, 2005; available online at: http://www.cbsnews.com/stories/2005/04/01/politics/main684601. shtml [accessed April 30, 2005].

66. National Public Radio Morning Edition, "What's a little pie in the face?" March 31, 2005; available online at: http://www.npr.org/templates/story/story.php?storyId=4569410 [accessed April 30, 2005].

67. Trifecta, "David Horowitz: Sissyboy racist," Daily Kos, April 7, 2005; available online at: http://www.volneysimmons.dailykos.com/story/2005/4/7/18654/18921.

68. The Party Plague,"Its just a fucking cream pie," Daily Kos, April 7, 2005; available online at: http://www.dailykos.com/comments/2005/4/7/18654/18921/19#19 [accessed April 30, 2005].

69. Robert Gavin, "Eyman, meet the piemen; popped with pastry while inside capitol," *Seattle Post-Intelligencer*, June 29, 2000, p. B1.

70. *Washington Times*, "Pie throwers and goon squads," April 11, 2005, p. A18.

71. Shannon Colavecchio-Van Sickler, "Bumper sticker evokes road rage," St. Petersburg Times (Florida), March 10, 2005, p. 1A.

72. Shannon Colavecchio-Van Sickler, "Businessman arrested in road rage case," St. Petersburg Times (Florida), March 12, 2005, p. 1B.

Chapter Four: They Don't Support Our Troops

1. Kurt Erickson, "Durbin hoping for middle ground," *The Pantagraph* (Bloomington, Ill.), December 19, 1998, p. A10.

2. Shailagh Murray, "Durbin Apologizes for Remarks on Abuse," *Washington Post*, June 22, 2005, p. A6

3. Amnesty International Report 2005, Speech by Irene Khan at Foreign Press Association, May 25, 2005; available online at: http://web.amnesty.org/library/index/ENGPOL100142005 [accessed July 7, 2005].

4. Adam Zagorin, Michael Duffy, "Inside the Interrogation of Detainee 063," *Time*, June 20, 2005; available online at: http://www.time.com/time/archive/preview/0,10987,1071284,00.html [accessed July 7, 2005].

5. Michelle Malkin, "Newsweek lied.* People died," michellemalkin.com, May 15,2005; available online at: http://michellemalkin.com/archives/002459.htm [accessed July 7, 2005].

6. United States Southern Command News Release on Koran Inquiry, June 3, 2005; available online at: http://www.voanews.com/mediaassets/english/2005_06/Other/pdf/PR050603a.pdf [accessed July 7, 2005].

7. For a strong argument relating to Durbin's lack of perspective, see Ed Morrissey, "Durbin Oddly Silent About The Torture Closer To Home," Captain's Quarters, June 17, 2005; available online at: http://www.captainsquartersblog.com/mt/archives/004735.php [accessed July 7, 2005].

8. Veterans of Foreign Wars of the United States, "VFW Demands Senator Apologize to Troops," June 16, 2005; available online at: http://www.vfw.org/index.cfm?fa=news.newsDtl&did=2655 [accessed July 7, 2005].

9. Anti-Defamation League press release, "ADL to Senator Durbin: Inappropriate Comparison to Nazi Tactics Unacceptable," June 16, 2005; available online at: http://www.adl.org/PresRele/HolNa_52/4734_52.htm [accessed July 7, 2005].

10. Dan Balz, "Durbin Defends Guantanamo Comments," *Washington Post*, June 17, 2005, p. A11.

11. Steve Gilliard, "Torture? No big deal. They deserved it.," The News Blog, June 16, 2005; available online at: http://stevegilliard.blogspot.com/2005/06/torture-no-big-deal-they-deserved-it.html [accessed July 11, 2005].

12. John Aravosis, "It's official. Right-wing smear and lie campaign in full swing against Senator Durbin," AMERICAblog, June 15, 2005; available online at: http://americablog.blogspot.com/2005/06/its-official-right-wing-smear-and-lie.html [accessed July 11, 2005].

13. Markos Moulitsas Zuniga, "The latest moronic Right-Wing smear attack," Daily Kos, June 15, 2005; available online at: http://www.dailykos.com/story-only/2005/6/16/25826/4241 [accessed July 11, 2005].

14. "Durbin's non-apology," New York Sun, June 23, 2005, p. 8.

15. Ed Morrissey, "Dick Durbin: The Ring Of Familiarity," Captain's Quarters, June 16, 2005; available online at: http://www.captainsquartersblog.com/mt/archives/004734.php [accessed July 7, 2005].

16. Elizabeth Hamilton, "Hillary Clinton Rallies Democratic Troops," *Hartford Courant* (Connecticut), April 29, 2003, p. B1.

17. Susan Jones, "Newsweek reporter asked to apologize for 'mercenary Army' comment," CNSNews.com, August 30, 2005; available at http://www.cnsnews.com/news/viewstory.asp?Page=%5CCulture%5Carchive%5C200508%5CCUL20050830b.html [accessed August 30, 2005].

18. Ken Hechtman, "We Support Our Troops...When They Shoot Their Officers," FrontPageMagazine.com, July 4, 2003; available online at: http://www.frontpagemag.com/Articles/ReadArticle.asp?ID=8744 [accessed July 7, 2005].

19. Jake Weyer, "Yellow ribbon magnets are bound to stick around," *Saint Paul Pioneer Press* (Minnesota), October 29, 2004 Friday, p .1E.

20. Associated Press Online, "Town Bans War Tributes on Public Property," March 28, 2003.

21. Adam Fifield, "Crackdown on yellow has town seeing red; Borough's ribbon ban generates a lot of anger, and lots more ribbons," *Philadelphia Inquirer*, March 29, 2003, p. A01.

22. "War briefs from California," Associated Press, April 10, 2003.

23. John Johnson, "War with Iraq; back home; town finds skater out of line; an antiwar woman blades down Carpinteria's main street, snipping yellow ribbons off trees and outraging neighbors," *Los Angeles Times*, April 15, 2003 Tuesday , part 2, p. 1.

24. Steve Chawkins, "War with Iraq; City Sorry for Untying Mom's Yellow Ribbons," *Los Angeles Times*, March 29, 2003, part 2, p. 1. Sadly, Freeman's son died in a car accident in January 2005 on his way back to his military base before his third deployment to Iraq.

25. Stacy Finz, Wyatt Buchanan, "Brouhaha over yellow ribbons; for and against in Burlingame," *San Francisco Chronicle*, April 4, 2003, p. A19.

26. Kim Vo, "City in knot over yellow ribbons; Burlingame mother's gesture sets off controversy over legality of display," *San Jose Mercury News*, April 5, 2003 Saturday PS1 edition, p B1.

27. City Administrator Gridley said ribbons would not be allowed on city-owned property. He was later overturned by the Common Council. See Associated Press, "Council reverses ban on yellow ribbons on city property," April 15, 2003.

28. Jerry Harkavy, "Tourist town awash in ribbons – and controversy," Associated Press, June 10, 2003.

29. Michelle Malkin, "The war on 'support our troops' stickers," michellemalkin.com, January 24, 2005; available online at: http://michelle-malkin.com/archives/001320.htm [accessed May 28, 2005].

30. Associated Press, "Dispute over 'Support Our Troops' magnet hits University of Oregon," January 25, 2005.

31. Nevy Wilson, "Robbery can't hurt patriotism at MTI," *Bradenton Herald*, April 5, 2003, p. 1.

32. Associated Press, "Military families upset over ribbon thefts ," August 29, 2004

33. Thomas Moen and Christine Moen, *Journal and Courier* (Lafayette, Ind.), September 18, 2004, p. 7A.

34. Richard Roeper, "Magnetic ribbons exercise powerful attraction," *Chicago Sun-Times*, December 23, 2003, p. 11.

35. "Police Briefs," Brattleboro Reformer (Vermont), November 15, 2004 Monday

36. Charity Vogel, "Amid patriotic fervor in wartime, ribbon magnets are phenomenon," *Buffalo News* (New York), November 28, 2004, p. B1.

37. Thomas Naughton, "No yellow ribbons here," *Daily Collegian*, February 23, 2005; available online at: http://www.dailycollegian.com/vnews/display.v /ART/2005/02/23/421beb6d96af4 [accessed May 28, 2005].

38. Jeff McMahan, "Supporting our troops?" December 6, 2004; available online at: http://left2right.typepad.com/main/2004/12/supporting_our_.html [accessed May 28, 2005].

39. Bob Sommers, "what is the real message of yellow ribbons on cars?" National Public Radio, February 14, 2005; audio available at: http://www.npr.org/templates/story/story.php?storyId=4498757 [accessed May 28, 2005].

40. Robert L. Jamieson, Jr., "Veteran gets rude welcome on Bainbridge," *Seattle Post-Intelligencer*, July 9, 2004, p. B1; available online at: http://seattlepi.nwsource.com/jamieson/181422_robert09.html [accessed May 28, 2005].

41. Michelle Malkin, "Welcoming home the troops," michellemalkin.com, July 15, 2004; available online at: http://michellemalkin.com/archives/000203.htm [accessed May 28, 2005].

42. Robert L. Jamieson, Jr., "An apology and—it is hoped—healing," *Seattle Post-Intelligencer*, July 16, 2004, p. B1; available online at: http://seattlepi.nwsource.com/jamieson/182359_robert16.html [accessed May 28, 2005].

43. Associated Press article posted online at: http://www.militarycity.com/valor/345583.html [accessed May 28, 2005]. See also Texas House of Representatives Resolution 380, available online at: http://www.capitol.state.tx.us/tlo/79R/billtext/HR00380F.HTM [accessed May 28, 2005].

44. Nbc5i.com, "Family Of Killed Soldier: Vigil Crowd Threatening," September 9, 2004; available online at: http://www.nbc5i.com/news/3719681/detail.html [accessed May 28, 2005].

45. Ibid.

46. Terry Horne, "Arrest made in memorial attack; Police skeptical of Danville teen's story that damage to heroes display was accident," *Indianapolis Star*, April 9, 2005, p. 1B.

47. Kris Kirschner, "Hoosiers react to monument vandalism," WTHR, March 30, 3004; available online at: http://www.wthr.com/global/story.asp?s= 3139133&ClientType=Printable [accessed May 28, 2005].

48. Stark and other left-wing congressmen wanted a stronger condemnation. See Brian Carnell, "Left Wing Democrats Vote Against Resolution Condemning Iraqi Prisoner Abuse," Brian.Carnell.Com, May 7, 2004; available online at: http://brian.carnell.com/archives/years/2004/05/000012.html [accessed July 7, 2005].

49. Letter was posted at The Command Post on May 7, 2004; available online at: http://www.command-post.org/oped/2_archives/012131.html [accessed May 28, 2005].

50. Audio available online at: http://images.radcity.net/5152/663017.wav [accessed May 28, 2005].

51. Josh Richman and Sandhya Somashekhar, "Stark's voice mail stirs big reaction; Congressman uses profanity, insults in message that winds up on national radio," *Daily Review* (Hayward, California), May 8, 2004.

52. Lisa Fernandez, "Old-time liberal Democrat outnumbered, still has fire," *San Jose Mercury News*, February 13, 2005.

53. Ibid.

54. Daily Kos received, on average, well over 300,000 visits per day during the first six months of 2004, according to SiteMeter statistics—far more than any other blog listed on the Truth Laid Bear traffic rankings See: http://www.sitemeter.com/default.asp?action=stats&site=sm8dailykos&report=36 [accessed July 7, 2005].

55. Markos Moulitsas, "Every death should be on the front page," April 1, 2004; comment in response to gregonthe28th, "Corpses on the Cover," Daily Kos, April 1, 2004; available online at http://www.dailykos.com/story/2004/4/1/144156/3224 [accessed May 28, 2005].

56. Kevin Dayton, "Ambush victim was a soldier's soldier," *Honolulu Advertiser*, April 7, 2004, p. 4B.

57. Associated Press, "Daughter of slain U.S. contractor in Iraq remembers her father," April 11, 2004.

58. Deborah Schoch, Julie Tamaki and Monte Morin, "Death Came Brutally to a Man Who 'Never Quit,'" *Los Angeles Times*, April 3, 2004, p. A1.

59. Lauren Howard, "Local man among four slain in Iraq," *Leaf-Chronicle* (Clarksville, Tennessee), April 2, 2004, p. 1A.

60. Scott Reeves, "Family members remember man killed in Iraq," Associated Press, April 10, 2004.

61. Jean Marbella, "A life taken in Iraq, a job left unfinished; family and friends of a security worker killed in attacks support the U.S. operation even as they mourn his death," *Baltimore Sun*, April 3, 2004, p. 1A.

62. Markos Moulitsas, "Mercenaries, war, and my childhood," Daily Kos, April 2, 2004; available online at: http://www.dailykos.com/story/2004/4/2/175739/8203?mode=alone%3bshowrate=1 [accessed May 28, 2005].

63. E-mail from Jess Fassler to Michael Friedman; available online at: http://michael-friedman.com/archives/000311.html [accessed May 28, 2005].

64. http://weeklystandard.com/content/public/articles/000/000/005/207exwra.asp

65. Congress Daily article cited in Hotline, "Battle for the Senate: is it time for the WH to start stepping; in?," June 7, 2005.

66. Barbara Boxer, "Thank you so much," Daily Kos, January 27, 2005; available online at: http://dailykos.com/story/2005/1/27/124226/410 [accessed May 28, 2005].

67. Edward M. Kennedy, "ON the Downing Street Minutes," Daily Kos, June 7, 2005; available online at: http://www.dailykos.com/story/2005/6/7/101849/4431 [accessed June 13, 2005].

68. Kris Oser and Ken Wheaton, "Blogs turn subversive into a big ad draw; Majority toil for free, but a few rake in up to $20,000 a month ," *Advertising Age*, October 18, 2004, p. 34.

69. Susan Paynter, "School's stage was set for a stark lesson," *Seattle Post-Intelligencer*, March 16, 2005, p. B1; available online at: http://seattlepi.nwsource.com/paynter/216092_paynter16.html [accessed May 28, 2005].

70. Brian Crouch, "Vet strikes back," Sound Politics, March 21, 2005; available online at: http://www.soundpolitics.com/archives/004019.html [accessed May 28, 2005].

71. Michelle Malkin, "Shameless in Seattle," michellemalkin.com, March 24, 2005; available online at: http://michellemalkin.com/archives/001843.htm [accessed May 28, 2005].

72. Ibid.

73. Michelle Morgan Bolton, "Colorful beads lead to court," *Times Union* (Albany, New York), February 17, 2005, p. A1.

74. Carol McAlice Currie, "Career day photo of soldier with gun puts school district in a bind," *Statesman Journal*, March 25, 2005; available online at: http://www.statesmanjournal.com/apps/pbcs.dll/article?AID=/20050325/COLUMN0101/503250306/1064 [accessed May 28 ,2005].

75. Ibid.

76. Deb, "Update!" Marine Corps Moms, March 31, 2005; available online at: http://marinecorpsmoms.com/archives/2005/03/update.html [accessed May 28, 2005].

77. Connie, "Zero tolerance? Let 'em know what you think," Marine Corps Moms, March 15, 2005; available online at: http://marinecorpsmoms.com/archives/2005/03/zero_tolerance.html [accessed May 28, 2005].

78. Bill O'Reilly, "The worst of Times," Newsday, June 21, 2004; available online at: http://www.nydailynews.com/news/ideas_opinions/story/204738p-176737c.html [accessed July 20, 2005].

79. Herald staff, "Globe caught with pants down: Paper duped into running porn photos," *Boston Herald*, May 13, 2004, p. 006.

80. John Hawkins, "The Iraqi 'Quagmire' In Quotes," RightWingNews.com, undated; available online at: http://www.rightwingnews.com/quotes/muddy.php [accessed July 20, 2005].

81. Michelle Malkin, "Guantanamo Bay: the rest of the story," michellemalkin.com, May 26, 2005; available online at: http://michellemalkin.com/archives/002566.htm [accessed July 15, 2005]; Michelle Malkin, "Gitmo detainees desecrate Quran," michellemalkin.com, June 3, 3005; available online at: http://michellemalkin.com/archives/002642.htm [accessed July 15, 2005].

82. "Iraq Antiquities Revisited," Iraqi Bloggers Central; available online at: http://jarrarsupariver.blogspot.com/2005/01/iraq-antiquities-revisited.html [accessed July 20, 2005].

83. See, for example, Daniel Pipes on Kudlow & Cramer, September 7, 2004; transcript available online at: http://www.danielpipes.org/article/2075 [accessed July 20, 2005].

84. See, for example, Tony Blankley, "Thank God for General Boykin ," townhall.com, October 22, 2003; available online at: http://www.townhall.com/columnists/tonyblankley/tb20031022.shtml [accessed July 20, 2005].

85. See, e.g., Moncia Davey, "Un-Volunteering: Troops Improvise to Find a Way Out," New York Times, March 18, 2005, p. A18. See also Democracy Now!, "U.S. Army War Resister Jeremy Hinzman: 'I Have a Duty to Disobey,'" December 13, 2004; available online at: http://www.democracynow.org/article.pl?sid=04/12/13/1457230 [accessed July 20, 2005].

86. "The Women of Gitmo," *New York Times*, July 15 ,2005; available online at: http://www.nytimes.com/2005/07/15/opinion/15fri1.html [accessed July 20, 2005].

87. Image is available online at: http://www.harpers.org/art/covers/2005-03_350x476.jpg [accessed July 20, 2005].

88. Sharon L. Bond, "The few, the proud - but surely not AWOL," *St. Petersburg Times*, March 26, 2005; available online at: http://sptimes.com/2005/03/26/outhpinellas/The_few__the_proud___.shtml [accessed July 20, 205].

89. Sharon L. Bond, "Magazine to clarify that Marines weren't AWOL," *St. Petersburg Times*, March 29, 2005, p. 3B.

90. See Easongate.com (http://billroggio.com/easongate), LaShawn Barber (http://lashawnbarber.com/archives/category/easongate/), and

michellemalkin.com (http://michellemalkin.com/archives/001489.htm) for background on the Eason Jordan controversy.

91. See FoleyGate.com (http://foleygate.com/) and Choose Honor (http://choose-honor.blogspot.com) for background on the Linda Foley controversy.

92. Justin Vaisse, "Blog De dAVOs: 26 - 29 janvier 2005," available online at: http://vaisse.net/BiblioJustin/Blog-de-Davos.htm [accessed July 20, 2005]; translated from French into English by Rodger Marrow, "Another Easongate eyewitness," This isn't writing, it's typing, February 7, 2005; available online at: http://writingcompany.blogs.com/this_isnt_writing_its_typ/2005/02/another_ea songa.html [accessed July 20, 2005].

93. Howard Kurtz, "Eason Jordan, Quote, Unquote; CNN News Chief Clarifies His Comments on Iraq," *Washington Post*, February 8, 2005, p. C01; available online at: http://www.washingtonpost.com/wp-dyn/articles/A6490-2005Feb7.html [accessed July 20, 2005].

94. Eason Jordan, 1999 Joe Alex Morris Jr. Memorial Lecture at Harvard University, March 10, 1999; available online at: http://nieman.harvard.edu/events/hon-ors/morris/EASON-Morris.html [accessed July 20, 2005].

95. Howard Kurtz, "CNN's Jordan Resigns Over Iraq Remarks; News Chief Apolo-gized For Comment on Troops," *Washington Post*, February 12 ,2005, p. A01; available online at: http://www.washingtonpost.com/wp-dyn/articles/A17462-2005Feb11.html [accessed July 20, 2005].

96. Michelle Malkin, "Easongate: David Gergen speaks," michellemalkin.com, Feb-ruary 7, 2005; available online at: http://michellemalkin.com/archives/001448.htm [accessed July 20, 2005].

97. Michelle Malkin, "Easongate: Barney Frank talks," michellemalkin.com, Febru-ary 7, 2005; available online at: http://michellemalkin.com/archives/001447.htm [accessed July 20, 2005].

98. Michelle Malkin, "Easongate: Chris Dodd speaks," michellemalkin.com, Febru-ary 7, 2005; available online at: http://michellemalkin.com/archives/001450.htm [accessed July 20, 2005].

99. Jake Ellison, "Anti-war group targets on-campus military recruiters," *Seattle Post-Intelligencer*, February 4, 2005, p. B1; available online at: http://seattlepi.nwsource.com/local/210741_protest04.html [accessed May 31, 2005].

100. Joseph R. Chenelly, "College students take aim; Recruiters become targets of campus anti-war hostilities," *Army Times*, February 7, 2005, p. 8.

101. Jake Ellison, "Anti-war group targets," op cit.

102. Socialist Worker Online, "Get the military out of our schools; how activists built the struggle; Seattle showdown," March 4, 2005; available online at:

http://www.socialistworker.org/2005-1/533/533_09_Seattle.shtml [accessed May 31, 2005].

103. Matt Rosenberg, "36th Dist. Dems Endorse Military Recruiting Ban at SCCC," Sound Politics, March 19, 2005; available online at: http://www.soundpolitics.com/archives/004004.html [accessed June 16, 2005].

104. Joseph R. Chenelly, "College students take aim; Recruiters become targets of campus anti-war hostilities," op cit.

105. Damien Cave, "For recruiters, antiwar protests raise perils on the home front," New York Times, February 21, 2005, p. B1.

106. WTOL11, "Military Recruiting Office Vandalized," February 2, 2005; available online at: http://www.wtol.com/global/story.asp?s=2887448&ClientType=Printable [accessed May 31, 2005].

107. Ibid.

108. Michael Wilson, "Metro Briefing New York: Manhattan: College Secretary Arrested," New York Times, March 14, 2005, p. B.6

109. Karen W. Arenson, "Metro Briefing New York: Manhattan: 3 Students Arrested At Protest," New York Times, March 10, 2005, p. B6.

110. Press & Sun-Bulletin, "Briefing," February 12, 2005, p. 1B.

111. IndyMedia Watch, "What makes an activist?," February 26, 2005; available online at: http://indymediawatch.blogspot.com/2005/02/what-makes-activist.html [accessed June 13, 2005].

112. Ibid.

113. Joseph R. Chenelly, "College students take aim; Recruiters become targets of campus anti-war hostilities," op cit.

114. "Bronx Community College Students Drive Out Military Recruiters!," The Internationalist, March 2005; available online at: http://www.internationalist.org/bccdriverecruitersout0503.html [accessed June 16, 2005]. See also Mike Burke, "Bronx Students Force Military Recruiters Off Campus For A Third Time," CounterRecruiter, April 16, 2005; available online at: http://rncwatch.typepad.com/counterrecruiter/counter_recruitment_protests/ [accessed June 16, 2005].

115. Erin Pursell, "Activists protest military on campus; group opposes recruiters at S.F. State University career fair," insidemayarea.com; available online at: http://www.insidebayarea.com/localnews/ci_2603424 [accessed May 31, 2005].

116. UW-Madison Stop the War, "Air Force ROTC cancels recruiting event in response to student protest ," May 1, 2005; available online at: http://www.campusantiwar.net/index.php?option=content&task=view&id=77 [accessed June 16, 2005].

117. Code Pink, "Recruiting Center Protest Guide," undated; available online at: http://www.codepink4peace.org/article.php?id=332 [accessed July 22, 2005].

118. Not Your Soldier web site; available online at: http://www.notyoursoldier.org/ [accessed July 22, 2005].

119. For more background, see Rocco diPippo, "The Left's War Against the Military At Home," FrontPageMagazine.com, July 11, 2005; available online at: http://www.frontpagemag.com/Articles/ReadArticle.asp?ID=18720 [accessed July 22, 2005].

120. Ted Rall comic strip, May 3, 2004; available online at: http://www.ucomics.com/rallcom/2004/05/03/ [accessed July 22, 2005].

121. Ted Rall, "Boycott the Military," July 13, 2004; available online at: http://www.informationclearinghouse.info/article6483.htm [accessed June 16, 2005].

Chapter Five: Campus Moonbats on Parade

1. Perry de Havilland, Samizdata blog glossary; available online at: http://www.samizdata.net/blog/glossary_archives/001981.html [accessed July 20, 2005].

2. Ward Churchill, "'Some People Push Back' On the Justice of Roosting Chickens," Pockets of Resistance, September 2001; reproduced online at: http://www.darknightpress.org/index.php?i=news&c=recent&view=9 [accessed May 31, 2005].

3. Ibid and Ward Churchill, On the Justice of Roosting Chickens: Reflections on the Consequences of U.S. Imperial Arrogance and Criminality (AK Press), 2003.

4. Ward Churchill, On the Justice of Roosting Chickens, op cit.

5. Ian Mandell, "Controversial speaker to visit Hill," *The Spectator* (Hamilton College, New York), January 21, 2005; available online at: http://spec.hamilton.edu/sports.cfm?action=display&news=476 [accessed May 31, 2005].

6. Michelle Malkin, "Ward Churchill: caught on tape advocating terrorism," michellemalkin.com, February 24, 2005; available online at: http://michelle-malkin.com/archives/001588.htm [accessed May 31, 2005].

7. Michelle Malkin, "Another bizarre twist in the Ward Churchill saga," michelle-malkin.com, Febuary 25, 2005; available online at: http://michellemalkin.com/archives/001596.htm [accessed May 31, 2005].

8. Ken Masugi, "Ward Churchill Whines: Fascist America UPDATED," The Claremont Institute: The Remedy, April 26, 2005; available online at: http://www.claremont.org/weblog/002964.html [accessed May 31, 2005].

9. Pirate Ballerina, June 26, 2005; available online at: http://www.pirateballerina.com/blog/entry.php?id=158 [accessed June 27, 2005].

10. Ibid.

11. John Hawkins, "The San Francisco Peace Protest: The Line Between Dissent & Treachery," rightwingnews.com, April 12, 2004; available online at: http://www.rightwingnews.com/category.php?ent=1936 [accessed May 31, 2005].

12. Lee Kaplan, "Intifada Against College Republicans," frontpagemagazine.com, November 2, 2004; available online at: http://www.frontpagemag.com/Articles/ReadArticle.asp?ID=15779; accessed May 31, 2005.

13. Lee Kaplan, "Jihad at San Francisco State," frontpagemagazine.com, November 8, 2004; available online at http://www.frontpagemag.com/Articles/ReadArticle.asp?ID=15855 [accessed May 31, 2005].

14. *London Review of Books*, October 4, 2001.

15. M. Shahid Alam, "America and Islam: Seeking Parallels," Dissident Voice, December 28, 2004; available online at: http://www.dissidentvoice.org/Dec2004/Alam1228.htm [accessed May 31, 2005].

16. Robert Jensen, "U.S. just as guilty of committing own violent acts," *Houston Chronicle*, September 14, 2001, p. A33.

17. Robert Jensen, "Ward Churchill: Right to Speak Out; Right About 9/11," Counterpunch, February 14, 2005; available online at: http://www.counterpunch.org/jensen02142005.html [accessed May 31, 2005].

18. Michelle Malkin, "Another nutty professor," michellemalkin.com, February 11, 2005; available online at: http://michellemalkin.com/archives/001484.htm [accessed May 31, 2005].

19. Assad Pino, "The world needs more Churchills to speak up," *Daily Kent Stater* (Ohio), April 7, 2005; available online at: http://www.stateronline.com/vnews/display.v/ART/2005/04/07/4254bd6d8ef9b?in_archive=1 [accessed May 31, 2005].

20. "Professor calls for 'million more Mogadishus;' Controversial comments at anti-war teach-in," CNN.com, March 28, 2003; available online at: http://www.cnn.com/2003/US/Northeast/03/28/sprj.irq.professor.somalia/ [accessed May 31, 2005].

21. "The Sontag Award," *The Weekly Standard*, October 22, 2001, p. 39.

22. Kay S. Hymowitz and Harry Stein, "Earth to Ivory Tower: Get Real!", *City Journal*, Autumn 2001, pp. 90-101; Vol. 11, No. 4.

23. Associated Press, "Colorado teacher kicks student for wearing GOP shirt off campus," October 30, 2004.

24. Nora Zamichow and Stuart Silverstein, "As Hate-Crime Concerns Rise, So Does the Threat of Hoaxes; Campuses often provide conditions that can cultivate

false reports of racist or anti-gay acts, experts say," *Los Angeles Times*, April 20, 2004, p. B1.

25. Michelle Malkin, "The boy who cried 'muslim,'" townhall.com, October 5, 2001; available online at: http://www.townhall.com/columnists/michelle-malkin/mm20011005.shtml [accessed May 31, 2005].

26. Sara Russo, "Hate Crimes Against Muslim Student at Arizona State a Hoax," Accuracy in Academia; available online at: http://www.academia.org/campus_reports/2001/nov_2001_2.html [accessed May 31, 2005].

27. Michelle Malkin, "Another hate crime hoax," michellemalkin.com, May 9, 2005; available online at: http://michellemalkin.com/archives/002382.htm [accessed June 2, 2005].

Chapter Six: "You Are One Sick Gook"

1. Greg Pierce, "Inside Politcs," *Washington Times*, November 7, 2003, p. A06.

2. Adam Cohen, "Editorial Observer; A New Kind of Minority Is Challenging Louisiana's Racial Conventions," *New York Times*, October 12, 2003, p. 10.

3. Scott Gold, "Louisiana Politics Show a New Face; An Indian American conservative's bid for governor underscores a break with the past," *Los Angeles Times*, October 3, 2003, p. A13,

4. Adam Nossiter ," In Louisiana, a candidate for governor who leads in polls despite breaking the mold," Associated Press, September 28, 2003.

5. Adam Nossiter, "Bobby Jindal: a dual pull, here and beyond, and its consequences," Associated Press, September 2, 2003; Adam Nossiter, "Did racism beat Jindal?" Associated Press, November 26, 2003.

6. Michelle Malkin, "Michelle Malkin is a c**t," michellemalkin.com, April 7, 2005; available online at: http://michellemalkin.com/archives/002024.htm [accessed July 20, 2005].

7. Kevin Drum, "Blog Civility," September 2, 2003; available online at: http://calpundit.com/archives/002048.html [accessed May 6, 2005].

8. E-mail from Kevin Drum to the author, April 7, 2005.

9. Margaret Cho herself engaged in this empty tactic against me in a diatribe about my last book, In Defense of Internment. See Margaret Cho, "In Defense of Michelle Malkin," September 27, 2004; available online at: http://margaretcho.net/blog/indefenseofmichellemalkin.htm [accessed May 6, 2005].

10. Ted Rall, "How Sad . . ." June 6, 2004; available online at: http://www.rall.com/2004_06_01_archive.html#108653231413264149 [accessed May 6, 2005].

11. Universal Press Syndicate home page; available online at: http://www.amuniversal.com/ups/index.htm [accessed May 6, 2005]

12. Ted Rall home page; available online at: http://www.tedrall.com/about.htm [accessed May 6, 2005].

13. Cartoon is available online at: http://www.ucomics.com/rallcom/2004/07/05/ [accessed May 6 , 2005].

14. Project 21 press release "Black Group Condemns Cartoonist for Racist Strip About Condoleezza Rice," July 19, 2004; available online at: http://www.nationalcenter.org/P21PRRall704.html.

15. Ibid.

16. Cartoon is available at
http://images.ucomics.com/comics/db/2004/db040407.gif [accessed May 6, 2005].

17. Cartoon is available at http://americandigest.org/mt-archives/002864.php [accessed May 6, 2005].

18. Jay Nordlinger, "Running dishonest, fearing a shift, a revolting cartoon, and more," National Review Online , October 12 ,2004; available online at: http://www.nationalreview.com/impromptus/impromptus200410120834.asp [accessed May 6, 2005].

19. See A Red Mind in a Blue State, "Jeff Danziger, Half Racist," October 12, 2004; available online at: http://redmindbluestate.blogspot.com/2004/10/jeff-danziger-half-racist.html [accessed May 6, 2005].

20. See, e.g., http://img.photobucket.com/albums/v89/mhking/blog/condicartoon_1.jpg [accessed July 20, 2005].

21. Michelle Malkin, "Vacant Lott," Creators Syndicate; available online at: http://www.townhall.com/columnists/michellemalkin/mm20021213.shtml [accessed May 6, 2005].

22. Ed Henry, "Heard on the Hill," Roll Call, April 7, 2004.

23. http://www.washingtonpost.com/wp-dyn/content/article/2005/06/18/AR2005061801105.html?sub=AR

24. Eric Pianin, "A Senator's shame," Washington Post, June 19, 2005, p. A01; available online at: http://www.washingtonpost.com/wp-dyn/content/article/2005/06/18/AR2005061801105.html [accessed July 7, 2005]. See also Michelle Malkin, "Senator Robert Byrd, ex-klansman," Creators Syndicate, March 7 ,2001; available online at: http://www.townhall.com/columnists/michellemalkin/mm20010307.shtml.

25. Ibid.

26. Randall Archibald, "Dodd Says He Regrets 'Poor Choice Of Words," New York Times, April 16, 2004, p. B6.

27. Associated Press, "Hillary Clinton 'truly regrets' Gandhi joke," January 7, 2004; available online at: http://www.cnn.com/2004/ALLPOLITICS/01/06/elec04.s.mo.farmer.clinton.ap/ [accessed July 22, 2005].

28. David Wissing, "Is Tom Daschle a racist?," The Hedgehog Report, May 24, 2003; available online at: http://www.davidwissing.com/index.php/501 [accessed July 22, 2005].

29. John Grogan, "Fumo's invective belies his words," Philadelphia Inquirer, October 11, 2004, p. B1.

30. Mario F. Cattabiani, "Fumo says he's sorry for using gay slur; The state senator said he lost his temper in a dispute with GOP leaders on the Senate floor," *Philadelphia Inquirer*, October 8, 2004, p. A1.

31. Ibid.

32. Ibid.

33. Quotation originally published in The Patriot News was reproduced at "WHAT Media Bias? Where? I Don't See it!!," Barking Moonbat Early Warning System, October 8, 2004; available online at: http://www.barking-moonbat.com/index.php/weblog/comments/what_media_bias_where_i_dont_se e_it/ [accessed July 4, 2005].

34. Michelle Malkin, "Fortney "Pete" Stark: Poster Boy for Democrat Double Standards," *Capitalism Magazine*, July 23, 2003; available online at: http://capmag.com/article.asp?ID=2964 [accessed July 7, 2005].

35. Ibid.

36. Ibid.

37. Karen Matthews, "Clinton says stories about GOP consultant are 'sad,'" Associated Press, April 11, 2005.

38. Remember when Gloria Steinem called Texas Republican Senator Kay Bailey Hutchison, mother of four children, a "female impersonator?" Or when curdled NOW leader Patricia Ireland instructed Democrats to vote only for "authentic" female political candidates? Or when Al Gore's fashion consultant Naomi Wolf described the foreign-policy analysis of Jeane Kirkpatrick as being "uninflected by the experiences of the female body?"

39. Joyce Howard Price, "Harris demonized in the media," *Washington Times*, November 20, 2000, p. A14.

40. Robin Givhan, "The eyelashes have it," *Washington Post*, November 18, 2000, p. C01.

41. Michael Getler, "Mascara smear," *Washington Post*, November 22, 2000, p. A26.

42. Hotline, "Kerry: stumping while stumped," October 20, 2004.

43. Answers.com, "Jesusland map," available online at: http://www.answers.com-topic/jesusland-map [accessed May 76, 2005].

44. Joseph Curl, "Blue states buzz over secession" *Washington Times*, November 9, 2004, p. A01.

45. http://www.kenlayne.com/2004/11/secret_jesusland.html

46. Media Matters, "Media overplayed 'moral values' as 'decisive' election issue," November 10, 2004; available online at: http://mediamatters.org/items/200411100010 [accessed May 6, 2005].

47. David Brooks, "The Values-Vote Myth," *New York Times*, Nov. 6, 2004, p. A19.

48. Gary Wills, "The day the enlightenment went out," *New York, Times*, Nov. 4, 2004, p. A25.

49. Maureen Dowd, "The red zone," *New York Times*, Nov. 4, 2004, p. A25.

50. Bob Herbert ,"Voting without the facts," *New York Times*, Nov. 8, 2004 ,p. A23.

51. Jane Smiley, "Why Americans Hate Democrats :A Dialogue," Slate.com, Nov. 4, 2004.

52. Tara Kadioglu, "NPR star Keillor tells of home life on a prairie," November 7, 2004; available online at: http://maroon.uchicago.edu/news/articles/2004/11/07/npr_star_keillor_tel.php [accessed July 7, 2005].

53. Joseph Curl "Blue states buzz over secession, op cit.

54. Hannity & Colmes, Fox News, "Iraq Election Results Only the Beginning, Rangel Defends Redneck Comments," Feb. 17, 2005.

55. Dana Milbank, "With Giant Spoon, Florida Woman Helps Stir Up Schiavo Protest Across From White House," *Washington Post*, March 28, 2005, p. A03; available online at: http://www.washingtonpost.com/wp-dyn/articles/A7802-2005Mar28.html [accessed May 6, 2005].

56. Paul Krugman, "What's going on?" *New York Times*, Mar. 29, 2005, p. A17.

57. Matt Taibbi, "The 52 funniest things about the upcoming death of the Pope," *New York Press*, May 4-1, 2005; available online at: http://www.nypress.com/18/9/news&columns/taibbi.cfm [accessed May 6, 2005].

58. Philip Blenkinsop, "New Pope served in Hitler Youth but was no Nazi ," Reuters, April 19, 2005; available online at: http://www.alertnet.org/thenews/newsdesk/L19376016.htm [accessed May 6, 2005].

59. Uew Siemon-Netto, "Commentary: Benedict abused as 'nazi pope,' " United Press International, April 21, 2005; available online at: http://washtimes.com/upi-breaking/20050421-040257-2592r.htm [accessed May 6, 2005].

60. Ibid.

61. Valerie Richardson, "Salazar's 'Antichrist' flap spotlights judicial battle," *Washington Times*, April 29, 2005; available online at: http://washingtontimes.com/national/20050428-115525-8515r.htm [accessed May 6, 2005].

62. *Denver Post*, "Salazar says he misspoke in calling Focus 'anti-Christ' Senator says 'un-Christian' fits Springs group," April 28, 2005, p. A2.

63. Scarborough Country, MSNBC, February 15, 2005.

Chapter Seven: The Hollywood Walk of Hate

1. George Rush and Joanna Molloy, "Punk the prez? Moby's anti-Bush tricks," *New York Daily News*, February 9, 2004; available online at: http://www.nydailynews.com/news/gossip/story/162588p-142554c.html [accessed June 1, 2005].

2. Ergun Mehmet Caner, "Moore's 'hate-riotism,'" jewishworldreview.com, June 24, 2004; available online at: http://www.jewishworldreview.com/0604/hate-riotism.php3 [accessed June 1, 2005].

3. Deborah Orin, "Howard's hatefest," *New York Post*, December 16, 2003.

4. Ibid.

5. Ibid.

6. "ACME Whoopi! What She Said!" Available online at: http://www.acmewebpages.com/whoopi/whoopisaid.htm [accessed June 1, 2005].

7. Jodi Wilgoren, "Kerry's celebrity fund-raiser is a huge Bash," *New York Times*, July 9, 2004, p. A1.

8. Ibid.

9. Mark Binelli, "Hollywood's hottest chick," rollingstone.com, September 4, 2001.

10. Michelle Goldberg, "A simple, poetic indictment," Salon.com, January 13, 2004; available online at: http://www.salon.com/news/feature/2004/01/13/moveon/ [accessed June 1, 2005].

11. Matt Drudge, "Raw rage at Bush during moveon.org awards; transcript revealed," Drudge Report, January 13, 2003; available online at: http://www.drudgereport.com/mattmo3.htm [accessed June 1, 2005].

12. Richard Leiby, "It's the F-Time Show With Chevy Chase," *Washington Post*, December 16, 2003, p. C03.

13. Ibid.

14. Matt Drudge, "Raw rage at Bush during moveon.org awards; transcript revealed," op cit..

15. Federal News Service, National Press Club Luncheon With Tim Robbins, Actor, And Thomas Andrews, Director, Win Without War, April 15, 2003, National Press Club Ballroom, Washington, D.C.

16. Sonya Ross, "Danny Glover Targeted for Anti-War Views Danny Glover targeted for anti-war views," Associated Press Online, May 18, 2003.

17. Associated Press, "Martin Sheen tapes mouth shut, joins protest," March 26, 2003.

18. Simon Hattenstone ,"Weekend: the devil and Miss Jones," *The Guardian*, October 18, 2003, Guardian Weekend Pages, p. 50.

19. BBC News, "Elton attacks 'censorship' in US," July 17 ,2004; available online at: http://news.bbc.co.uk/2/hi/entertainment/3902833.stm [accessed June 25, 2005].

20. MarkSteyn, "Bring on the war - for everyone's sake," *National Post* (Canada), March 10, 2003, p. A14.

21. Mugger, "Round One Begins," Jewish World Review, January 2, 2002; available online at: http://www.jewishworldreview.com/cols/mugger010302.asp

22. The O'Reilly Factor, Fox News, December 17, 2003.

23. Scarborough Country, MSNBC, July 10, 2003, transcript # 071000cb.471.

24. *Los Angeles Daily News*, "Madonna bashes Bush administration," January 10, 2004, p .N2.

25. "Sandra Bernhard," washingtonpost.com, February 25, 2003; available online at: http://discuss.washingtonpost.com/wp-srv/zforum/02/entertainment_bernhard022502.htm [accessed June 25, 2005].

26. "Bush/Hitler Image Removed From Ozzfest Video Montage," MTV News, July 22, 2004; available online at: http://www.mtv.com/news/articles/1489619/20040722/story.jhtml [accessed June 25, 2005].

27. Media Research Center CyberAlert, August 21, 2003; available online at: http://www.mediaresearch.org/cyberalerts/2003/cyb20030821.asp [accessed June 25, 2005].

28. U.S. Senate Roll Call Votes 107th Congress - 1st Session, Vote Number 313, October 25, 2001; available online at: http://www.senate.gov/legislative/LIS/roll_call_lists/roll_call_vote_cfm.cfm?congress=107&session=1&vote=00313 [accessed June 25, 2005].

29. Matt Drudge, "Raw rage at Bush during moveon.org awards; transcript revealed," drudgereport.com, January 13, 2003; available online at: http://www.drudgereport.com/mattmo3.htm [accessed June 1, 2005].

30. Beth Gillin, "Acting out: Hollywood antiwar sentiment is loud and clear. And so is the opposition," *Philadelphia Inquirer*, February 20, 2003; available online at: http://www.philly.com/mld/philly/5218882.htm? template=contentModules/printstory.jsp [accessed June 25, 2005].

31. Elysa Gardner, "Linda Ronstadt, hummin' an outraged tune," *USA Today*, November 17, 2004, p. 6D.

32. Simon Hattenstone ,"Weekend: the devil and Miss Jones," *The Guardian*, October 18, 2003, Guardian Weekend Pages, p. 50.

33. Associated Press Online, "Streisand Chides Democratic Leaders," April 3, 2001.

34. Lloyd Grove, "The reliable source," *Washington Post*, March 8, 2002, p. C03.

35. Bill Cotterell, "Actor compares 2000 election to September 11; Alec Baldwin says disputed vote damaged democracy," *Tallahassee Democrat*, March 8, 2002, p. B3.

36. Phil Sutcliffe, "Pop Music; Bad boys to men," *Los Angeles Times*, June 13, 2004, p. E31.

37. Dennis Cauchon and Jim Drinkard, "Special report: Florida voter errors cost Gore the election; Bush still prevails in recount of all disrupted ballots, using two most common standards," *USA Today*, May 11, 2001, p. 1A.

38. Joe Heim, "Rapper Ups the Anti on Bush and 9/11," *Washington Post*, July 17, 2004, p. C01.

39. Rashaun Hall, "Beats & Rhymes: Jadakiss Single Courts Controversy," *Billboard*, July 17, 2004, p. 22.

40. Joe Heim, "Rapper Ups the Anti on Bush and 9/11," op cit.

41. Michelle Malkin, "Giving the U.S. a bad rap," *Washington Times*, December 30, 2001, p. B3.

42. Ibid.

43. Michael Kane, "Hip-Hop and the 9/11 Truth Movement," Guerilla News Network, December 22, 2004; available online at: http://gnn.tv/articles/1016/Hip_Hop_and_the_9_11_Truth_Movement [accessed June 26, 2005].

44. Ali Asadullah, "Rapper, Paris, Unleashes A 'Sonic Jihad,'" IslamOnline.net, August 1, 2003; available online at: http://www.islamonline.net/English/artcul-ture/2003/01/article07.shtml [accessed June 26, 2005].

45. Seeklyrics.com, "Know Your Enemy Lyrics," available online at: http://www.seeklyrics.com/lyrics/Dead-Prez/Know-Your-Enemy.html [accessed June 26, 2005].

46. Soren Baker, "Dead prez runs with a militant, anti-war agenda," *Chicago Tribune*, February 15, 2003, p. N38.

47. Michael Kane, "Hip-Hop and the 9/11 Truth Movement," Guerilla News Network, December 22, 2004; available online at: http://gnn.tv/articles/1016/Hip_Hop_and_the_9_11_Truth_Movement [accessed June 26, 2005].

48. Ibid.

49. Ibid.

50. "Eminem Lyrics; Mosh," available online at: http://www.azlyrics.com/lyrics/eminem/mosh.html [accessed June 27, 2005].

51. *Detroit Fress Press*, "Eminem and Dr. Dre join anti-Bush ranks for new album," October 22, 2004.

52. Ibid.

53. Matt Drudge, "Cher issues Bush warning at disco," Drudge Report, October 23, 2004; available online at: http://www.papillonsartpalace.com/cheWr.htm [accessed June 28, 2005].

54. Matt Drudge, "Cameron Diaz: 'if you think rape should be legal, then don't vote,'" Drudge Report, September 30, 2004; available online at: http://www.drudgereportarchives.com/data/2004/09/30/20040930_164619_flash5.htm [accessed June 25, 2005].

55. The Oprah Winfrey Show, transcript; available online at: http://www.oprah.com/tows/slide/200409/20040929/slide_20040929_104.jhtml [accessed June 25, 2005].

56. Jessica Callan, Eva Simpson, Suzanne Kerins, "3am: Woody's on side; U.S. actor defends George Michael's anti-Bush single," The Mirror (United Kingdom), August 9, 2002, pp. 8-9.

57. John McCaslin, "Inside the Beltway," Washington Times, October 11, 2002,. A08.

58. Steve Dunleavy, "Victory will shut up H'wood blowhards," New York Post, March 24, 2003, p. O20.

59. Agence France Presse, "Former Dallas star slams US president over Iraq," February 20, 2003.

60. Robyn-Denise Yourse, "Life - arts etc.; taking names," Washington Times, November 4, 2003, p. B05.

61. Brian Reade, "Our stupidity is embarrassing. 60 per cent of young Americans don't even know where Great Britain is on a map," The Mirror, November 3, 2003, pp. 16-17.

62. Michelle Malkin, "The Hollyweird world of Gwynnie Paltrow," Philadelphia Daily News, January 26, 2004, p. 21.

63. "Brits winners attack war plans," BBC News, February 21, 2003; available online at: http://news.bbc.co.uk/1/hi/entertainment/music/2781653.stm [accessed June 1, 2005].

64. Sharon Waxman and Randy Kennedy, "The 2004 election: Hollywood; the gurus of what's in wonder if they're out of touch," New York Times, November 6, 2004, p. A14.

65. Stephanie Mansfield, "Producing a Hollywood flop," Washington Times, November 4, 2004, p. A01.

66. Barbra Streisand, Barbra Streisand Statements, available online at: http://barbrastreisand.com/statements.html [accessed June 25, 2005].

67. Ronald Bailey, "Joan Baez and Me: She gwine tell de folks how dat ol' missuh prez'dent be a debbil!," Reason Online, November 4, 2004; available online at: http://www.reason.com/links/links110404.shtml [accessed June 25, 2005].

68. Newsmax.com, "Michael Moore Bedridden by Bush Win," December 6, 2004; available online at: http://www.newsmax.com/archives/ic/2004/12/6/101145.shtml [accessed June 25, 2005].

69. "Jones trashes 'View' co-hosts," *New York Post,* November 17, 2004, p.12

Chapter Eight: Assassination Fascination

1. Sarah Vowell, *Assassination Vacation* (New York: Simon & Schuster), 2005, p. 6.

2. USC Title 18, Part I, Chapter 41, Section 871; available online at: http://straylight.law.cornell.edu/uscode/html/uscode18/usc_sec_18_00000871———000-.html [accessed June 8, 2005].

3. Vowell, *Assasination Vacation,* op cit., p. 7.

4. Vowell, *Assasination Vacation,* op cit., p. 8.

5. "Assassins Soundtrack Lyrics," available online at: http://www.stlyrics.com/lyrics/assassins/everybodysgottheright.htm [accessed June 8, 2005].

6. "Assassins Soundtrack Lyrics," available online at: http://www.stlyrics.com/lyrics/assassins/gunsong.htm [accessed June 8, 2005].

7. Vowell, *Assasination Vacation,* op cit., p. 6.

8. Michael Feingold, "Second Shots: Sondheim and Weidman hail the chief-killers; Larry Kramer uses rant to fight the plague," (*Village Voice*/April 27, 2004; available online at: http://www.villagevoice.com/theater/0417,feingold,53024,11.html [accessed June 8, 2005].

9. Michelle Goldberg, "Is this play illegal?," Salon.com, October 29, 2003; available online at: http://www.salon.com/ent/feature/2003/10/29/president/index1.html [accessed June 8, 2005].

10. William Cook, "Stars and slights," *The Guardian,* March 6, 2003; available online at: http://www.guardian.co.uk/arts/columns/laughingmatters/story/0,12231,907376,00.html [accessed June 8, 2005].

11. Nicholson Baker, *Checkpoint: A Novel* (New York: Alfred A. Knopf, Inc.) August, 2004, p. 103.

12. PR Newswire, "Newsweek: Nicholson Baker Says Idea for His Controversial Novel 'Checkpoint,' About a Plot to Assassinate President Bush, Came From Fury Over Iraq; 'Suddenly This Thing Speared Into My Life and It Just Took Me Over'; Wept While He Typed; 'I'd Never Had That Experience Before,'" August 1, 2004.

13. Ted Anthony, "Nicholson Baker treads the political line with 'Checkpoint,' an assassination what-if," Associated Press, August 6, 2004.

14. Baker, *Checkpoint*, op cit.

15. Benjamin Strong, "W: The Broken Pickle," *Village Voice*, August 11-17, 2004; available online at: http://www.villagevoice.com/books/0432,strong, 55819,10.html [accessed June 8, 2005].

16. Timothy Noah, "Assassination Porn: Nicholson Baker's irate new novel," Slate, August 5, 2004.

17. Cited in Hillel Italie, "Public spurns novel about man who wants to kill Bush," Associated Press, August 31, 2004; available online at: http://www.southcoast-today.com/daily/08-04/08-31-04/b01li169.htm [accessed June 8, 2005].

18. "Secret Service inspects exhibit," *Chicago Tribune*, April 13, 2005, p. 5.

19. Kari Lydersen, "An Artist's Controversial Stamp Acts," *Washington Post*, May 15, 2005, p. N05.

20. Charles Hurt, "'Kill Rumsfeld' ad withdrawn," *Washington Times*, April 14, 2004; available online at: http://www.washingtontimes.com/national/20040414-123947-2345r.htm [accessed July 9, 2005].

21. Ibid.

22. Peronet Despeignes, "Brits' campaign backfires in Ohio," *USA Today*, August 4, 2004; available online at: http://www.usatoday.com/news/politicselections/vote2004/2004-11-04-brits-letters_x.htm [accessed June 8, 2005].

23. "Screen Burn, The Guide," *Guardian*, October 24, 2004; available online at: http://www.guardian.co.uk/theguide/tvradio/story/0,14676,1335307,00.html [accessed June 8, 2005].

24. Dean E. Murphy, "Can History Save the Democrats?," *New York Times*, November 7, 2004, Section 4, p. 1.

25. Charles Johnson, "NYT Responds to 'Act of God' Article Outrage," Little Green Footballs, November 8, 2004; available online at: http://www.littlegreenfoot-balls.com/weblog/?entry=13510_NYT_Responds_to_Act_of_God_Article_Out-rage [accessed June 8, 2005].

26. BBC News, "Kill Bush' rappers rapped by US," November 4, 2004; available online at: http://news.bbc.co.uk/1/hi/world/europe/3983541.stm [accessed June 8, 2005].

27. Paula Span, "Radio Waves," *Washington Post*, September 12, 2004, p. W11; available online at: http://www.washingtonpost.com/ac2/wp-dyn/A3763-2004Sep7?language=printer [accessed June 8, 2005].

28. Matt Drudge, "Air America Radio Investigated After Bush 'Gunshots,'" Drudge Report, April 27, 2005.

29. John Mainelli, "Air America Shoots Off An Apology," *New York Post*, April 28, 2005, p. 111.

30. Evan Coyne Maloney, "Oh, Those Peace-Loving New York Liberals!," Brain Terminal, April 14, 2005; available online at: http://brain-terminal.com/posts/2005/04/14/peace-loving-ny-liberals [accessed June 8, 2005].

31. Michelle Malkin, "Unhinged Liberal Products For Sale," michellemalkin.com, April 12, 2005; available online at: http://michellemalkin.com/archives/002059.htm [accessed June 8, 2005].

32. After my blog exposed the products on April 12, Café Press removed the products. See Michelle Malkin, "'Kill Bush' Products—Killed," michellemalkin.com, April 14, 2005; available online at: http://michellemalkin.com/archives/002080.htm [accessed June 8, 2005].

33. Victor Davis Hanson, "Brace Yourself," National Review Online, September 2, 2004; available online at: http://www.nationalreview.com/script/printpage.p?ref=/hanson/hanson200409022149.asp [accessed June 8, 2005].

Afterword

1. Associated Press, "Text of Senator John Kerry's concession speech," November 3, 2004; available online at: http://www.usatoday.com/news/politicselections/vote2004/2004-11-03-kerry-concession-speech_x.htm [accessed July 12, 2005].

2. Paul Krugman, "What's going on?," New York Times, March 29, 2005, p. A17.

3. Eric Krol, "Durbin: U.S. won't leave Iraq for years," Daily Herald, July 6, 2005; available online at: http://www.dailyherald.com/story.asp?id=70177 [accessed July 12, 2005].

4. Lloyd Grove, "Rangel in 'Holocaust' firestorm," New York Daily News, June 9, 2005; available online at: http://www.nydailynews.com/front/story/317351p-271348c.html [accessed July 12, 2005].

5. Christina Almeida , "Reid Calls Bush 'A Loser,' Then Apologizes," May 6, 2005; available online at: http://apnews.myway.com/article/20050507/D89U0RBO0.html [accessed July 12, 2005].

6. Michelle Malkin, "The 7/7 attacks: reactions from the American left," michellemalkin.com, July 7, 2005; available online at: http://michellemalkin.com/archives/002945.htm [accessed July 12, 2005].

7. Michelle Malkin, "Anarchy in San Francisco," michellemalkin.com, July 11, 2005; available online at: http://michellemalkin.com/archives/002975.htm [accessed July 12, 2005].

8. Hunter, "Long attacks: open thread," Daily Kos, July 7, 2005; available online at: http://dailykos.com/story/2005/7/7/111317/2427 [accessed July 12, 2005].

9. Shmooth, "George Bush's Wet Dream, Part II," Daily Kos, July 7, 2005; available online at: http://dailykos.com/comments/2005/7/7/55748/30370/570#570 [accessed July 12, 2005].

10. Markos Moulitsas Zuniga, "The conspiracists," Daily Kos, July 8, 2005; available online at: http://dailykos.com/story/2005/7/8/114856/8349 [accessed July 12, 2005].

11. Matt Drudge, "REVEALED: INSIDE A MOVEON SUPREME COURT HOUSE PARTY; TAKE 'BUSH LIAR' T-SHIRTS OFF," Drudge Report, July 10, 2005; available online at: http://drudgereport.com/flash8.htm [accessed July 12, 2005].

Back Cover

i   E-mail from Escobarcut@aol.com dated May 4, 2005.

ii   E-mail from vinnie9holes@optonline.net, March 29, 2005.

iii   http://sadlyno.com/cgi-bin/shizzle.cgi?entry_id=1276

iv   E-mail from A1ACHILLES@aol.com, April 12, 2005.

v   Cited in http://www.softgreenglow.com/mt/archives/2005/05/blind_or_hypocr.html. Originally published at http://www.isthatlegal.org/archive/2005/05/nine_months_lat.html#comments.

vi   http://majikthise.typepad.com/majikthise_/2005/04/michelle_malkin.html

vii   http://roxanne.typepad.com/rantrave/2005/04/mm_dishonest_sh.html

viii http://sadlyno.com/cgi-bin/shizzle.cgi?entry_id=1276

ix   http://sadlyno.com/cgi-bin/shizzle.cgi?entry_id=1276

x   E-mail from Rossen3@aol.com dated July 26, 2005.

A

ABC, 44, 103, 126

Aberdeen News, 126

abortion, 58–59

Abovitz, Rony, 91

Abu Ghraib prison, 83, 90, 121

Academy Awards, 136

ACLU. *See* American Civil Liberties Union

ACORN. *See* Association of Community Organizations for Reform Now

ADL. *See* Anti-Defamation League

AFL-CIO. *See* American Federation of Labor-Congress of Industrial Organizations

The Agency, 143

Aguilar, Esmeralda, 56

AHA. *See* American Health Association

AIDS, 3

Air America, 8, 143, 162, 163

al Jazeera, 41

al Qaeda, 70, 142, 148, 165

Alam, M. Shahid, 104

Alaska, 61

Albright, Madeleine, 32–33, 100, 168

Algeria, 106

Alien, 2

Allen, Norman, 85

Alterman, Eric, 19–20, 112

Alvicar, Lenny, 56

Amazon.com, 98
America Coming Together, 52
AMERICAblog, 71
American Civil Liberties Union
    (ACLU), 136
American Federation of Labor-Con-
    gress of Industrial Organizations
    (AFL-CIO), 52, 56, 57
American Health Association
    (AHA), 3
American Indian Movement, 100
American Psychological Association,
    1
American Revolution, 106
Amnesty International, 54, 70
Aniston, Jennifer, 139
Anthony, Ted, 158
anti-Americanism: on college cam-
    puses, 97–111; Hollywood, 134,
    135–51
Anti-Defamation League (ADL), 71,
    133
AP. *See* Associated Press
Apple Valley High School, Minn., 29,
    64
Aravosis, John, 71
Ardolino, Bill, 46, 59
Arizona, 61
Arizona, University of, 45, 59
Arizona Daily Wildcat, 47
Arizona State University (ASU),
    110–11
Army Times, 93

Arnett, Peter, 91
Ashcroft, John, 20–22, 112
Assassination Vacation (Vowell), 153
Assassins, 155–57
Associated Press (AP), 4, 27, 33, 74,
    76, 80–81, 83, 113, 126, 130,
    141, 158
Association of Community Organiza-
    tions for Reform Now (ACORN),
    52
ASU. *See* Arizona State University
Austin, Steve, 16
"Axis of Evil, the Secret History of
    Sin," 158

B

Bacon, Kenneth, 26–27
Baez, Joan, 150–51
Bailey, Ronald, 150
Baker, Nicholson, 157, 160
Baker, Pete, 75
Baldwin, Alec, 144
Baldwin, James, 107
Barnes, J., 88–89
Baron, Sally, 27
Bataan, 136
Batalona, Kristal, 85
Batalona, Wesley, 84–85
The Battle of Midway, 136
Bazian, Hatem, 103–4
Beastie Boys, 144
Bechtel, 103
Beckel, Bob, 131

Benedict XVI, 133

Bergreen, Nicholas, 94

Berkshire Theatre Festival, 155, 156

Bernhard, Sandra, 142, 144

Billboard.com, 144

bin Laden, Osama, 44, 68, 78, 112, 142; Bush, George W. and, 10, 31–32, 32–33, 168; Democratic conspiracy theories and, 31–33, 41–42; Reagan, Ronald and, 23; Republican Party and, 41–42; Rove, Karl and, 41–42

"BitchAboutBush.com," 17

Black, Duncan, 11, 118

Black Liberation Army, 100

Black Panthers, 106

BlackBoxVoting.org, 48

blacks. *See* racism

Blackwater Security, 84–85

Blackwell, Kenneth, 49

Blair, Tony, 170

blogosphere. *See* Internet

Bloomsbury Review, 98

Boca Raton News, 5

Booker, Charlie, 160–61

Booth, John Wilkes, 155, 160

Boston Globe, 57, 90

Boston Herald, 57

Boucek, Simona, 89

Boxer, Barbara, 49, 50, 86, 152

Bradenton Herald, 76

Brawley, Tawana, 108, 109, 111

Brock, David, 11, 25, 118

Bronx Community College, 95

Brooks, Renana, 3

Brown, Corrine, 126

Brown, Jerry "Moonbeam," 70

Bryn Mawr College, 118

Buchanan, Pat, 64–65

Buffalo News, 77

Burkett, Bil, 36

Burnam, Lon, 81

Bush, Barbara, 126

Bush, George H. W., 123, 156

Bush, George W., 16–19, 36, 113; assassination fantasies and, 8, 112, 153–54, 156–59, 161–65; bin Laden, Osama and, 10, 31–32, 32–33, 41–42, 168; Democratic conspiracy theories and, 31–52; draft and, 44–47; evangelical Christians and, 130; Hitler, Adolf and, 10, 143; Hollywood and, 140–44, 148–49, 149–51; homosexuality and, 146–47; Iraq War and, 10; liberal hatred of, 1, 2, 8, 13–18, 27–28; military service of, 35–41; September 11 and, 3, 33–34, 35, 144–46, 152, 168; women and, 147–48

Bush, Jeb, 48, 132

Bush, Laura, 126, 128

Bush Derangement Syndrome, 34, 35, 172

"Bush Survival Bible" (Stone), 6

Bush v. Gore, 10

Butler University, Ind., 65
BuzzFlash.com, 41
Byrd, Robert "KKK," 124–29

C
CafePress, 163, 164
Caldwell, Lewis G., 63
California, 14, 74–75
California, University of, Berkeley, 101, 103
California, University of, Irvine, 118
California Institute of Technology, 49
Cal State Monterey Bay, 101
Campus Report (ASU), 111
Canada, 6, 46
Caner, Ergun Mehmet, 137
Capital Times, 4
Caplis, Dan, 99
Capra, Frank, 135
Captain's Quarters, 72
Carlyle Group, 103
Carr, Joshua, 74
Castro, Fidel, 95
CBS, 126
CBS News, 35, 36–41, 46, 125
celebrities. *See* Hollywood
Central Committee for Conscientious Objectors, 96
Chait, Jonathan, 15
Chaney, Lon, 138
Charles, Bruce C., 29, 64
Chase, Chevy, 140
Chavez, Hugo, 8

Checkpoint (Baker), 157
Cheney, Dick, 8, 25–27, 138, 140
Cheney, Lynne, 138
Cheney, Mary, 138
Cher, 68, 146–47
Chevron, 103
Chicago, University of, 130
Chicago Maroon, 130
Chicago Sun-Times, 77
Chicago Tribune, 28
China, 70
Cho, Margaret, 139–40, 143
Christian Broadcasting Network, 8
Churchill, Ward, 97–103, 105
Cincinnati, Ohio, 55
City College of New York, 94
City Journal, 106
Civil Rights Act of 1964, 124
Clanton, Chad, 37
Claremont College, 101
Claremont McKenna College, 108
Cleland, Max, 45
Clennon, David, 143
Cleveland Plain Dealer, 50
Clift, Eleanor, 73, 112
Clinton, Bill, 26, 27, 69, 70, 127, 131, 172
Clinton, Chelsea, 20
Clinton, Hillary, 51, 72, 125, 126, 127, 128, 172
Clooney, George, 149
CNN, 14, 41, 91, 103, 125, 131
Cocco, Beverly, 46

Code Pink, 10–11, 95
Cohen, Adam, 113
ColdPlay, 149
college campuses: anti-Americanism on, 97–111; anti-war movement on, 92–96; hate crime hoaxes on, 108–11; liberals on, 8
College Democrats, 113
College of New Jersey, 110
College Republicans, 57, 59, 104, 108
Colmes, Alan, 16
Colorado, 62
Colorado, University of, 97, 101
Columbia College, 158
Columbia University, 105–6
Columbine High School, Colo., 156
CommonDreams.org, 48
Comstock, Gary, 107
conservative media. *See* media
Conservative Political Action Conference (2005), 16
conservatives: as crazy, 1; Hollywood and, 137; liberals and, 1, 19–27; patriotism and, 164–65; PEST and, 6; religion and, 164–65; Republican Party and, 1
Conyers, John, Jr., 48
Corn, David, 48
Cornell University, 49, 52
Cottle, Michelle, 131–32
Coulter, Ann, 25, 59, 65, 116
Counterpunch, 105
CountTheVote.com, 47

Couric, Katie, 117
Cox News Service, 27
Crawford, Craig, 43
Cronkite, Walter, 41, 112
Crouch, Brian, 87–88
Cuba, 42, 70–73, 96
Cutler, Jonathan, 106–7

D
Daily Kos, 65, 71, 170
Daley, Richard, 71, 170
Dallas Peace Center, 81
Danziger, Jeff, 112, 122–23
Daschle, Tom, 125, 140
"DC Media Girl," 11
Dean, Howard: assassination fantasies and, 152, 165; conspiracy theories and, 32, 45, 52; conspiracy theories of, 33–35; Democratic Party and, 8; Democratic vandalism and, 64; Hollywood fundraising and, 138; liberal craziness and, 1, 10, 16, 19, 29; military and, 84, 86
DeBusk, Darrell, 60
De Genova, Nicholas, 105–6
de Havilland, Perry, 97
de Luna, Michael Hernandez, 159
"Democracy Now," 28
Democratic Farm Labor (DFL) Party, 57
Democratic Party, Democrats: anti-Bush death notices and, 27–28; assassination fantasies of, 8;

Democratic Party, Democrats
(continued): attacks of, 53–67;
conspiracy theories of, 8, 10,
31–52; Election 2004 and, 3–8,
53–67; media and, 2; mental
health crisis of, 3–8; patriotism
and, 72–73; people's rejection of,
167–68; PEST and, 3–8; platform
of, 53; racism and, 123–29; van-
dalism and, 8. *See also* liberals
Democratic Underground (DU), 20,
22, 24, 169
Democrats.com, 49
Denver Post, 133
Department of Dirty Tricks, 42, 44,
52
Derse, Susan, 88
Des Moines Register, 5
DFL. *See* Democratic Farm Labor
Party
Diaz, Cameron, 68, 146, 147–48
Diebold Corporation, 32, 47–48, 150
Dobson, Jim, 133
Dodd, Christopher, 92, 123–24, 170
Dole, Bob, 123
Donahue, Deirdre, 158
D'Onofrio, Vincent, 68, 151
Doonesbury, 122
Douglas, Timothy, 156
Dow, Daniel, 82–83
Dowd, Maureen, 128, 130, 155
Dowling, Robert, 150
Drago, Ed, 110

Drake, Chad, 80–81
Drennan, Suzanne, 4
Drudge, Matt, 171
Drudge Report, 57, 160, 163
Drum, Kevin, 119–21
Due, Jeff, 92–93
Dunn, Kerri, 108–9
Durbin, Dick, 69–73, 152, 168, 170

E

Edmiston, Suanne, 58
Edwards, Elizabeth, 24, 26, 169
Edwards, John, 10, 24, 47, 62, 139,
140
Eibensteiner, Ron, 57
Eichmann, Adolf, 97, 102
Elder, Larry, 14
Election 2000, 10
Election 2004: conspiracy theories
and, 47–52; Democratic violence
and, 53–67, 63–67; electoral fraud
in, 10, 32, 47–52, 150; Holly-
wood and, 149–51; PEST and,
3–8; September 11 and, 3
Eminem, 146
Emmerson, Karen, 5
"Eschaton," 118
ESPN, 122
Esquire magazine, 19
evangelical Christians, 129–31
Everett, Wash., 55
Everett Herald, 55
Eyman, Tim, 65

F

FactCheck.org, 45–46

Fahrenheit 9/11, 137

Family Circus, 36

Fassler, Jess, 86

Fazio, Charles, 171

Feingold, Michael, 156

Fernandez, Michael, 65–66

Fetzer, James, 41

Finkelstein, Arthur, 127

First Amendment, 65, 141

First Motion Picture Unit, 135

First Persian Gulf War, 73, 156

Fisher, Jeff, 48

Florida, 29; Democratic violence in, 56, 58; Election 2000 and, 10; Election 2004 and, 48–49; war on ribbons in, 75–76

Flying Tigers, 136

Focus on the Family, 133

Foley, Linda, 91

Foner, Eric, 106

Ford, Gerald, 155

Fortuyn, Pim, 65

Fort Worth Star Telegram, 4

Founding Fathers, 106

Fourmyle, Maia, 6

Foxman, Abraham H., 133

Fox News Channel, 4, 10, 14, 16, 32, 39, 90, 126, 127, 140

Fox News Sunday, 34, 124

Frank, Barney, 92, 170

Franken, Al, 8, 16, 112

Freeman, Brenda, 74

Free Republic, 26–27

Frenk, Clara, 11

Frohnmayer, Dave, 75

Front Page Magazine, 104

Frost, Martin, 86, 170

"FucktheSouth.com," 17–18

"FuckYouBush.com," 17

Fulbright committee, 72

Full Metal Jacket, 151

Fumo, Vincent, 126–27, 152

Fund, John, 57

fundraising, political, 137–40

Furbert, Raven, 88–89

Furgess, John, 70

G

Gable, Clark, 135, 136

Gainsville, Fla., 56

Gandhi, Mahatma, 125

Gannon, Jeff, 116

GAO. *See* Government Accountability Office

Garfield, James, 153, 155

Garms, Roger, 4

Garofalo, Janeane, 68, 138, 143

Gatas Parlament, 162

Gawker, 59

General Union of Palestinian Students (GUPS), 104

George Washington University, 58

Gergen, David, 92

German TV, 149

Getler, Michael, 128

Gibson, Charlie, 44

Gibson, Mike, 94

Gilliard, Steve, 71

Gilson, Jason, 78–80

Gil-White, Francisco, 105

Glover, Danny, 140–41

Godfather, 15, 162

Gold, Judy, 138

Gold, Scott, 113

Goldberg, Bernard, 20

Goldberg, Whoopi, 138–39

Gone With the Wind, 122

Goodman, Amy, 28

Google.com, 11

Gore, Al, 2, 34–35, 70, 144

Government Accountability Office
    (GAO), 48

Grant, Bobbie, 75

Grenada, 23

Gridley, Clint, 75

Grosvenor, Kim, 76

Guantanamo Bay, Cuba, 168, 170;
    abuses at, 42, 70–73, 90; Koran
    desecration at, 42; liberals and, 96

Guardian, 143, 160

Guiteau, Charles, 155

H

Hackney, Douglas, 77

Hagman, Larry, 149

Hall, Rich, 157

Hall, Richard Melville. *See* Moby

Halliburton, 31, 96, 103, 172

Hamilton College, 98

Hamilton Spectator, 98

Hannity, Sean, 39–40, 143

Hannity and Colmes, 39–40

Hanson, Victor Davis, 165

Harper's, 6, 90

Harrelson, Woody, 148

Harris, Bev, 47

Harris, Katherine, 29, 58, 128

Hartocollis, Anemona, 27

Harvard University, 49

hate crime hoaxes, 108–11

Hawaii, University of, 101

HBO, 20

Helvenston, Scott, 84–85

Herbert, Bob, 130

The Hill, 43

Hinchey, Maurice, 35, 37–41, 152

Hinckley, John, Jr., 155, 160

Hispanics, 2, 139. *See also* racism

Hitler, Adolf, 10, 22, 140, 143

Hitler Youth, 133

Hoard, Greg, 60

Hofstadter, Richard, 31

Holiday, Jamal, 55

Hollings, Ernest, 45

Hollywood: anti-Americanism of,
    134, 135–51; Bush, George W.
    and, 140–44, 148–49, 149–51;
    conservatives and, 137; Election

2004 and, 149–51; international media and, 148–49; Iraq War and, 140–44; liberals in, 8; military and, 135–36; political fundraising and, 137–40; War on Terrorism and, 148

Hollywood Reporter, 150

homosexuality: Bush, George W. and, 146–47; liberal bigotry and, 126–27

Honolulu Advertiser, 85

Horn, Travis, 56

Horowitz, David, 65

Howell, Justin, 63

Huffington, Arianna, 25–26, 42

Human Rights Campaign, 127

Husar, Michael, 29, 57–58

Hussein, Saddam, 78, 91, 142; capture of, 31, 33, 152; Iraq War and, 86

Hymowitz, Kay, 106

Hynde, Chrissie, 142

Hynde, Chrissy, 68

I

Illinois, 61, 76

IMF. *See* International Monetary Fund

Immoral Technique (Tech), 145–46

Imus, Don, 16

The Incredibles, 155

INDC Journal, 46, 59

Indiana, 65

Indianapolis Star, 82

Ingraham, Laura, 16, 24–25

International Monetary Fund (IMF), 107

Internet: liberal craziness and, 2; political activism and, 3; racism and, 114–21

Interview magazine, 141

Iowa, 76

Iran-Contra affair, 23

Iranian hostage crisis, 73

Iraq War, 154, 169; Bush, George W. and, 10; Bush draft and, 44–47; Hollywood and, 140–44; Hussein, Saddam and, 86; purpose of, 10

"Is Bush Wired?," 43

Isikoff, Michael, 42

Israel, 31–32

J

Jackson, Jesse, 49, 172

Jadakiss, 144

Jamieson, Robert, 78–79

Jensen, Robert, 105

Jews, 31–32, 104

Jindal, Bobby, 113–14

John, Elton, 141

John Paul II, Pope, 132–33

Johnson, Diane, 74

Johnson, Nancy, 83

Jones, Rickie Lee, 141, 143

Jordan, Eason, 91–92, 112
Journal and Courier, 76

K
Kaiser, Dan, 13–14
Kane, Michael, 145–46
Kansas, 61
Karamcheti, Indira, 106
Kean, Tom, 34
Keillor, Garrison, 130–31
Kennedy, Jacqueline, 18
Kennedy, John F., 8, 41, 157
Kennedy, Robert F., Jr., 172
Kennedy, Ted, 35, 86
Kent State University, 105
Kerry, John, 167; assassination fantasies and, 159–60; Democratic violence and, 55, 62; Hollywood fundraising and, 138–39; Vietnam War-era testimony of, 72
Kerry, Teresa Heinz, 18, 45, 47, 128, 152
Khan, Genghis, 72
Khmer Rouge, 72
King, Larry, 41
King, Martin Luther, Jr., 125
King, Michael, 122
KING-TV, 55
Kirsanow, Peter, 50
KKK. *See* Ku Klux Klan
Klebold, Dylan, 156
Klein, Jonathan, 14, 16
Knopf, 157

Kohut, Andrew, 130
Kondracke, Morton, 32–33
Koran, 42
Kordonowy, Darlene, 80
Krauthammer, Charles, 34
Kristol, Bill, 64, 65
Krugman, Paul, 90, 132, 168
Kucinich, Dennis, 32
Ku Klux Klan (KKK), 124, 138, 150
Kurtz, Howard, 131–32

L
Lambert, Katherine, 56
Landrieu, Mary, 172
Lang, Carol, 94
Lange, Jessica, 148
Laos, 91
Laqueur, Thomas, 104
Larson, Lars, 89
Las Vegas Review Journal, 121
Lato, Chris, 63
LA Weekly, 18
Layne, Ken, 129
Leab, Chris, 73
League of Women Voters, 51
LeBron, Anthony, 77
Left. *See* liberals
Left2Right, 78
Leguizamo, John, 139
Lenin, Vladimir, 42
Lexington Herald-Leader, 121
liberalism. *See* liberals
liberals: assassination fantasies of, 8,

112, 153–65; Bush, George W. and, 2, 13–18; Bush, George W., hatred of, and, 2; Bush-bashing and, 16–18; on college campuses, 8; conservatives and, 1; as crazy. *see also* Democratic Party, Democrats; Guantanamo Bay, Cuba and, 70–73; hatred of, 8; hatred of conservatives of, 19–27; Hollywood, 8, 68, 135–51; homosexuality and, 126–27; Internet and, 2; media, 112; military and, 8, 69–96; patriotism and, 1; portrait of, 8–9; profanity of, 16–19, 119–21; racism and, 2, 112; racism of, 113–34; Reagan, Ronald and, 2; religion and, 129–31, 132–34; veterans and, 8, 80–82, 84–86, 96; War on Terrorism and, 1, 10; women and, 8, 57–60, 128–29; Yellow Ribbons and, 96. *See also* Democratic Party, Democrats
Liberals Gone Wild, 10, 13
Lieberman, Joe, 2, 72
LifeNews.com, 58
Limbaugh, Rush, 19–20, 57, 122, 141, 158
Lincoln, Abraham, 153, 154, 155, 161
Liponis, Mark, 6
Little Green Footballs, 37
Lizon, Peter, 62
Lockhart, Joe, 37
London Daily Mirror, 149

London Review of Books, 104
London School of Economics, 118
Lopez, Jennifer, 126
Lopez, Jonna, 47
Los Angeles Times, 3, 74, 85, 109, 113, 121
Lott, Trent, 123

M

M1 and Stickman, 145
Matthews, Chris, 2, 19
McAuliffe, Terry, 36, 37
McBride, Bill, 48
McCall, Edna, 160
McCally, David Philip, 29, 56
McClure, Mike, 4
McDermott, Jim, 33, 80, 152
McGovern, George, 149
McInnis, Scott, 83, 127
McKay High School, Ore., 89–90
McKinley, William, 153, 154, 161
McKinney, Cynthia, 35, 152
McMahan, Jeff, 78
Madison, Wisc., 29
Madonna, 142
Maher, Bill, 14, 16, 20, 112, 134
Mailer, Norman, 42
Maine, 75
mainstream media. *See* media
Malheiro, Sharon, 5
Malkin, Michelle, 11; hate mail sent to, 114–21
Maloney, Evan Coyne, 163

Manatee Technical Institute, 75–76
Mandel, Ian, 98
Manhattan College, 94
Manhattan Institute, 106
Mapes, Mary, 36–37
Marcos, Ferdinand, 116
Marine Corps Moms, 89
Marshall, Elizabeth, 4
Martin, Chris, 149
Massachusetts, University of, 77
Massachusetts Daily Collegian, 77
Massachusetts Institute of Technology
    (MIT), 49
MCI, 140
Mebane, Walter, Jr., 52
media: Bush draft and, 46; conserva-
    tive, 2; Democratic Party and, 2;
    Democratic violence and, 53. 63;
    liberal racism and, 125; military
    vs., 90–92; religion and, 130;
    Republican Party and, 8
Media Bloggers Association, 16
Media Matters for America, 118
Medlin, Josh, 64
Medved, Michael, 16
Mellencamp, John, 139
Melucci, Giulia, 91
Mesnick, Samuel, 65
Michigan, 57
Miklaszewski, Jim, 46
Mikulski, Barbara, 72
Milbank, Dana, 132
military: as "baby-killers," 78–80;

Democratic violence and, 8,
    81–82; fragging and, 101–2; Hol-
    lywood and, 135–36; media vs.,
    90–92; public schools and, 88–90;
    recruitment and, 92–96; smearing,
    84–86, 87–90; yellow ribbons
    and, 73–78
Miller, Glenn, 136
Miller, Leah, 109
Milwaukee, Wisc., 29
Miner, Joshua M., 81–82
Minnesota, 57, 61, 64
minorities. *See* racism
Mirror (Britain), 148
Missouri, 57
MIT. *See* Massachusetts Institute of
    Technology
Mitchell, Patrick, 11
Moby, 136–37, 139
Moen, Thomas and Christine, 76
Mohammad, Lavelle, 63
Montana, 61
Moore, Gwen, 63
Moore, Michael, 8, 10, 31, 54, 68,
    104, 136, 137, 149, 151
Morning Sentinel, 62
Morrissey, Ed, 72
Mother Jones, 43
Motion Picture Association, 136, 137
Moulitsas Zuniga, Markos, 34–35,
    71, 84–86, 112, 170–71
MoveOn, 139, 140, 171
Moynihan, Daniel Patrick, 8

MSNBC, 2, 20, 43, 126, 131, 134, 149

MTV, 45, 144

Munch, Edward, 172

Murphy, Dean, 161

Myers, Charlotte, 85

Mystic River, 142

N

NAACP. *See* National Association for the Advancement of Colored People

NABJ. *See* National Association of Black Journalists

Nadler, Jerrold, 48

NARAL Pro-Choice America, 58

Nasim, Ahmad Saad, 110–11

National Association for the Advancement of Colored People (NAACP), 52, 122, 125

National Association of Black Journalists (NABJ), 122

National Lawyers Guild, 104

National Press Club, 141

National Public Radio (NPR), 33, 65, 78, 130, 155

National Review, 122

National Voter Fund (NAACP), 52

Naughton, Thomas, 77

Nazis, 10, 23, 71, 72

NBC, 126

NBC News, 16, 81, 103

NBC Nighly News, 46

Nelson, Robert M., 43

Newark Star-Ledger, 121

New Jersey, 74, 94

New Republic magazine, 15, 131

Newspaper Guild, 91

Newsweek, 42, 73, 112, 126, 157

New York, 63, 77, 88, 94–95

New York Daily News, 136

New York Post, 138, 151

New York Press, 132

New York Sun, 6

New York Times, 8, 27, 54, 63, 90, 113, 122, 126, 128, 130, 132, 133, 153, 161, 168

Nielsen SoundScan, 144

Nixon, Richard, 123, 149

Noah, Timothy, 158

Nordlinger, Jay, 122

Noriega, Roger, 126

North Carolina, 63

North Dakota, 62

Northeastern University, 104

North Korea, 70

Northwestern University, 109

Nossiter, Adam, 113

NOW Legal Defense and Education Fund, 28

NPR. *See* National Public Radio

O

O'Donnell, Lawrence, 131, 149

O'Donnell, Mark, 108

Ogletree and Deakins, 10

Ohio, 94; Democratic violence in, 55, 61; Election 2004 and, 10, 49–52, 150

"Ohio Voter Suppression News," 47

Olbermann, Keith, 43

Oliphant, Pat, 122

Ollee, Mildred, 93

Omokunde, Sowande Ajumoke, 63

O'Neill, John, 16, 149

Operation Iraqi Freedom, 154

Oregon, 61

Oregon, University of, 75

O'Reilly, Bill, 19, 68, 90, 140, 142

O'Reilly Factor, 10

Orin, Deborah, 138

Orlando, Fla., 56

Osbourne, Ozzy, 143

Oswald, Lee Harvey, 157, 160

P

Pacifica radio, 35

Pacific University, Ore., 29, 64

Palestine, 103–4

Paltrow, Gwyneth, 149

Paris, 145

Party Music, 144–45

Patriot Act, 68, 143

"Patriot Act," 158–59

patriotism: conservatives and, 164–65; Democratic Party and, 72–73; liberals and, 1

Paxton, Stacie, 61

PBS, 14, 125

Penn, Sean, 68, 136, 142

Pennsylvania, University of, 105

People Against the Draft, 46

People magazine, 139

Perle, Richard, 29, 64, 65

PEST. *See* Post-Election Selection Trauma

Pew Research Center, 130

Pheiffer, Sherman, 4

Philadelphia Gay News, 127

Philadelphia Inquirer, 74

Piccola, Jeffrey, 126–27

Pino, Assad, 105

Planned Parenthood, 58

Polite, Nelson, 6–7

political fundraising, Hollywood and, 137–40

Pol Pot, 69, 73, 152, 168

Poor People's Economic Human Rights Campaign, 55

Post-Election Selection Trauma (PEST), 3–8, 164

Pratt, Marvin, 63

Pratt, Michael, 63

The Pretenders, 142

Princeton University, 161

Project 21, 122

public schools, anti-military mindset in, 88–90

Purdue University, 76

Q

Quayle, Dan, 163

R

racism: Byrd, Robert and, 123–29; Democratic Party and, 123–29; hate mail and, 114–21; Internet and, 114–21; of liberals, 113–34; liberals and, 2, 112; Malkin, Michelle and, 114–21; Rice, Condoleezza and, 121–23

Radio Pennsylvania Network, 126

Ragsdale, Lynda, 29, 74

Rainbow/PUSH Coalition, 122

Raj, Ajai Prasad, 29, 59

Rall, Ted, 23, 96, 112, 121–23

Rangel, Charles, 45, 47, 131

Rangel, Charlie, 169

Rather, Dan, 35, 37, 43, 111

Rathergate, 35, 152

Rathergate and, 42, 44

Ratzinger, Cardinal, 133

Reagan, Ronald, 117, 155; bin Laden, Osama and, 23; death of, 22–23, 121; liberals and, 2; September 11 and, 23

Reed College, 101

Rehm, Diane, 33–34

Reid, Harry, 72, 86, 169

Reliable Sources (CNN), 131

religion: conservatives and, 164–65; liberal bigotry and, 129–31, 132–34; media and, 130

Reno, Janet, 48

Republican Party, Republicans: bin Laden, Osama and, 32, 41–42; conservatives in, 1; Department of Dirty Tricks of, 42, 44, 52; Hispanics in, 139; media and, 8; PEST and, 5–6; in South, 17–18

Rhodes, Randi, 8, 112, 162–63

Rice, Condoleezza, 112, 121–23

Rich, Frank, 90

Riecke, Bill, 89

Riecke, Connie, 89–90

Riecke, Shea, 89–90

Riley, Boots, 144

Robbins, Tim, 68, 141

Robertson, Pat, 8

Robertson, Ravid, 125

Rodriguez, Justin, 94

Roll Call, 32

Rolling Stone magazine, 139, 146

Ronstadt, Linda, 143

Roosevelt, Franklin D., 136

Roper, Richard, 77

Rose, Charlie, 14

Ross, Dave, 33

Rove, Karl, 112, 152, 170, 172; bin Laden, Osama and, 41–42; conspiracy theories and, 36–44, 52; Democratic Party and, 32; Democratic violence and, 54; liberal bigotry and, 116; liberal craziness and, 10; Rathergate and, 35–41

The Ruckus Society, 95–96

Rumsfeld, Donald, 159–60

Russell, Michael, 55

Russert, Tim, 16
Ryan, Tim, 45

S

Saide, Jaime Alexander, 109–10
Saint Paul Pioneer Press, 73
Salazar, Ken, 133–34
Salon.com, 43, 156
Samuels, Lynn, 163
San Francisco State University, 95, 104, 109
San Jose Mercury-News, 121
Santana, Carlos, 149
Sarasota, Fla., 29, 58
Sarasota Herald-Tribune, 58
Saudi Arabia, 152
Savage, Michael, 141
Scarborough, Joe, 134
Schaeffer, Beth, 62
Schiavo, Terri, 131–32
Schlesinger, Richard, 46
Schlessinger, Laura, 141
Schooler, Douglas, 5
Schumer, Charles, 72
Scott, Linda, 125
Sears, Tony, 3
Seattle Central Community College, 92–93
Seattle Post-Intelligence, 78, 80
Secret Service, 43, 59, 162, 163
Segal, David, 144–45
Segal, Mark, 127

Selective Service System (2004), 45
Seltzer, Barry, 58
September 11, 143; Bush, George W. and, 3, 33–34, 35, 144–46, 152, 168; Election 2004 and, 3; Israel and, 31–32; Jews and, 31–32; Reagan, Ronald and, 23; smearing victims of, 97–103, 105–7
Shahbander, Oubai, 111
Shanahan, Virginia R., 28
Sharpton, Al, 111
Sheehan, Casey, 11
Sheehan, Cindy, 10–11
Sheen, Martin, 68
Shelton, Hilary, 125
Shinawatra, Thaksin, 149
Shinebaum, Mryna, 133
Silverman, Craig, 99
Sinton, Jon, 163
60 Minutes, 36, 100
Slate.com, 130
Slate magazine, 6, 158
Smiley, Jane, 130
Smith, Liz, 151
Smith, Phillip Edgar, 59
Smith, Ray, 126
Snow, Tony, 124
The Socialist Worker, 93
Society of Professional Journalists, 121
Somalia, 105
Sommers, Bob, 78
Sondheim, Steven, 155, 160

So Proudly We Hail!, 136
sorryeverybody.com, 7
South, Republican Party in, 17–18
Southern California, University of, 7
Special Report with Brit Hume, 32
Spero, Maria, 108
Spokane, Wash., 61
Stachelberg, Winnie, 127
Stanford University, 49
Stark, Pete, 82–84, 127, 152
Statesman Journal, 89
Stein, Harry, 106
Steltzer, Barry, 29
Stern, Howard, 68, 142
Stevenson, Adlai, 8
Stevenson, Frederick, 62
Stewart, Jimmy, 135, 136
Stiles, Julia, 68, 140, 141
Stoltzfus, David, 6–7
Stone, Gene, 6
Stone, Oliver, 31
Stop the War, 95
St. Petersburg Democratic Club, 159
St. Petersburg Times, 91
The Stranger, 18
Streep, Meryl, 139
Streisand, Barbra, 136, 143–44, 150
Strong, Benjamin, 158
Students Against War, 93
Students for Dean, 47
"Supreme Solar Allah". *See*
    Omokunde, Sowande Ajumoke

Sutton, John, 111
Swift Boat Veterans, 2
Swift Boat Veterans for Truth, 37

T
Tacoma News Tribune, 14
Tailwind scandal, 91
Tamalpais High School, Cali., 111
Tampa, Fla., 29, 56
Teague, Mike, 84–85
Teague, Rhonda, 85
Tech. *See* Immoral Technique
Tennessee, 60, 62
Texas, University of, Austin, 59, 105
Thailand, 149
Thomas, Evelyn, 125
Thomas, Helen, 2–3
Thomas, Terry, 87–88
Thurman, Andrew, 62
Thurmond, Strom, 123–25
Tillman, Pat, 96
Time magazine, 16, 126
Tinseltown. *See* Hollywood
Tor, Jeremy, 46–47
Trudeau, Garry, 122
Tubbs-Jones, Stephanie, 49–50
Tully, Mary Jean, 27–28
Tyler, Edward, 74, 152

U
Unfit for Command (O'Neill), 16
unhinged liberals. *See* liberals

United Press International, 6, 133
Universal Press Syndicate, 121
Université Catholique de Louvain, 118
universities. *See* college campuses
Urtel, Scott, 75–76
U.S.A. Magnets and More, 73
USA Today, 126, 128, 158
U.S. News and World Report, 126

V
Valentine, Perry, 55
Vanity Fair, 59
Veteran Feminists of America, 28
veterans, liberal attacks on, 8, 80–82, 84–86, 96
Veterans of Foreign Wars (VFW), 70
VFW. *See* Veterans of Foreign Wars
Vietnam War, 35, 72, 88
Village Voice, 156, 158
Votescam.com, 47
Voting Technology Project, 49
Vowell, Sarah, 153–55, 157, 160, 165

W
Wake Island, 136
Wallace, Chris, 34
Wall Street Journal, 57
Walsh, Brendan, 95
Wanger, Walter, 136
War on Terrorism: Hollywood and, 148; liberals and, 1, 10
War Resisters League, 96

Washington Monthly, 119, 121
Washington Post, 31, 43, 50, 63, 121, 126, 128, 132, 144, 162, 171
Washington State, 13–14, 55, 61, 63, 78
Washington Times, 65, 129, 150
Weekly Standard, 64, 86
Wellstone, Paul, 26, 41, 146
Wesleyan University, Conn., 106
West, Kanye, 172
Western Michigan University, 64–65
West Seattle High School, 87–88
West Wing, 149
Wexler, Robert, 48
Why We Fight, 135
Wilentz, Sean, 161
Wills, Gary, 130
Winfrey, Oprah, 147–48
Winkler, Nathan, 29, 66–67
Wisconsin, 29, 57, 62, 75, 95
Wisconsin-Madison, University of, 95
Wissing, Dave, 125
Wolcott, James, 59
Wolff, William Zachary, 59
women: Bush, George W. and, 147–48; liberals and, 8, 57–60, 128–29
World Bank, 107
World Economic Forum, 91
World War I, 136
World War II, 135, 136
Wray, Derek, 104
WTOL-TV, 94

Y

Yankee Doodle Dandy, 136
Yatovitz, Seth, 75
yellow ribbons, 73–78
Young Republicans, 56

Z

Zetlen, James, 7
Zimbleman, Corwyn (Cory) William, 28
Zovko, Jerry, 84–85

Get a FREE chapter
of Regnery's latest bestseller!

Visit us at

www.Regnery.com

- Hot New Releases

- Upcoming Titles

- Listings of Author Signings
  and Media Events

- Complete Regnery Catalog

- Always a Free Chapter
  of a Brand-New Book!

Since 1947
REGNERY
PUBLISHING, INC.

An Eagle Publishing Company • Washington, DC
www.Regnery.com